eventy years ago, Chicago White Sox fans
earned their team had taken bribes to
hrow the 1919 World Series. The day the
ews broke, baseball legend has it, a crowd
f South Side boys begged outfielder "Shoe-
ss Joe" Jackson to "Say it ain't so!" Jackson
nswered with the candor and shame that
ter generations have often lacked. "I'm
fraid it is, boys," he said. "I'm afraid it is."

n *Winning Is the Only Thing,* Randy Roberts
nd James Olson take a hard look at the dark
de of American sports. The scandals. The
ole of organized crime. How politicians and
usinessmen exploit the Olympics. Who
ets rich and who goes broke. Why the fit-
ess craze has nothing to do with fitness.
nd how TV sports czars like Roone
rledge—inventor of the "instant replay"—
ctually dictate how games are played.

hese are the sports stories you won't find
n the record books. Before landing in a
tate mental hospital in 1956, middleweight
illy Fox "wins" 50 of 51 bouts, all by KOs,
nost of them fixed, some against imaginary
pponents in fights that never took place.
ut-of-work math whiz Charles K. McNeill
urns his talents to bookmaking during
World War II—and invents the "point
pread." Howard Cosell, after receiving
ountless death threats from irate listeners,
roadcasts Monday Night Football from a
ooth protected by FBI agents. Nebraska
rm boy George Wagner dyes his hair plat-
num, dons an ermine robe, parades into a
ew York wrestling ring in 1943 to the tune
f "Pomp and Circumstance," and becomes
Gorgeous George," the first modern pro
restler.

With measure of common sense, son argue that none of this developed in a vacu-
um. The cold war shaped the Olympic
Games. Racial integration of U.S. sports
teams helped spearhead the civil rights
movement. College basketball's point-
shaving scandals belonged to a decade of
crooked disk jockeys and rigged quiz shows.
Jackie Robinson, Billy Jean King, and Len
Bias are as much a part of America's postwar politics as are Gloria Steinem, Martin
Luther King, and Richard Nixon. For better
or for worse, America's leisure pastimes
reflect—and influence—the values of our
society at large.

# Winning Is the Only Thing

# Winning Is the Only Thing

## Sports in America since 1945

• • •

**RANDY ROBERTS and
JAMES S. OLSON**

*91-455*

The Johns Hopkins University Press

Baltimore and London

The Johns Hopkins University Press
701 West 40th Street, Baltimore, Maryland 21211
The Johns Hopkins Press Ltd., London

The paper used in this publication meets the minimum requirements of American National Standard for Information Sciences—Permanence of Paper for Printed Library Materials, ANSI Z39.48–1984.

Library of Congress Cataloging-in-Publication Data

Roberts, Randy, 1951–
   Winning is the only thing: sports in America since 1945 / Randy Roberts and James Olson.
       p.     cm.—(The American moment)
   Bibliography: p.
   Includes index.
   ISBN 0-8018-3830-4
   1. Sports—United States—History—20th century. 2. Sports and state—United States. I. Olson, James. II. Title. III. Series.
GV583.R6   1989
796'.0973—dc 19                                                      89-1689
                                                                      CIP

*Frontispiece:* Welterweight champion Benny "Kid" Paret, fatally injured in a title fight with Emile Griffith before a nationwide TV audience in 1962. (Courtesy of the University of Notre Dame)

To Suzy, Alison, Kelly, and Craig

# • Contents

Pro-basketball hopeful Len Bias (#34) ended life and an illustrious college career with an accidental drug overdose, a few days before graduation. (Credit: Larry Crouse, University of Maryland, College Park)

# • Preface

Len Bias, the All-American basketball star from the University of Maryland, had just signed a multimillion dollar professional contract with the Boston Celtics. He took the shuttle back from Boston to Washington, D.C., and went straight to his dorm room at College Park. Bias partied with some friends for a few hours, accompanied one of them out to the parking lot, and then returned to his room and died of a cocaine overdose. Everyone agreed that it was a tragedy. Larry Bird said, "It's the cruelest thing I've ever heard." Bias's friends assured reporters that the All-American did not use drugs, or at least not before that fatal night. "I swear on my life, I hope to die if this kid ever used drugs before," remarked Celtics general manager Red Auerbach. Bias, they said, was not like the athletes who had drug problems—not like Mercury Morris, Michael Ray Richardson, John Lucas, Quentin Dailey, Terry Furlow, Tim Raines, Hollywood Henderson, Bob Hayes, Dave Parker, Darrell Porter, Tony Peters, Aaron Pryor, Steve Howe, Dock Ellis, or the other athletes who had abused drugs. Throughout 1986 and 1987, as the investigation into Bias's death reached a grand jury, it became clear that the Terrapin star had not been a casual cocaine user. He too had a drug problem.

Journalists agreed that the drug problem in sports was out of control. In the summer of 1988, All-Pro linebacker Lawrence Taylor of the New York Giants was suspended for thirty days when he tested positive for cocaine. Even though he knew that a mandatory urine test would be required at training camp, he was unable to kick the habit, threatening his playing career. From the professional level through college ball and even into the high school ranks, drug abuse had become an endemic problem in the 1980s.

Twenty-three years separated the heroin overdose of football great Big Daddy Lipscomb and Bias's death. Big Daddy's death was written off as an anomaly. Not so with Bias: reporters said Bias was more a victim of the times than of himself. Few writers, however, asked if sports was to blame. Certainly Bias, who had for the first time to deal with the very real world of sports business, was in an anxious and confused state before his death. His moods fluctuated, and the constant talk of negotiations—with the Celtics, the Reebok shoe company, and his agent—left him restless. Bias's short career was not that unusual. Pampered in high school and college, he found adjustment to a world outside of the gym difficult.

Bias, of course, does not represent all world-class athletes. Yet his tragedy does underscore America's misplaced emphasis on sports. Priorities are out of whack. Sports increasingly occupy to an unwholesome degree the attention of millions of Americans. For example, in 1973 a Denver Broncos fan watched his team fumble seven times in a losing effort against the Chicago Bears. It was too much for him to take, and after the game he attempted suicide. His suicide note read: "I have been a Broncos fan since the Broncos were first organized, and I can't stand their fumbling anymore."

Money is one indication of the incredible changes in the world of sports. John McEnroe, for example, has become a multinational corporation. He has an entertainment division, which includes exhibitions at a going rate of $75,000 and up per night. His personal appearance division, as Tony Schwartz noted in 1983, "books corporate functions and autograph sessions, and also fields philanthropic requests." The licensing division insures that the McEnroe name appears on T-shirts, hats, posters, and other such wearables. The endorsement division decides which tennis racquets, clothes, shoes, toothpaste, pens, and other products will receive John's official blessings. And then, of course, there is the tournament division, which is not really much of a money-maker. Some tennis insiders have suggested that with McEnroe's money-making ability and his father's skillful money management, the tennis star may have made as much as $1 million a week in his prime. That may be a slight exaggeration, but it is probably in the ballpark (or tennis complex).

Tennis and boxing undoubtedly have the richest athletes, but participants in team sports can also afford to buy homes. Millionaires in baseball are as common as .200 hitters. In 1970 the average major league salary was $29,204; by 1986 it climbed to $431,521. By position, the highest-paid players in 1986 were outfielder George Foster, $2 million; outfielder Dale Murphy, $1.8 million; outfielder Jim Rice, $1.96 million; first baseman Bob Horner, $1.8 million; second baseman Willie Randolph, $860,000 (an impoverished position); shortstop Ozzie Smith, $1.94 million; third baseman Mike Schmidt, $1.94 million; catcher Gary Carter, $1.96 million; right-handed pitcher Fernando Valenzuela, $1.6 million. Throw in relief pitcher Bruce Sutter ($1.73 million) and manager Pete Rose ($1 million), and the players would form the nucleus of an expensive baseball team.

Years ago Bernard Baruch commented that when the financial news muscled onto the front page, the time had come for people to worry. After he made the remark, the stock market crashed, and his fears were realized. Today sports, another inside section, is forcing its way onto page one. In fact, the sports section is losing its significance. Rather than containing all the important sports news, it has been given the secondary role of keeping the reader up to date on batting averages, won-lost records, conference standings, and the like. The important news—scandals, strikes, cocaine charges, francise shifts, stadium-building bonds, and ownership changes—is front-page fodder. Perhaps it is nothing to worry about, this inordinate concern Americans have for sports. As Willie Davis told reporters after making three errors in one inning in a World Series game, "It's not my wife and it's not my life." But as a cultural indicator, it is enough to give us pause.

There was a time in United States history, back in the pre–World War II era, when sports knew its place in American culture. It was a pastime, diversion, leisure, recreation, play—fun. In sports people found relief from the real things of the world and their own lives—wars, unemployment, social conflict, politics, religion, work, prices, and family. But after World War II, sports assumed an extraordinary significance in people's lives; games became not only a reflection of the changes occurring in the United States but a lens through which tens of millions Americans interpreted the significance of their country, their communities, their families, and themselves. Americans came to take sports very seriously, and they watched and played for the highest economic, politic, and personal stakes.

For tens of millions of Americans, sport was not leisure anymore. Nor was it a distraction from the pressing demands of real life. Sport had become a national obsession, a new cultural currency, a kind of social cement binding a diverse society together. Instead of work, family, or religion, increasingly large numbers of Americans were choosing sport as the focus of their lives. In the 1970s and 1980s, modern America worshipped sport, not only in global arenas but inside the home as well.

We would like to acknowledge the debts we incurred in writing *Winning Is the Only Thing*. Without the encouragement of Stanley Kutler the book would not have been written; he was an ideal editor, friendly, supportive, perceptive, and a fund of knowledge. Henry Tom displayed heroic patience. We thank both men. Our work is a synthesis, which means we have often depended upon the research of others. Scholars such as Benjamin Rader, Allen Guttmann, James Riordan, Richard Espy, and David Voigt have analyzed with insight different aspects of modern sports. We would like to thank Charles C. Alexander for his careful reading of the book; his willingness to sacrifice his time to help other historians demonstrates the continued vitality of the scholarly community. And such journalists as Charles Rosen, Howard Cosell, David Wolf, and Barney Nagler have gone far beyond the simple chronicling of games won and lost. We thank these people, and the others who work in their fields, for their books and articles. The dedication page expresses our thanks to those whose special help was most important of all.

# Winning Is the Only Thing

Track stars like Avery Brundage became innocent cold warriors for the U.S. against the Soviet Union in international sporting events. (Credit: Avery Brundage Collection, University of Illinois)

# • The World That Hiroshima Created

## The Olympic Games and the Cold War

*[Amateur sports] is recreation, it is a pastime or a diversion, it is play, it is action for amusement, it is free, spontaneous and joyous—it is the opposite of work.*
—AVERY BRUNDAGE

The smell of a new age was still in the air. At 9:15 on the morning of August 6, 1945, the bombardier of the B-29 *Enola Gay* pressed his toggle and released a single missile over Hiroshima, a Japanese city of 344,000 people. The bomb dropped for less than sixty seconds, then detonated. At 9:16 A.M. more than 60,000 people in Hiroshima were dead, and the United States had become the first country to use an atomic weapon against another country. Three days later the United States dropped another atomic bomb on Japan, this time on Nagasaki. It destroyed—a more accurate word than killed—over 35,000 people. The two bombs ended the Second World War and ushered in a new age, one characterized by intense nationalism and an uneasy, fearful vision of the future.

Less than two weeks later, a group of distinguished men met in London for a four-day conference. London was suffering from the effects of war and hard times. But most of these men were millionaires, and some were aristocrats by birth. They were the Executive Board of the International Olympic Committee, and they were products of a different age and a different set of values. They believed in the progress of mankind and maintained that amateur sport could serve as a shining example for all nations, lighting the path toward internationalism, humanity, and fair play. For them, the

**1**

recently concluded war had not so much shattered their ideals or created a new system of beliefs as it had simply interrupted the march of Olympic progress. So they met—to rekindle the flame, light the torch, and choose the sites for the 1948 winter and summer Olympic Games. The Olympic motto "Citius, Altius, Fortius" ("faster, higher, stronger") was for the leaders of the IOC a metaphysical as well as an athletic ideal. As one of the men said later about a different event, one he understood no better than the Second World War, "The Games must go on."

They picked London to host the summer Games and Saint-Moritz to host the winter Games. London especially held symbolic significance for the IOC. Although the modern Olympics was the handiwork of Frenchman Baron Pierre de Coubertin, its inspiration was largely English. Coubertin was thoroughly Anglophile. As a youth he had read Hippolyte Taine's *Notes sur Angleterre* and Thomas Hughes's *Tom Brown's School Days* and had developed a deep passion for England. He particularly admired the English public school system, which attempted to develop the mind, body, and soul of all the youths who passed through it. Compared to the dreary routines of French schoolboys, the students at such English institutions as Rugby School seemed to have achieved a higher state. The more Coubertin examined the different national educational systems, the more he was convinced that unless France altered its course, it would be unable to compete against England, Germany, and the United States in its various national rivalries.

The result of Coubertin's study, ideas, and organizational skill was the Olympic Games. In part it was nationalistic. From the time of the first modern Games in 1896 in Athens, national flags and national anthems played a prominent role. Influenced by the writings of French and English Social Darwinists, Coubertin readily accepted that life was a struggle and that the strongest would and should prosper. Indeed, his mission was to make France fitter, if not the fittest. At the same time, the visionary side of Coubertin was drawn to the theme of internationalism. He conceived of the Olympic Games as an athletic World Fair promoting international harmony in sports and by extension political goodwill. Coubertin's Social Darwinism was never ruthless and chaotic; instead it was rule-bound, clothed in the notion of fair play.

An aristocrat, Coubertin visualized the Olympics as a contest where class, sex, and station still mattered. Amateurism, the very core of the Olympic movement, was class-oriented. There had been no such concept in the ancient Olympic Games. For hundreds of years, the Greeks had rewarded and honored their best athletes with money and prizes. In turn, their outstanding athletes devoted themselves to sport. The notion of amateurism originated in Victorian England. For late-nineteenth-century moralists, athletes participated in sport to build character, in pursuit of Muscular Christianity, or simply for sport's own sake—but not for financial gain or as a means of existence. As Allen Guttmann has argued in *The Games Must Go On* (1984), the amateur code was partially an expression of the concept of the Renaissance man, who was proficient in many things but an expert in none of them. "Amateurism in this sense can be traced back to the Renaissance, to the world of Baldassare Castiglione's *Il Cortegiano*, to the courtier who danced, wrote sonnets, played the lute, and commanded armies on the field of battle, who was, however, neither a dancer nor a poet nor a musician nor a soldier." Needless to say, during the late nineteenth century, as during the Renaissance, only the aristocrat could afford the time and expense to be the ideal intellectual, artistic, and athletic dilettante.

For wealthy Victorians, then, sporting activity assumed a casual and social air. They certainly did not have to use sports to achieve any economic ends. This, after all, brought them in contact with professional athletes, men from the lower classes who boxed, ran, and peddled for lucre. In order to prevent the mingling of classes they institutionalized the amateur code. In its purest form, it prohibited competition between wealthy men of leisure and ambitious men from the lower classes. The regulations of the Henley Regatta of 1879 made this point painfully clear: "No person shall be considered an amateur oarsman or sculler . . . who is or has been by trade or employment for wages, a mechanic, artisan, or laborer." It was this rule which prohibited John Kelly, whose daughter Grace became the princess of Monaco, from rowing in the regatta.

Although Coubertin and the other IOC officials dropped the overtly class element of amateurism, they attempted to keep the aristocratic tone of the code. They envisioned athletes as Renaissance men who competed effortlessly and joyously. A competitor could come from any class or occupation as long as he (and later she) did not earn any money as a result of sports. Perhaps the ideal athlete of this school was John Pius Boland. On leave from Oxford, he traveled to Athens in 1896 to watch the first Olympic Games. Once there, he decided to enter the competition and won a gold medal for Great Britain in the singles tennis event. Then when Fritz Traun's doubles partner fell ill, Boland joined the German to capture the gold medal in the doubles competition. Graceful and well-mannered, Boland later became a well-known barrister, politician, and author.

Amateurism was not the only code Coubertin endorsed. He and his fellow IOC members agreed that Olympic competition should be an all-male affair. In this instance, the ancient Greeks had set the precedent. They prohibited women from watching the Olympic Games, and their athletes ran and wrestled in the nude. Although the IOC's Hellenism stopped short of the naked body and did not bar women from watching the Games, it did prohibit female participation in the athletic events. Like most Victorians, Coubertin and his followers believed that female athletes could and should be graceful and stylish, but not competitive.

During the generation after 1896 the IOC permitted females to move from the grandstand to the playing fields. The movement was painfully slow and opposed at every step. Coubertin was one of the leading opponents. As Mary Hanson Leigh noted in her examination of the subject, Coubertin "had not planned for the admission of women, did not want women to be admitted, and fought against their admission for more than thirty years." During the Olympics of the first two decades of the twentieth century, the IOC allowed women to compete in gymnastics and swimming—sports considered suitable for them—but not until 1928 did the IOC agree to sanction female track and field in the Olympics.

And even then the organization found reason to second-guess its decision. The 800-meter race created a nightmare of controversy. It was a good race, a fast and competitive race. The winner, Lina Radke of Germany, broke the old world record by almost three seconds. After the strenuous race, several of the competitors collapsed in exhaustion and had to be given aid. That was enough for antifeminists. Newspapers quoted doctors who said that women who took part in "feats of endurance" would "become old too soon." The IOC debated whether or not it should prohibit female competition in future Games. Women stayed in the Olympic Games, but the 800-meter event was dropped from the female track program until 1960.

The IOC that prepared for the 1948 Olympic Games had changed little from the days of Coubertin. Princes, counts, barons, and marquesses still wielded remarkable influence. And not one female member had ever been elected. It was altogether a singular international organization of wealthy and aristocratic men whose minds and hearts were still locked in the comfortable notions of the nineteenth century. But they were soon to face, however reluctantly, the world that Hiroshima created.

• • •

As the IOC was preparing for the 1948 Olympic Games, the United States and the Soviet Union were exchanging bitter accusations. Before the United States dropped an atomic bomb on Nagasaki the two countries had been wartime allies. The uneasy alliance, more the result of a common enemy than common national concerns, ended soon after the United States signed surrender accords with Japan. Russian control of Eastern Europe and American control of atomic energy divided the two powers as much as ideological differences had before World War II. By early 1946 the battle of words had started. In February 1946 Soviet leader Joseph Stalin warned Russians that there could never be a lasting peace with capitalism. He said that the Soviet Union must prepare to meet the capitalist challenge. Supreme Court Justice William Douglas called the speech "the declaration of World War III." The following month Winston Churchill delivered his "iron-curtain" address in Fulton, Missouri. In vivid and condemnatory language, he remarked that "from Stettin in the Baltic, to Trieste in the Adriatic, an iron curtain has descended across the Continent allowing 'police governments' to rule Eastern Europe." He urged Americans to use their atomic strength to free Europe. Stalin labeled Churchill's speech "a call to war with the Soviet Union." In Russia, Stalin began to purge all Western influences. In the United States, Congress began its attack on "un-American" forces. The Cold War had begun.

International organizations supplied the battlegrounds for the war of words. From the United Nations to the World Bank the Cold War raged. The Olympic Games almost inevitably became involved in Cold War politics. Although in theory the Games had been designed to promote internationalism, in practice they had been used consistently as a showcase of national achievement and power. The Greek government had used the 1896 Olympic Games in Athens as a demonstration of the revival of Greek nationalism, and so it continued as politics, athletic accomplishments, and national pride jostled each other for supremacy every four years. The Berlin Olympics of 1936 climaxed this pre-World War II development. During the Nazi Olympics Hitler demonstrated to the world the beauty, athleticism, power, and vision of his "New Germany." Some visitors—although surprisingly few—also managed a glimpse of another, more dangerous and unsettling, side of Hitler's Germany.

The Berlin Games also demonstrated that the Olympics could be employed to justify a repressive state. Amid the pagan festivity of the 1936 Olympics—a festivity that owed more to the Nuremberg rallies than to any Hellenistic model—Hitler bedazzled the world. Torchlight ceremonials and oceans of waving, smiling youths obscured the reality of Nazi Germany. It was as Hitler planned. Announcing a pre-Olympian holiday, the German Labor Front ordered: "The coming eight days will be days of jollity and cheerfulness. Prior to the strain of the Olympic weeks, Berliners should take stock of themselves, then with merry hearts and friendly expressions on their faces, receive their Olympic guests. None should miss this chance." The vicious Nazi newspaper *Der Angriff* agreed: "We must be more charming than the Parisians, more easygoing than the Viennese, more vivacious than the Romans, more cosmopolitan than London, and more practical than New York." As Richard Mandell observed in *The Nazi Olympics*, Berlin "had been cleaned and dressed for a whole series of festivals that had the common intention of convincing the Germans and their foreign guests that the new Germany was, as it claimed to be, a savior and a creator of culture." And in the end, evil as well as pigeons was released by the Nazi Olympics.

The Second World War forced the cancellation of the 1940 and 1944 Games. Nevertheless, the lessons of Berlin survived the war intact. Politics and sports did and would again mix. It took a while for the Soviet Union to learn the lesson. Czarist Russia had participated in the Olympics, but the Soviet regime spurned "bourgeois" sports and withdrew from the Games. For a short time, the Soviets sponsored a rival to the Olympics, the Rote Sport-Internationale, but it failed to attract much international attention or interest. For Soviet athletes it was like laboring in the minor leagues.

By the mid-1940s the Soviets were ready to return to the major leagues. The Olympic Games were too important of an international forum for the Soviets to reject. During the Cold War, when seemingly insignificant events were transformed by the media into major ideological victories or defeats, the Soviets could not afford to ignore the Olympic Games. They soon discovered, however, that "bourgeois" sports were easier to reject than to join.

The Soviets had to overcome several prickly procedural problems. First, in order to participate in the Olympics, they had to have a recognized national Olympic committee that was politically independent from their own government. Under the Stalinist regime, of course, this was an impossibility. The IOC settled this problem by deciding to ignore the true nature of Soviet sports. Through a fiat by the IOC, the state-controlled Soviet Olympic committee was recognized as a politically independent organization. It was comforting fiction and an easy solution.

An even more vexing problem was the status of the Soviet athletes themselves. Were they professionals or amateurs? Clearly the state supported them and paid them for their victories in international competition and for setting world records. Both government support and cash prizes were in violation of IOC rules. But the IOC wanted Soviet participation; it desired an all-inclusive Olympic Games. Once again an official blindness supplied the most convenient solution. "State amateurism," like "independent" national Olympic committees, became another comforting fiction of international sport.

In 1955 IOC head Avery Brundage recalled the problem with admitting the Soviet Union into the Olympic movement: "There was little that could be said or done on the question of state subsidization of the [Soviet] program. Under Olympic rules, national committees must be independent and autonomous. In communist countries, where everything is subservient to the state, no organization can be independent and autonomous." Of course, something could have been done; the IOC could have demanded changes in the Soviet sports system or denied admission. But in the end, the Olympic ideal of universalism won out over nonpolitical amateurism.

After considerable debate, controversy, and compromise, the

IOC welcomed Soviet athletes into the pure world of amateur sporting competition. But the invitation came after the 1948 Olympic Games. The Russians were not invited to the London Games. Nor, for that matter, was the Israeli team. If the Russian question was complex, the issue of Israeli participation was hopelessly Byzantine. Faced with a threatened Arab boycott if the Israeli flag was flown at the Olympics, the IOC declared Israel ineligible to participate in the London Games.

With a sense of relief, the IOC turned from the pre-Olympics political controversies to the Games themselves. After the Second World War and Hiroshima, and cast against the backdrop of the Berlin Blockade and the Chinese Civil War, the London Games seemed a throwback to simpler times. There were moments of real athletic beauty and even innocence. Bob Mathias, a teenager from Tulare High School in California, amazed the world by becoming the youngest man ever to win the decathlon. When asked how he planned to celebrate his victory, he replied, "I'll start shaving, I guess."

Older and more experienced, Francina "Fanny" Blankers-Koen inspired a hungry Western Europe. At the age of 18, she had competed for Holland at the Berlin Games. Now, twelve years older, married, and mother of two children, she again ran for Holland. Running in the rain and mud of London, she won gold medals in the 100-meter, 200-meter, 80-meter hurdles, and 400-meter relay races. When she returned to Holland, her neighbors gave her a bicycle "so she won't have to run so much."

The heroics of Blankers-Koen and Mathias and the other athletes could not obscure, however, the fundamental fact of the modern Olympics. They were as much a political event as an athletic one. Even the United States's offer to feed all the athletes at the London Games was enlarged into a political issue. The Soviet magazine *Ogonyak* called the offer a trick by American capitalists to turn European hunger into easy profits. Nevertheless, compared to later Olympics, the 1948 Games would be considered uncomplex and nonpolitical.

• • •

In the world of international sports, as in the arena of international political relations, a fundamental shift in responsibilities occurred during the late 1940s and early 1950s. Increasingly, Western Europe looked to the United States as the leader of the democratic nations. In international relations, the shift was obvious. In late 1947 English officials informed the U.S. government that Great Britain could no longer provide sufficient aid to the democratic governments of Greece and Turkey. If those two countries were to be saved from Communist takeovers, the United States would have to provide the desperately needed money. President Truman accepted the new responsibilities for America. Congress responded quickly with the Truman Doctrine, which provided aid for Greece and Turkey, and then with the Marshall Plan, which extended the aid to Western Europe.

The shift was just as evident in international sports. Since 1894 every president and vice-president of the IOC had been European. Then at the first postwar meeting of the IOC, Avery Brundage of the United States was elected vice-president. In 1952 President Sigfrid Edstrom, a tough-minded, short-tempered Swede, decided it was time to retire. Brundage wanted the vacated office, and he had Edstrom's support. But he was an American, and the IOC was a European association. As Prince Axel of Denmark explained to Brundage, "No American should be President of the IOC." Nevertheless after a close vote, Brundage became the first non-European president of the IOC.

It is perhaps ironic that the most important person in world sports during the twentieth century was not a sinuous, fleet athlete but a pudgy, near-sighted administrator. Avery Brundage was as complex as his times. He was an idealist and a hypocrite, a man more comfortable with universal abstractions than with fallible individuals. During his life critics accused him of being an anti-Semite, a Nazi sympathizer, and a Communist stooge. And in fact, there was more than a shred of truth in each accusation.

Brundage was Horatio Alger in gym shorts. His father left home when Avery was five, and his mother went to work to support the family. Avery too worked, but he also went to school and practiced sports. Drawn to track and field, he became a successful high school and college athlete. In 1912 he competed in the Stockholm Olympic Games in the decathlon and pentathlon. Although he failed to qualify for the finals in the decathlon, he finished sixth in the pentathlon. His fellow countryman Jim Thorpe won both events.

After the Olympics Brundage, a trained engineer, went to work. In time, he started his own construction company. Known for his honesty—he once returned the money on a contract he finished on schedule and under cost—by 1927 he had become a millionaire. Although he lost a fortune during the Great Crash of 1929, shrewd real estate investments, especially in California, soon made him again wealthy.

For a man with no real passion for making money, Brundage's success was remarkable. His true love was amateur sports. He competed as long as his body allowed and then channelled his organizational skill into sports administration. By 1928 he was president of both the Amateur Athletic Association (AAA) and the American Olympic Association (AOA). In both organizations he demonstrated unusual administrative skill and tact.

Brundage's failure was that his passion for amateur athletics was too deep. It blinded him to the world around him. The Olympic movement became his religion, and any attack on it he interpreted as blasphemy. When thoughtful and sincere Americans called for the United States to boycott the 1936 Berlin Games as a protest against Nazi discrimination against Jews, Brundage reacted angrily. The boycott movement, Brundage said, was the work of Communists and Jews. As the debate intensified, Brundage became a vitriolic anti-Semite and hardened anti-Communist. It should be emphasized, however, that his hatred both of Jews and Communists was not ideological but, rather, the result of his belief that both groups threatened the Olympic movement.

Brundage even placed his commitment to Olympism above his personal life. Although Brundage's public image was decidedly prudish, he enjoyed the company of women. He seldom allowed his marriage to inhibit his amorous adventures. His longest-lasting affair was with Lilian Dresden, daughter of Karl Gustav Wahamaki, an Olympic gymnast from the 1912 Stockholm Games. Brundage was the father of her two sons. He acknowledged his paternity and set up a trust fund for both children under the stipulations that Lilian and the boys keep the affair secret and that they renounce all further claims to his estate. It appears that Brundage's primary fear was not that the exposure of his affair would destroy his marriage but that it might taint the Olympic movement and crush his chances of being elected president of the IOC. Frederick J. Ruegsegger, Brundage's business manager and closest friend, noted, "In most things, A.B. was a thoroughly honest and honorable man. But during those years in the 1950s, when he was terrified that the truth might come out, that he'd then be forced out of his IOC position, . . . he felt no guilt at all."

As an Olympic administrator, Brundage was committed to the nineteenth-century world of Coubertin. Although a self-made millionaire, he became fawning and obsequious around European aristocrats. Once at lunch with two leading American sports administrators, Brundage noticed the marquess of Exeter and Prince Axel of Denmark enter the restaurant. Allen Guttmann says that "Brundage rose and, with scarcely a word of apology, abandoned his American colleagues in order to join the influential Europeans." It was almost as if he wished to return to the deferential class system of earlier centuries.

Consistent with this attitude, his view of sports mirrored Baron de Coubertin's. Brundage believed in pure amateur sport unsullied by commercialism or ulterior motives. He was not opposed to professional sports, which he viewed as "a branch of the entertainment business." He simply drew his own iron curtain between amateur and professional activities. Whereas professional sport was a job performed by "a troop of trained seals," amateur sport embraced "the highest moral laws." As Brundage commented, amateur sport "is recreation, it is a pastime or a diversion, it is play, it is action for amusement, it is free, spontaneous and joyous—it is the opposite of work." Throughout his years on the IOC, he strenuously opposed any attempt to pollute the pure amateurism which he believed was embodied in the Olympic code. Given the trend toward state amateurism and other assaults on the division between professionalism and amateurism, Brundage's attitude guaranteed conflict within the Olympic movement.

In time Brundage would have to fight battles over creeping commercialism in amateur sports. But during the late 1940s and early 1950s political battles overshadowed commercial conflicts. The admission of the Soviet Union into the IOC solved only one problem. Other, more complex issues confronted the organization. None were more emotional than the issue of politically divided nations. In a world in which twin Chinas, Germanies, and Koreas coexisted uneasily, the IOC found it increasingly difficult to be nonpolitical.

Chinese participation presented an interesting but not unique challenge for the IOC. The Chinese had competed in the prewar Olympics, and three members of the IOC were Chinese. But the Communist victory in China in 1949 created problems. None of the Chinese IOC members followed Chiang Kai-shek to Taiwan. One went to Hong Kong, another to New York, and the other stayed in Peking. Nevertheless, both Nationalist China and the People's Republic of China formed national Olympic committees, picked national teams, and wanted to participate in the 1952 Helsinki Games.

The IOC listened to the arguments of both Chinas and searched for a way out of the messy political and procedural problem. Which team and national committee represented China? Any answer would embroil the IOC in a political nightmare. Finally it struck upon a totally unsatisfactory compromise. The IOC decided that it would not recognize either national Olympic committee but would allow both Chinas to compete in the Helsinki Olympics.

Neither Nationalist China nor the People's Republic of China was satisfied by the decision. Upon hearing the verdict, the Nationalist Chinese promptly protested and withdrew their "team" (composed of a single competitor) from the Games. The larger team from the People's Republic of China received the IOC decision on the way to Helsinki. Whether the team planned to compete or not is difficult to say. It arrived at the Olympics ten days after the start of the Games, too late to participate in any of the events in which it had athletes. In short, no Chinese competed in 1952, and the problem of Chinese recognition was still a long way from settled.

To some extent, the Germany controversy overshadowed the Chinese question. Both the Federal Republic of Germany (West Germany) and the German Democratic Republic (East Germany) formed national Olympic committees, sought recognition by the IOC, and desired to compete in Helsinki. And on its part, the IOC wanted German participation. But the political issues were staggering. The Federal Republic insisted that it represented all Germans, East as well as West, and the Democratic Republic maintained that it was an independent state. Under IOC rules, an individual country could only be represented by a single national Olympic committee.

The question facing the IOC was: Is there one or two Germanies? The answer was bound to arouse political controversies.

The IOC decided that the best solution would be to try to bring the two Germanies together for Olympic purposes. Negotiations started, ended abruptly, commenced again, and ended just as quickly. It was an idea whose time had simply not yet come. By the time of the Helsinki Games the two teams had not been brought together. As a result, West Germany, whose national Olympic committee had earlier been recognized by the IOC, competed in the 1952 Games, but East Germany did not.

The political wranglings before the Games did not end in Helsinki. A mood of struggling nationalism replaced the feeling of joyous competition for many athletes. Spectators, press, and athletes alike focused on the duals between East and West, the Soviet Union and the United States, communist and democratic. Bob Mathias, who won another gold medal in the decathlon, recalled that in Helsinki, "There were many more pressures on American athletes because of the Russians than in 1948. They were in a sense the real enemy. You just love to beat 'em. You just had to beat 'em. It wasn't like beating some friendly country like Australia. This feeling was strong down through the entire team, even [among] members in sports where the Russians didn't excel."

East as well as West encouraged this new and decidedly un-Olympic attitude. The Russians approached the Olympics with a warlike spirit. Soviet leaders believed, as James Riordan noted in his classic study *Sport in Soviet Society*, that "victories over bourgeois states would demonstrate the vitality of the Soviet System." As early as 1949, Andrei Zhdanov, the Party spokesman responsible for ideological and cultural affairs, urged Russian athletes to "win world supremacy in the major sports in the immediate future. . . . Each new victory is a victory for the Soviet form of society and the socialist sports system; it provides irrefutable proof of the superiority of socialist culture over the decaying culture of the capitalist states."

The Soviets traveled to Helsinki prepared to compete and to win, and they were not particularly interested in Olympic fellowship. The only Olympic symbolism they cared about was that which came with gold medals. Before the Games the Kremlin had refused to allow the Olympic torch to be hauled over Soviet territory. And once in Helsinki, the Soviets scorned the common Olympic housing and isolated themselves near the Russian naval base at Pochkalo. Yet Soviets competed in every Olympic event save field hockey, and they performed remarkably well. In a scoring system that awarded points to the top six places, the Soviet Union tied the United States for first place in the Helsinki Games.

For the Western press, the athlete who most visibly represented the Communist system was Czechoslovakian Emil Zatopek. The best distance runner in the world, he ran as if he were in pain or as if he were driven by the demons of the State. He won the 10,000- and 5,000-meter races, and then announced that he would run the marathon. He ran with the same tortured style. At the 15-mile point, he supposedly remarked to the favored English runner James Peters, "Excuse me, I haven't run a marathon before, but don't you think we ought to go a bit faster?" He then picked up the pace and won the race by over two minutes.

The entrance of Cold War politics and emotions into the Olympic Games had several results. In purely athletic terms, nationalistic athletes raised the level of their performance in pursuit of ideological as well as individual glory. In addition, the ideological clash between East and West increased the level of public interest in the Games. The world press fully exploited the symbolism. Each event became a titanic struggle between the Free World and Communism, between State Socialism and Bourgeois Capitalism. In the public mind, the fates of national Olympic teams and Cold War controversies began to intertwine. Soon they would be inseparable.

• • •

Avery Brundage hated this trend, but he was powerless to prevent it. Even within the halls of the IOC, he could not shut out the winds of the Cold War. The election of Soviet officials to the IOC ended the cozy insularity of that aristocratic body. In theory, IOC officials were autonomous. They represented the IOC in their respective countries; they were not supposed to represent their countries in the IOC. To maintain their independence, the wealthy IOC members paid their own expenses to meetings and remained aloof from any political pressure from their own countries.

The Soviet Union shattered that cozy practice. Soviet members of the IOC were first and foremost bureaucrats of the Soviet Union— paid by, loyal to, and instructed by their government. Once inside the IOC, Soviet officials introduced purely political topics and sought a political reorganization of the entire body. Konstantin Andrianov, the leading Russian IOC member, envisioned an IOC that would resemble the United Nations, where each country had one vote and bloc voting prevailed. Although most of his reorganization schemes failed, bloc voting soon took hold in the IOC.

As the IOC prepared for the 1956 Games in Melbourne, Australia, it faced a series of old and new political questions. The organization had yet to decide the Olympic fate of Germany and China—or the Germanies and the Chinas. For the Soviet members of the IOC, the recognition of an independent East German Olympic Committee was the most important issue. Andrianov pressed the issue, and the IOC members debated it for several years. Finally, the IOC recognized the East German Olympic committee, but it insisted that East and West Germany compete in the 1956 Games as a single German team. East Germany agreed. Brundage believed it was a great accomplishment for the Olympic movement. As he told his fellow IOC members, "We have obtained in the field of sport what politicians have failed to achieve."

The Chinese issue was not so easily settled. In 1954 the IOC decided to recognize the Olympic committees of both Nationalist China and the People's Republic of China and invite both countries to the 1956 Games. Neither the Communists nor the Nationalists, however, was very happy with the solution. Once in the IOC, representatives of the two countries initiated a series of bitter and petty squabbles. In the 1955 meeting in Paris, for example, Brundage discovered that someone had crossed out the words "Formosan China" from the attendance list that had been passed around. In his biography of Brundage, Allen Guttmann described the seriocomic scene: "When [Brundage] complained about the schoolboy trick, Jung Kao-tung of the Communists' national Olympic committee rose to proclaim that there was only one China, which represented the entire Chinese people: Formosa ought to be erased. And Formosa too." It was hardly a high point in the Olympic movement, but the event was indicative of the politicization of the IOC and the erosion of the Olympic spirit.

The bickering continued. The Communists demanded that the IOC bar Formosa from the Melbourne Games. The IOC refused. In protest, the People's Republic of China boycotted the Games. Yet when the Nationalists arrived in Melbourne, the Communists' flag was raised over their quarters. This led to more protests. In all, it was strikingly like a scene from a Marx Brothers' movie.

But there was nothing comic about the mood of the world on the eve of the Games. In late October and early November 1956, less than a month before the Melbourne Games began, a series of tragic and potentially very serious conflicts disrupted the uneasy status quo of the Cold War. The first started in Egypt, where President Gamal Abdel Nasser was struggling to remain above the Cold War and strike a neutral course for his country. Since both the United States and the Soviet Union eyed neutrals with suspicion, Nasser faced a difficult task. Trying to win his favor, the United States offered him a $56 million loan for the construction of the Aswan High Dam on the Nile. The proposed loan, however, did not prevent Nasser from pursuing amicable relations with Russia and the People's Republic of China. Upset by what he interpreted as ungrateful behavior, on July 19, 1956, Secretary of State John Foster Dulles publicly cancelled the American loan to Egypt.

Nasser soon struck back. On July 26 he nationalized the Suez Canal and announced that Israel would not receive protection for its shipping. The action threatened not only Israel but also England and France, which depended upon access to the canal for most of their oil supplies. A crisis atmosphere hung over London and Paris. Something had to be done. But what? Short on sound ideas, English prime minister Anthony Eden, French premier Guy Mollet, and Israeli premier David Ben-Gurion hatched a complicated plot. According to the Tripartite Declaration of 1950, Britain and France could take over the Suez Canal if war broke out between Israel and Egypt. For the three leaders, the course was clear.

On October 29, Israel invaded Egypt. Two days later, English bombers attacked Egyptian airfields, preparatory to a joint Anglo-French invasion of the Suez. All was going according to the plan. On November 5 British paratroopers secured the north end of the canal. Soviet Premier Nikolai Bulganin was furious. He threatened a Soviet military response. In the United States, President Dwight Eisenhower was just as enraged. He had to interrupt his campaign for reelection to return to Washington, and, as one observer reported, "The White House crackled with barracks-room language." For once, America and Russia were on the same side, and the thought made Eisenhower uncomfortable. Unsure of what the Soviets might do, the president put the Strategic Air Command on alert and warned the military, "If those fellows start something, we may have to hit 'em—and, if necessary, with everything in the bucket."

He did not use the bucket, for Russia was not about to act. Serious problems closer to home had Soviet leaders looking for their own buckets. While the Royal Air Force attacked the canal zone, Hungarian revolutionaries were actively involved in anti-Soviet demonstrations. Imre Nagy, the nationalistic premier of Hungary, moved rapidly. He denounced the Warsaw Pact, which tied Hungary to the Soviet defense community, and announced plans for a truly independent and democratic Hungary.

The Kremlin reacted with brutal swiftness. Sweeping into Budapest, the Red Army used bullets to end the anti-Soviet demonstrations. Hundreds of Hungarian revolutionaries died in the streets. The world could only watch the slaughter. A Soviet veto froze any United Nations action, and Bulganin ignored all official and unofficial protests.

Neither the Suez Crisis nor the Hungarian Revolution disrupted the status quo of the Cold War. Eisenhower ended the Suez Crisis by condemning the coordinated Israeli, British, and French invasion of Egypt. On election day, November 6, Prime Minister Eden informed Eisenhower that England and France were ending their invasion. The Kremlin's use of unbridled force doomed the Hungarian Revolution.

Two weeks after the crises concluded, the Melbourne Games started. The atmosphere was heavy, and signs of protest were visible. Several nations boycotted the Games altogether. Egypt, Lebanon, and Iraq wanted no part of any Games that included Britain, France, and Israel. Holland and Spain boycotted the Games in protest of the Soviet invasion of Hungary. How, their protest implied, could the world think of sports and peaceful competition against the Russians when the streets of Budapest were still red with the blood of Hungarian patriots?

IOC President Avery Brundage attempted to explain. "Every civilized person recoils in horror at the savage slaughter in Hungary, but . . . the Olympic Games are contests between individuals and not between nations." In fact, he continued, "In an imperfect world, if participation in sport is to be stopped every time the politicians violate the laws of humanity, there will never be any international contests." Brundage had a point, but few people could take such a dispassionate attitude toward the separation of sports and politics.

Tensions during the Games often ran high. The most dramatic moments of the Olympics occurred in a water polo match between Hungary and the Soviet Union. Although the match started conventionally enough, athletic competition soon gave way to a form of aquatic warfare. The Hungarian players were the best in the world, but they sought more than simply victory; they wanted to physically hurt the Russians. Blood spilled into the water as the two teams tore into each other. Finally, with Hungary leading 4–0, the referee halted the brawl, awarding the game to Hungary. Afterward, Olympic officials had to summon the police when angry spectators tried to exact further revenge on the Soviet players.

Even when the athletes appeared friendly, the competition was ferocious. This was particularly true in events which displayed power and strength. Because of the symbolism inherent in producing the strongest men and women, Soviet sports leaders emphasized the weight events in track and field, boxing, wrestling, and weightlifting more than most other events. And in these events, Soviet athletes made remarkable gains. They were, however, paying an equally remarkable price.

By 1954 the Soviet sports establishment had discovered the athletic uses of testosterone, a male-produced hormone. In that year, Dr. John B. Ziegler, a U.S. national team physician during the 1950s, noticed the improvements Soviet weightlifters were making. He noticed other things as well: "What caught my attention was the young athletes having to get catherized, which is a tube they insert into the urinary tract so they can urinate. This procedure is usually used for old men who have prostate trouble." A friendly Soviet physician explained to Ziegler the reasons for the improved performances and prostate problems. The Russians were taking straight testosterone, which helped to build muscle mass and strength. Upon his return to the United States, Ziegler worked with CIBA Pharmaceutical to develop the original anabolic steroid, an artificially produced derivative of testosterone. By the end of 1956, the marriage between drugs and athletics had been made both in the Soviet Union and the United States.

To be sure, testosterone was not the sole reason for the Russian victories in the Melbourne Games. By then it was clear to most ob-servers that the Soviet achievement was the result of careful plan-ning and painstaking effort. Russian physicians had transformed athletic success into an exacting science. They studied blood oxy-genation in long distance runners and examined psychological stress on sprinters. They left as little to chance as possible as they coached, trained, and pampered their athletes. Using the resources of the state, they forged a winning team. In 1956 the Soviet team won 98 medals, compared to 74 for the United States. Neither Russians nor Americans ignored these results. After decades of athletic domi-nance, the United States found itself second best.

The harmonious ending of the Melbourne Games did not obscure this point. The athletes might mix in a warm and spon-taneous celebration of youth and competition—as they did during the closing ceremonies—but the older, more cynical politicians at home were busy calculating the propagandistic value of the Games. In their games athletes were pawns, and they were the principal players. International sport was simply another nonmilitary means of achieving diplomatic and strategic goals.

The overtly political nature of the 1956 Olympics did not de-tract from the Games. Rather, it heightened interest in them. For Americans and Soviets, each event became an athletic contest and a morality play, a struggle between the forces of light and darkness, capitalism and communism. The American-Russian competition during the Olympic Games may also have had a cathartic effect on the citizens of both countries. Each little peaceful war served as a focus for pent-up emotions, anxieties, and hostilities. As a result, after the Games, United States and Soviet track officials announced a tentative agreement to hold joint track and field meets each year. Athletic warfare, they had decided, served the ends of the state.

Even after the dual meets began, the Olympics remained the centerpiece of international sports. By 1956, the Games had become predictable; each followed a set pattern. First came inter-Olympic political maneuvering and name-calling. This was followed by the Games themselves, during which competition was furious but out-wardly harmonious. Athletes competed as national soldiers of sport, then embraced their enemy after they had completed their mock war.

Almost as if they were following a script, the members of the

IOC prepared for the 1960 Olympics, to be held in Rome. The old political problems once again took the floor. Reluctantly, the two Germanies agreed to form a single team. Other countries, however, were not so agreeable. In particular, the People's Republic of China approached the Games in a mood of deep suspicion.

The relationship between Brundage and Tung Shou-yi, the PRC's representative to the IOC, wavered between farce and tragedy. Always an idealist when it came to the Games, Brundage insisted that Tung keep politics out of the increasingly politicized Olympics. The two men exchanged vituperative letters. Tung noted that Brundage, not he, had introduced politics into the Games. And besides, "There is only one China in the world and that is the People's Republic of China." Finally in August 1958 the heated exchange reached its climax. Tung accused Brundage of being "a faithful menial of the U.S. imperialists bent on serving their plot of creating two Chinas." He added that the IOC president had stained the Olympic spirit and violated the Olympic charter. With that said, Tung resigned from the IOC. The resignation was part of a general Communist Chinese withdrawal from international sports. Anti-Western forces were growing stronger, as was the crusade to purge Western influences in China, and the Olympic Games were certainly a Western influence. For almost two and a half decades, Communist China ignored most international sports.

The Communist Chinese were gone, but the Nationalist Chinese stayed in the IOC, a fact the Soviets greatly deplored. Essentially, the Russians argued that the IOC should withdraw recognition from the Chinese National Olympic Committee in Taiwan because it did not represent China, which was not an island but a country of some 600 million people. After a long debate, the IOC reached a compromise. The organization altered its own rules to state that Olympic committees could be recognized by the IOC only "under the name of the territory in which they operate." The Republic of China could compete in the Olympics, but only under the banner of Formosa. In the United States, journalists and politicians accused Brundage and the IOC of abandoning tiny Formosa. Once called an imperialist and a Nazi and a capitalist, Brundage was now labeled a Communist stooge. Nevertheless, the IOC verdict was a wise one. It laid the groundwork for future recognition of such countries as East Germany and North Korea. Over a decade after the Cold War had started, the IOC was beginning to come to terms with its realities.

But as the IOC solved one political issue, others, like mushrooms, seemed to emerge full-grown overnight. The most pressing of the new problems concerned South Africa. The Soviets accused the South African National Olympic Committee (SANOC) of violating Olympic rules against free and equal competition. Quite correctly, Andrianov, the leading Soviet member of the IOC, charged that the South African apartheid policy in sport was a clear violation of the Olympic charter. South African officials tried to evade the thrust of the charge by claiming that blacks of Olympic caliber would not be discriminated against. As far as Brundage was concerned, that settled the problem. If the IOC representative from South Africa said that discrimination did not exist in his country's Olympic committee, then it did not exist. After all, Brundage and the IOC had accepted Andrianov's word that none of the Soviet athletes were professional.

For the 1960 Games the case was closed. But the Soviets had probed a sensitive spot. Apartheid was an embarrassment for the West and a burning issue in Black Africa. By harping on the issue, Andrianov placed Brundage in the uncomfortable position of having to wink at blatant racism and at the same time raised the image of the Soviet Union in the eyes of Black African nationalists. In the years to come, South Africa would replace China as the single greatest problem for IOC officials.

By 1960 the Olympic movement that Brundage so loved had all but died. White, Western, aristocratic dominance was on the wane. Even among the IOC members themselves, amateurism was declining. The marquess of Exeter, an English aristocrat who spoke for the future, proposed a 5 percent surcharge on tickets to the Olympics, with the proceeds going to the IOC and the international sports federations. He believed that the IOC tradition of members paying all their own expenses was anachronistic, particularly as the IOC accepted poorer countries into its fold. What was wrong with the IOC raising money to help pay expenses for its less affluent members? In addition, Exeter maintained, an independent IOC-controlled expense fund would combat the growing influence national governments exerted over their IOC members. Brundage strenuously opposed Exeter's plan. It had no place in his ideal world of pure amateurism.

Television would soon destroy the last vestiges of amateurism. It also increased the level of nationalism. Increased media exposure raised the value of the Olympic Games as a propagandistic tool. Now the world could watch as well as read about a Soviet triumph in wrestling or an American victory in track. The battle between capitalism and communism became more visible and therefore more important. National rivalries ran higher than ever in Rome. Few spectators lamented the loss of internationalism. As a *Sports Illustrated* editorialist noted, "Like sex, you can't make nationalism unpopular." He viewed a bit of the old flag-waving as a healthy sign: "We don't feel at all abashed about urging our boys in Rome to go out and beat the pants off the Russians and everyone else."

Unfortunately for the American partisans, Soviet and other athletes presented a formidable challenge. In both the summer and the winter Games, Soviet performers won the most medals. Americans offered a wide variety of excuses. Some blamed the judges; others criticized American athletes who sampled too much of the nightlife of Rome. *Sports Illustrated* noted that Roman water created problems for American athletes. The excuses offered, however, were less important than the fact that they were offered at all. As far as most Americans were concerned, the "American system," more than individual American athletes, was the real loser at Rome.

Nationalism was not restricted to the United States and the Soviet Union. Athletes from other countries also battled for Olympic gold medals. Germans—and particularly East Germans—recorded victories in glamorous events. Perhaps the most memorable event of the Rome Games, however, was the marathon. Running barefoot, Ethiopian Abebe Bikila, a guard at Haile Selassie's palace, won in a stunning upset. As he ran up to Via dei Trionfi toward the floodlit Arch of Constantine it became clear that the Olympic Games were for all nations—big and small, rich and poor, powerful and weak. Ethiopia as well as America and Russia could transform Olympic gold into rich propagandistic advantages.

By the conclusion of the Rome Olympics, the course of the modern Games was set. The cement of the Games was national self-interest. In the future East, West, and the Third World would fully exploit the Olympics for the ends of the state. Athletes were on the road toward becoming pawns and employees of the state. Increasingly they would be paid and trained by the state. To improve their performances, they would dedicate their lives to their sports and risk their health by taking dangerous, performance-improving drugs. A latecomer in the Olympics, television would accelerate and dramatize these trends. Like arms dealers, it would turn Cold War tensions into the basis of a profitable business. And old, crotchety Avery Brundage would increasingly become the voice in the wilderness.

Jackie Robinson found that the baseball diamond was more accepting of black Americans than most of the other places in the nation.
(Credit: UPI/Bettmann Newsphotos)

# ● The Integration of American Sports

*Perhaps there should be an asterisk after the record of every athlete who competed before 1946, before Jackie Robinson.*
—DAVID HALBERSTAM

**N**ot just the Olympics were being politicized. In the ideologically charged atmosphere of the Cold War, sports became a new vehicle for the Horatio Alger rags-to-riches legend, a way for Americans to reassure themselves about their destiny and project their values on a global scale. Generations of immigrants, beginning with the original colonists, had looked to the New World as the land of opportunity—a place free enough of tradition and vested institutions to give ambition and ability full play. With the Soviet Union and Communism predicting the demise of capitalism and the triumph of collectivism as the wave of the future, Americans put a premium on equality of opportunity, the right of any individual to become prosperous if he or she had the necessary abilities.

But the condition of black people in the United States, as it had done so often in the past, contradicted the ideology of opportunity, and Soviet propaganda exploited the discrepancy. The rhetoric of opportunity had a peculiarly hollow ring for black people. Not only did they suffer from poverty and gross political discrimination; they could not even get on the same baseball diamond, basketball court, or football field with whites in America. Professional sport was still segregated. It was hardly a new problem. As far back as the American Revolution the hypocrisy of fighting for freedom while allowing slavery to exist had bothered many consciences, and more recently the Japanese had tried to exploit negative American attitudes toward minority groups. The United States was about to witness once again a confrontation between the rhetoric of freedom and the reality of racism and discrimination. The drama began on a baseball diamond in New Jersey.

On April 18, 1946, the sports world focused on Jersey City. Not since Jack Dempsey knocked out Georges Carpentier there in 1921 had the city on the banks of the Passaic River attracted so much national interest. Mayor Frank Hague, "the Boss," was there, as were curious fans and sportswriters from New York, Philadelphia, Baltimore, and cities further west. It was opening day for the Jersey City Giants of the International League. But that wasn't the reason for the interest. Professional baseball, "organized baseball," was about to be integrated. Playing second base for the Montreal Royals, the Brooklyn Dodgers' leading farmteam, was Jack Roosevelt Robinson, a pigeon-toed, thick-necked, highly competitive, and marvelously talented black athlete.

Robinson's debut came when he walked toward the batter's box with one out in the first inning. He was greeted by a polite, slightly reserved applause. He was nervous, recalling later that his hands were "too moist to grip the bat." Warren Sandell, a promising pitcher, threw the ball. Robinson didn't swing. Sandell threw four more pitches, and four more times Robinson stood motionless. On the next pitch Robinson swung, hitting a grounder to the shortstop who threw Jackie out at first. It was a start—of sorts.

Integration of the major leagues brought white people face to face with their most entrenched racial attitudes. Racial stereotypes had long histories, reaching back to the first confrontation of Englishmen and Africans in the sixteenth century. Two hundred years of slavery reinforced the initial judgments. During the antebellum era and after the Civil War, the "Sambo" image captivated white America, convincing an entire nation that blacks were hopelessly different, instinctive rather than thoughtful, physical rather than intellectual, complacent rather than ambitious. Strong and rhythmical, libidos unrestrained, spirits dominated by the flesh, blacks seemed almost animal-like in their preoccupations, given to song and dance and games. But a genetic predisposition to play did not, according to the prevailing mythology, prepare blacks for American sports. Sambo loved to play, not compete; he was an adult child, afflicted with a short attention span, low intelligence, infantile dependency, deeply ingrained laziness, and a tropical inclination to lethargy. Black skills were natural but undisciplined and unreliable. The manifest talent of Bill "Bojangles" Robinson would always be undermined by the outrageous shortcuts of the Kingfish, the incompetence of Butterfly McQueen, or the slow-motion dim-wittedness of Stepin-Fetchit.

Whites considered blacks incapable of organized team sports, where raw talent and brute strength were secondary to mental acuity, careful planning, and coordinated execution. Hit-and-run plays, sacrifice bunts, full-court presses, line-of-scrimmage audibles, formation shifts, diagrammed movements, and memorized playbooks required skills in short supply, it was thought, among black athletes. Imagine Sambo trying to master Knute Rockne's single-wing shift or a Tinkers-to-Evans-to-Chance double play. Nor could whites imagine blacks playing with the intensity of Ty Cobb, the dedication of Lou Gehrig, or the dignity of Joe DiMaggio. Nature had designed them to laugh, sing, dance, and play but not to sacrifice, train, work, compete, and win. Why should they be any more successful in sports than they had been in life?

Ultimately blacks were judged inferior to white athletes, who were viewed as more intelligent, more competitive, and sounder in the basics of a given sport. About this mythology there was a certain speciousness. In large part, black athletic inferiority was based upon the fact that they were invisible athletes. First whites legally excluded them from big-time professional sports; then, because no blacks played in these contests, whites concluded that blacks were inferior athletes. So powerful was the grip of racism in America that few questioned the logic behind such assumptions. Larry King, reflecting on his West Texas boyhood in the 1930s in *The Confessions of a White Racist*, remembers visiting the town's black high school football games, the white boys "swaggering in our purple and gold letter jackets, sure of our superiority as men and athletes." When the black school's team bus pulled away after a game, at the white school's field, a young black man loudly proclaimed the superiority of the black team over any white team. "We stood rooted, amazed at his black audacity. . . . Burton, a wild and wiry little wingback, recovered sufficiently to shout, 'Piss on you, you boog fuckers'—for which withering witticism we young gentlemen roundly congratulated him."

Even in boxing, the one professional sport where whites and blacks competed against each other at all levels, the myths were still strong. When Jack Johnson battled Tommy Burns for the heavyweight crown in 1908, whites implored Burns to "hit the coon in the stomach." Whites assumed—indeed, scientists said they had "proved"—that blacks had weak stomachs and lacked the superb conditioning of white fighters. Their only advantage, a hard head, was the result of a greater inferiority. Blacks were said to have thicker skulls because they had smaller brains. And even though Johnson exploited the myths by allowing Burns to pound away at his midsection, the myths like unwanted guests lingered.

By the 1930s and 1940s the myths had been refined but remained unchanged in their essentials. Jesse Owens, the son of Alabama sharecroppers, flirted with white adulation after winning four gold medals at the 1936 Olympics in Berlin, despite Adolf Hitler's predictions of Aryan superiority. Owens was acclaimed throughout the country. But journalists did more than describe Owens' feats; they felt compelled to explain them as well. His success posed a threat to segregated America, and the public needed reassurance. They resorted to racial explanations. James Kieran of the *New York Times* wrote that "it takes time to work up endurance, but speed comes by nature." Frederick Lewis Allen claimed that "Negroes are especially well fitted emotionally for the sort of brief, terrific effort which sprints and jumps require." And Grantland Rice, the dean of American sportswriters, thought Owens and the other black Olympians had "easily, almost lazily, and minus any show of effort, . . . turned sport's greatest spectacle into the 'black parade of 1936'."

Worse was still to come. The day after winning his fourth gold medal, Owens began a tour of Europe on behalf of the Amateur Athletic Union, running eight times in ten days on a starvation-level per diem allowance. Tired of it, he refused to go to Sweden and run some more. Avery Brundage, a member and future dictator of the International Olympic Committee, was outraged. Owens went home and was soon stripped of his amateur status, ending his chance for a track and field scholarship to finish college. Back in the United States, Jesse's parents were turned away from the Hotel New Yorker in Manhattan because they were black. To make some money off his athletic feats, Jesse was reduced to a national tap-dancing tour with comedian Eddie Cantor and racing exhibitions against trains, motorcycles, and horses, proving he was like an animal or a machine.

The other black hero of the 1930s and 1940s was Joe Louis, whose rise to greatness was incredibly swift. Sportswriters transformed Louis into the very symbol of primordial man. Grantland Rice wrote:

> For he is part of years long lost, back in an age-old beat,
> Where strength and speed meant life and love—and death ran with
>   defeat
> For those who slugged the dinosaur, or lived on mammoth's meat.

Louis, and blacks in general, was thus seen as atavistic, a visible reminder of man's uncivilized past. Bill Corwin, writing for the *Chicago Sunday Herald and Examiner* after Louis knocked out Max Schmeling in the first round of their 1938 rematch, sounded a near-univeral white note: "Nobody will ever beat the Louis you saw last night. Not a Joe Louis who still is young, well-trained—and mad. . . . When the animal in this placid, quiet Negro boy surges into his fists, . . . hc's a killer supreme."

A killer, but a black killer, which whites interpreted as one who lacked heart and intelligence. When Louis was defeated by Schmeling in their first fight, reporters were quick to comment that his "heart just quit sooner" than his white opponent's. And throughout his career Louis was criticized for his poor showings against "clever" (always white) boxers. This was ascribed to Louis's weak mind. Dan Daniel, a leading boxing writer, noted, "When the mental giants of the ring are listed by posterity, the name of Joe Louis Barrow will be found quite a distance below Jim Corbett, Bob Fitzsimmons, and the erudite [Gene] Tunney." By implication, Daniel not only questioned Louis's intelligence but also Johnson's, one of the cleverest champions in the history of the ring, who was left out of the writer's short list of "mental giants."

Everything about white America's attitude toward Louis had overtones of racism. His nicknames—the Brown Bomber, the Dark Destroyer, the Sepia Socker—emphasized equally his race and his ability. Sometimes he was portrayed as a destructive machine—cold, ruthless, unemotional. He was "the greatest fighting machine" or "the closest approach to a human robot one ever saw."

Occasionally he was pictured as a jungle animal—stalking, pouncing, killing. He was a panther, a lion, a jungle cat. He was a machine and he was an animal. He was everything but a man. It was an attitude not too far removed from that of Richard Ligon, a white slavetrader in Barbados in the 1650s, who felt Africans were "neer the beast, setting aside their souls."

So to most whites the rules against blacks playing in the major leagues was more a recognition of fundamental differences between the races than any outright discrimination. White Americans, already conditioned by radio and film images like "Amos and Andy," were more comfortable watching black athletes who conformed to less threatening stereotypes—Sambos in sweats, clowns whose antics, tricks, and mischief were more in place on a vaudeville stage than a field or arena. The Harlem Globetrotters were a perfect symbol. They were the most famous sports team in the world during the 1940s and 1950s, and several players—Goose Tatum, Meadowlark Lemon, Marques Haynes, Choker Red Harrison, and Sweetwater Clifton—enjoyed celebrity status. Since Abe Saperstein founded the group in 1927, the Trotters had performed on every continent, from Madison Square Garden and the Boston Garden to cracker-box high school gymnasiums in the South to black-top outdoor courts in Africa and South America. In the guise of American liberalism, even a sincere liberalism, Saperstein touted the Trotters as ambassadors for the United States, symbols of American success, racial justice, and the reality of the Horatio Alger story. The Trotters were perfect advertising copy for Cold War propaganda, an image of American virtue. International tours, command performances for royalty, feature movies, and television contracts gave the Globetrotters extraordinary exposure, and throughout the world they became known as the "Clown Princes" of basketball.

Clowns they were, innocent caricatures of American racism, vaudevillians not competitors, contemporary Sambos "Uncle Tomming" to the strains of "Sweet Georgia Brown" with the paternalistic Abe in the background orchestrating their wide-eyed, toothy, lip-curling smiles and court and camera mugging. White audiences loved it—Marques Haynes dribbling circles around his hapless white opponents while the rest of the Trotters stretched out on the floor feigning sleep; Meadowlark Lemon hiding the basketball under his jersey and sneaking down the court to make a basket; Goose

Tatum slam-dunking while reading a comic book; all of them cavorting around with deflated, lopsided, or balloon balls, throwing confetti-filled water buckets on a indulgent crowd, deviously getting away with every conceivable infraction of the rulebook.

Saperstein consciously played to the racial expectations of white ticketbuyers and television viewers. Although the Globetrotters were headquartered in Chicago, Abe claimed Harlem as home. In the mid-1920s, the Harlem Renaissance in the arts and education was giving the black ghetto in Manhattan increasing visibility and, for many whites, an amusing notoriety, and Saperstein exploited it. He wanted good athletes, but more than that he wanted entertainers who could delight whites with a good show—sporting facsimiles of Rochester, Andy, Uncle Remus, and Buckwheat. Saperstein also thought whites got a kick out of "ugly Negroes," and he expressed preferences for what he considered "ugly": Ubangi-like lips, Stepin Fetchit eyes, and Neanderthal brows. On a tour through the small towns of the South, Saperstein once noticed a particularly "ugly" black man walking along the road, stopped the bus, and immediately pressed him into service as a Globetrotter, even though the man had never played basketball. In that instance ugliness was a greater asset than talent.

Abe had only three hard rules for "his boys": never get caught romancing white women, contradicting white men, or driving Cadillacs. Saperstein was acutely aware that Globetrotter popularity was a fragile thing. White people wanted to see "happy darkies," not "uppity niggers," and Abe felt the line between the two was exceedingly fine. For most Americans in the 1940s and 1950s, the Harlem Globetrotters, the "Clown Princes of basketball," epitomized black athletes: hilariously funny, naturally talented, but temperamentally unsuited for commitment and competition in the big leagues. Few white parents ever urged their sons to grow up and be like the Goose or Meadowlark.

The Harlem Globetrotters, though the most visible, was not the only black sports team trapped by racial stereotypes. Although most black baseball teams played serious ball, a number of them in the 1930s and 1940s used comedy and burlesque to boost ticket sales, especially if there was any chance of tapping into a sizeable white audience. Pregame antics included acrobatics and dancing, exaggerated black English, minstrel slapstick, and grinning, lots of grinning. The Indianapolis Clowns pushed it to the point of absurdity in the late 1930s and early 1940s, coming on field in grass skirts and body paint, sporting outlandish names, and engaging in as much comedy as baseball. Not surprisingly, the Clowns barnstormed around the country until 1968, the last of the all-black baseball teams. How could any reasonable person expect major league performances out of people playing baseball in grass skirts and war paint?

But here was Jackie Robinson stepping up to the plate in the third inning for his second at-bat, testing history once again. With runners on first and second and nobody out, Robinson lashed out at the first pitch and hit a line-drive home run over the left field fence. In the fifth inning he had a bunt single, stole second, advanced to third on a ground ball, and, faking an attempt to steal home, forced a balk and scored anyway. The crowd went wild. In the seventh, Jackie singled to right field, stole second, and scored on a triple. One inning later, he bunted safely again, advanced two bases to third on an infield hit, then forced a second balk and scored. He was tough, intense, fast, and smart, the equal of any white ballplayer, and the world knew it right away.

The time was ripe for change. For the previous five years the country had been in the middle of a vast struggle against fascism, and the second-class status of black people in the United States had become painfully apparent, providing the Nazis with more than enough fuel for their propaganda machines. As World War II turned into the Cold War, the Soviet Union offered the same criticism: the United States was hardly the land of equality and equal opportunity. A million blacks had fought for their country in the army and navy during the war, only to return home and find Jim Crow firmly in place. But there were differences too. Millions of blacks had relocated to northern cities in the previous thirty years, gaining a political power they had not enjoyed since Reconstruction. The urban machines of the Democratic party needed black votes, and the mass-production unions of the Congress of Industrial Organizations needed their support. Blacks were becoming the most loyal Democrats in the country and less and less patient with segregated schools, restaurants, theaters, housing, and parks. In 1944 the Supreme Court outlawed white primaries in the South, and two years later it prohibited segregation in public buses crossing state lines.

Self-conscious and vulnerable, millions of whites were ready for change.

Branch Rickey, the Dodger general manager, saw an opportunity to take advantage of changing attitudes, and in Jackie Robinson he made the perfect choice. Intelligent and hardworking, a high school graduate with almost four years of college at UCLA, a veteran army officer, and an active Methodist, Robinson was not a smoker, drinker, or womanizer. And he was so physically gifted. He came to UCLA from a junior college in 1940 and starred in four sports. He was the leading scorer for two years playing basketball in the Pacific Coast Conference and an All-American halfback on the football team. Robinson won the Pacific Coast Conference golf championship and the swimming championship at UCLA. He played tennis too, making it all the way to the semifinals in the national tournament for blacks. Jackie Robinson was perfect for the assault on the color line—Jesse Owens and Booker T. Washington rolled into one and suited up in Dodger blue. Jackie hit .347 with Montreal in 1946 and led the team to the Little World Series championship.

But Robinson was not alone in 1946. Branch Rickey was carefully planning the integration of baseball, and when he put Jackie up in Montreal, he placed Roy Campanella, a 5 foot 9, 200-pound catcher from the U.S. All-Stars who could also steal bases, and 6 foot 4 pitcher Don Newcombe, on the rosters of Nashua, New Hampshire, in the New England League; and pitchers John Wright and Roy Partlow at Three Rivers in Quebec for the Canadian-American League. Because Robinson came up to the majors first, he was by far the most prominent of the first blacks to play in the big leagues.

But baseball was not the only sport which was changing. Integration also came to football, basketball, bowling, and tennis. The color line had started to fade. The Cleveland Rams relocated their franchise to Los Angeles in 1946, and to boost ticket sales, they signed Kenny Washington and Woody Strode, Robinson's former UCLA teammates, to professional contracts. Paul Brown, head coach of the new Cleveland Browns in the All-American Football Conference, signed Bill Willis, a lineman from Ohio State, and fullback Marion Motley of Nevada. In July 1947 Bill Veeck, the new owner of the Cleveland Indians, crossed the color line in the American League and gave a contract to hard-hitting Larry Doby of the Newark Eagles in the Negro Leagues. The National Basketball League integrated in the 1946–47 season, when the Rochester Royals signed William "Dolly" King to a contract. The National Basketball Association did not sign its first blacks until 1950, when the Boston Celtics gave Chuck Cooper of Duquesne a contract and the New York Knicks took Nat "Sweetwater" Clifton, despite Abe Saperstein's bitter protests, away from the Harlem Globetrotters. The American Bowling Congress opened the lanes to blacks in 1949, and in 1950 Althea Gibson broke the color barrier in the U.S. Tennis Association's national tournament at Forest Hills.

Branch Rickey's decision to integrate the major leagues triggered diverse reactions throughout the country. Blacks were ecstatic. Black newspapers, black churches, and groups like the NAACP and the National Urban League transformed Jackie Robinson into a new hero, rivaling Jesse Owens and Joe Louis in the sports pantheon. The Brooklyn Dodgers became *the* baseball team of black America, and every morning in the spring and summer blacks throughout the country wondered "how Jackie had done" the day before. They also flocked to the ball parks, to the segregated bleachers of minor league teams in the South, spring training camps, and the major stadiums of the North. Baseball attendance broke all previous records in 1947, and the Dodgers drew 1.8 million fans to watch Jackie Robinson take Rookie of the Year and the "Bums" win the National League pennant.

Other reactions were far more mixed. At a 1946 meeting, major league owners voted 15 to 1 in opposition to Rickey's proposal to integrate. Owners worried that attendance would falter, that white fans would not show up to watch black players or sit next to large numbers of black fans in the bleachers. In Baltimore and Newark in 1946, blacks accounted for more than 50 percent of the crowd, and Larry MacPhail of the Yankees claimed integration might dramatically reduce the net worth of their franchises. They also worried that the Negro Leagues would decline if the best black talent was siphoned off to the majors. Although Branch Rickey didn't do it, most club owners made a good deal of money renting their stadiums to black professional teams. Yankee Stadium alone brought $100,000 a year in rentals from Negro League teams to Yankee owner Dan Topping. In the height of self-serving paternalism, a number of owners expressed concern about the fate of black athletes not good enough to make the major leagues who would certainly be unemployed if integration destroyed the Negro Leagues.

The managers of black franchises were in the most difficult position of all. Although most of them wanted Jackie Robinson to succeed, they knew that integration could destroy their franchises. Reserve clauses in black contracts were rare, and major league teams could "raid" their franchises without compensating them for the players signed. Black owners also knew that attendance would suffer, that given the choice between Negro League teams and integrated major league teams, black fans would choose the latter. They were right. Attendance for the Newark Eagle dropped from 120,000 in 1946 to only 57,000 in 1947. The Negro National League dissolved after the 1948 season. The Negro American League had six teams in 1949, only four in 1953. The Negro American League was dead by 1960, and only the Indianapolis Clowns, with their grass skirts, were barnstorming. According to their owner, "We are all show now. . . . We clown, clown, clown . . . like the Harlem Globetrotters in basketball."

Despite their self-interest, however, most of the black owners applauded integration. Abe Saperstein, owner of the Harlem Globetrotters, was a different story. As a white owner of a black team, his thoughts turned to his own pocketbook. When the Celtics and Knicks signed black players in 1950, especially Sweetwater Clifton, Saperstein threatened to boycott their games. At the time the Globetrotters frequently played preliminary games before regular NBA match-ups to help boost attendance. Abe's threat was empty, but his fears were well-founded. The presence of black players in the NBA diverted attention away from the "Clown Princes," just as Jackie Robinson and Roy Campanella and Larry Doby did in the National and American Leagues. The Globetrotters and the teams of the Negro League went into declines from which they never recovered.

White reactions were mixed. In Nashua, New Hampshire, Roy Campanella and Don Newcombe were astounded at their reception by the Dodger farm team. Walter Alston, destined to become the longtime skipper of the Brooklyn and Los Angeles Dodgers, welcomed them to the team, and the whole town responded in kind. Campanella and Newcombe were popular figures in Nashua, accepted socially and hailed as saviors for the franchise. Restaurants, clubs, theaters, schools, and neighborhoods were all open to them. After a few weeks Alston named Campanella second-in-command and chief adviser. The two players encountered some hostility on the road from opposing fans and players, but in Campanella's own words it was "nothing compared to what Jackie was going through."

Robinson endured a great deal. When he came to Montreal and performed so well in 1946, Southern players on the Brooklyn Dodgers, lead by Bobby Bragan and popular outfielder Dixie Walker, circulated a petition opposing his promotion to the majors. The petition foundered when shortstop Pee Wee Reese, a Southerner and team captain, refused to sign and Branch Rickey agreed to trade any player upset with having Jackie around. Most of the players, worried about their jobs or upset with racist rhetoric, wanted nothing to do with the petition, and the organized opposition to Robinson dissipated. Only a threat of immediate suspension by National League president Ford Frick put a stop to a St. Louis Cardinal promise to boycott games with the Dodgers. On the field in 1946 and 1947, Robinson faced racist catcalls, hate mail, death threats, dust-offs, bean balls, spikes, and extraordinary humiliation, seething inside but remaining faithful to Rickey's demand for patience and long-suffering. Robinson's public demeanor was extraordinary. He was patient, witty, and quick to forgive, and he became a genuine American hero, but not without a price. Throughout the 1946 and 1947 seasons Jackie was plagued by headaches, bouts of depression, nausea, and nightmares.

Some players had more serious troubles. Stuck in the American League cellar, 27 games out of first place, the St. Louis Browns tried to integrate at mid-season in 1947. They signed three players, but none of them lasted out the year. Hank Thompson and Willard Brown came from the Kansas City Monarchs and Piper Davis from the Birmingham Black Barons. Owner Richard Muckerman wanted to boost attendance by attracting black fans and turning the team into a winner. Muckerman was desperate, however, and did none of the planning Rickey had put into integrating the Dodgers. Hank Thompson, although a gifted player, was a chronic alcoholic with a criminal record and a penchant for carrying a gun. Brown had claimed to be twenty-six years old but was actually past thirty, with his skills eroding. Brown hit only .179 and Thompson .256, and both were cut in August. Davis was never brought up because he refused to spend any time on a St. Louis farm team. Thompson and Brown had the dubious distinctions of being the first blacks cut from a major league team.

The pressure on black players was also intense because of the unwillingness or inability of whites to understand what they were going through. Jackie Robinson was outraged when a number of journalists attributed his leg injuries in 1947 to "lack of endurance." Nor were black athletes allowed to have normal feelings. Althea Gibson, a native of South Carolina who had grown up in Harlem, went to Florida A&M on a tennis scholarship, and in 1949 she was invited to several U.S. Lawn Tennis Association tournaments. In 1950 she played at Forest Hills. She had a mercurial career until 1957, when she won both Wimbledon and the U.S. Open at Forest Hills. Althea's "problem," however, was her streetwise confidence, pride, and suspicion of strangers. In a white athlete, her attitude would have earned such descriptions as "self-assured," "tough," or "competitive." Instead, the white press saw Althea as "arrogant," "moody," "temperamental," "sullen," and "tactless," a "Ted Williams without his skills," or a "Jackie Robinson without charm."

The elite group of black athletes had to deal with difficult political and personal situations as well; they were pawns in the Cold War struggle between the United States and the Soviet Union and in the battle for athletic supremacy constantly raging throughout America. The public juxtaposition of Paul Robeson and Jackie Robinson, and the public mortification of Connie Hawkins are prime examples. Paul Robeson, a Phi Beta Kappa graduate of Rutgers, played football there between 1915 and 1918 and won All-American recognition his senior year. Robeson also earned eight letters in three other sports at Rutgers. He played professional football for five years after graduating, but quit in 1923 to pursue a theatrical and singing career. But as he performed throughout the United States and in Europe, his hatred of American racism intensified, and in 1949, as a member of the Communist party, Robeson claimed in Paris that American blacks would never bear arms against the Soviet Union as they had against the Japanese and Germans in World War II.

Robeson could not have spoken at a more inauspicious time. Nineteen forty-nine was a bad year. The Soviet Union had detonated an atomic bomb long before anyone expected, China had fallen to Mao Tse-tung and the Communists, and Alger Hiss, former adviser to President Franklin D. Roosevelt, was on trial for perjury on espionage charges. The United States was caught in the midst of a painful identity crisis, and the need for reassurance was overwhelming. The American Communist party was having a field day claiming that segregation in American sports, especially baseball, was proof of white oppression, and Robeson's comments were widely publicized. To refute him, the House Un-American Activities Committee invited Jackie Robinson to testify. Rickey urged him to cooperate. It was a painful moment for Robinson. In his opinion, Robeson had only told the truth about the humiliation Jim Crow imposed on black people, but he had foolishly exaggerated in claiming blacks would not fight for their country. After denouncing racism in American life, Robinson then said: "I've got too much invested for my wife and child and myself in the future of this country, and I and other Americans of many races and faiths have too much invested in our country's welfare, for any of us to throw it away for a siren song sung in bass." When the press printed the quote again and again without any reference to his remarks on racism, Robinson felt embarrassed and used. For the rest of his life he looked back on the appearance before HUAC as one of the lowest points in his career.

With blacks proving they could compete successfully in professional team sports, Americans at least felt reassured about their own identity and the ideology of opportunity. Black athletic prowess proved a point: the United States was still a place where a talented individual could succeed. Like politics and organized crime, sports became a ladder out of poverty and discrimination for a few blacks and new immigrants. During the 1920s, for example, Lou Gehrig found in baseball the acceptance his German-American parents had never experienced. Italian-Americans like Joe DiMaggio and Rocky Marciano had reaped extraordinary public adulation in the 1930s, 1940s, and 1950s even while many Americans held their heritage in suspicion. An ethnic succession functioned in American sports, with Irish domination in the early twentieth century giving way to a strong Italian profile in the 1930s and 1940s, and then to the profound presence of blacks and Hispanics in the 1960s, 1970s, and 1980s. What Joe DiMaggio had done for Italians, Jackie Robinson did for blacks—positively projecting himself and his people into the public consciousness. American propagandists made the most of it.

But there was a dark side to the success model; exploitation was never far away. Jackie Robinson had felt its sting from the House Un-American Activities Committee, but he was certainly not the last black athlete to be exploited. In the rush for talent in the 1950s and early 1960s, thousands of black athletes found themselves in impossible positions. Connie Hawkins was one of them. In 1959 he was the top high school basketball player in America. Born in the Bedford-Stuyvesant ghetto of New York City in 1942, Hawkins possessed unprecedented talent, a fluidly coordinated body 6 feet 7 inches tall, and a hand eleven inches wide from the tip of the thumb to the tip of the little finger. By the time he attended Boys High in New York, he could beat recognized NBA players in one-on-one games on blacktop courts. Poor, shy, and functionally illiterate, Hawkins, noted his biographer David Wolf, "was so intimidated by the printed word that he did not get a driver's license until he was 28" because he felt he couldn't handle the written test. Although he scored only 65 on standardized IQ tests, before tutors substantially improved his score, more than 250 colleges recruited him in 1961. He finally opted for the University of Iowa when they promised him room, board, books, tuition, and $150 a month under the table.

Iowa City was a thousand miles distant and culturally several worlds away from Bedford-Stuyvesant. Hawkins found himself bewildered in classes where he could barely understand the lectures and could not fathom the textbooks. Filled with white men and women from the Iowa and Dakota farms, the university offered Connie no social life, especially after his roommate warned him on his first night in the dorm that "people around here think Negroes ought to be screwin' Negroes and that's it." But there were few "Negroes" around. Except when the athletic department paid a young black woman to come in from New York or Chicago to spend a weekend, Hawkins had no dates, and he passed lonely days in the student union drinking Cokes or going to movies. Connie retreated into a lonely shell and was miserable in Iowa.

But there was worse to come. During the summers Hawkins had innocently spoken with and taken money from New York City gamblers, and when the 1961 basketball point-shaving scandals erupted, Hawkins was implicated, even though he had just been a freshman at Iowa and hadn't played in any varsity games. Supposedly Connie was an intermediary, introducing friends to known gamblers for a fee. At the end of April, New York City detectives came out to Iowa City to question Hawkins about the scandal, talking to him about grand juries, convictions, and point-shaving, even though he didn't have the faintest idea what any of them meant. They questioned him for days, believing most of his story because they found "the kid too stupid to lie." Connie denied wrongdoing again and again, but they kept insisting he knew more and threatened him with a jail sentence. Eventually, Hawkins pleaded guilty for one reason: "I decided I'd never get out if I kept telling the truth." Although he was not formally charged, he was mentioned in four indictments of other individuals, and his career was ruined. On May 10, 1961, Iowa rescinded his scholarship and the NBA blacklisted him. It took eight years for Hawkins to clear his name. Although he was the most spectacular example of exploitation in college athletics, he was by no means an isolated example.

The pace of integration in the 1950s varied from sport to sport. Professional football had the fewest problems. Throughout the 1920s black college recruits had joined professional teams, and as late as 1933 Jack Lillard had played with the Philadelphia Eagles. The history of segregation in football was short. After the Rams signed Washington and Strode, there was a rush throughout the National Football League to sign the best black athletes. Perhaps the nature of the game made it easier. With twenty-two people on a more than 50,000 square foot field, it was difficult for one player to dominate the game. Fans also watched at quite a distance from the action. They never really got a close glimpse of the players, whose bodies were hidden in helmets, face masks, shoulder pads, hip pads, thigh pads, large jerseys, and high-top shoes. A black face was rarely seen, even from the best seat on the fifty-yard line. Integration didn't seem to have the same impact as it had in baseball and basketball.

Players were more visible in baseball, even though the fans watched from a considerable distance. But baseball was the national pastime, with virtually all the teams doing their spring training in the warm southern climate. Despite Robinson's extraordinary season in 1947, there were only four black players in the majors in 1948: Jackie Robinson and Roy Campanella in Brooklyn, and Larry Doby and Satchel Paige in Cleveland. Paige, the legendary and aging pitcher, filled ball parks throughout the American League for a month in late July and early August, running up a 5–1 record with a league-leading 1.33 earned run average. Paige's personal life, however, was another story. Bill Veeck found Paige a problem because of his womanizing, drinking, curfew-breaking, and general demeanor. Larry Doby was just the opposite. Young and anxious to succeed, Doby worked hard, despite real problems in the outfield, and ended up the year with a .301 average, 14 home runs, and 65 RBIs. The Indians won the pennant and the World Series, and jammed 2.7 million people into Municipal Stadium in 1948, setting a league attendance record.

The success of Doby and Paige proved that Robinson was no fluke, and during the off-season scouts began combing through the winter leagues looking for talented black players. In 1949 black players began pouring into organized baseball. But except for the Dodgers and Giants in New York, the Cleveland Indians, and the Chicago Cubs, blacks were confined to the minors. They were so successful on the major league teams that a new stereotype about blacks entered the white community. Nobody believed anymore that they were inferior athletically to whites, but their image as naturally talented, gifted in quickness, reflex, and strength, but short on brainpower and reason, deepened. By the early 1950s, fears of a black takeover appeared. Major league teams had an unwritten rule never to put more than four blacks in the starting lineup. Walter Alston broke that tradition in 1954 when he regularly started Jackie Robinson, Roy Campanella, Junior Gilliam, Don Newcombe, and Sandy Amoros. In 1959, the National League had twice as many black players as the American League, and the results were clear to even the most skeptical observers. The National League won the World Series ten times between 1954 and 1969, and between 1950 and 1985, they won twenty-nine of thirty-six All-Star games.

When Jackie Robinson retired in 1957, thirteen major league teams had black players; only the Philadelphia Phillies, Detroit Tigers, and Boston Red Sox held out. The Phillies purchased the contract of John Kennedy from the Kansas City Monarchs late in 1957, and the Tigers integrated in 1958 when the Briggs Stadium Boycott Committee, a civil rights group, threatened to stay away from Detroit games until a black player was on the club. In June they brought up third baseman Ossie Virgil from Charleston to play. The Red Sox were the last because of owner Tom Yawkey, whose own racism made it next to impossible for him to countenance a black athlete. But in 1958 and 1959 Boston civil rights groups began demanding an end to the color barrier, and Yawkey surrendered by bringing Elijah Green in from Minneapolis. The major leagues were integrated.

In basketball, black takeover of the sport was more than just a fear; it quickly became a reality. For a while in the early 1950s, basketball too had a quota system. Team owners had an unwritten rule to have no more than four blacks on the roster. But it didn't last long. Blacks advanced into the NBA and changed it from relatively low-scoring affairs to the fast-break, high-scoring games of the 1960s. Bill Russell joined the Boston Celtics for the 1956–57 season, and Wilt Chamberlain became a Philadelphia Warrior in 1959. The two men dominated the game, changing it into one of great power, speed, and defense. Chamberlain's 100-point game on March 2, 1962, highlighted the new era in professional basketball.

Myths of black athletic inferiority, in basketball at least, were dead, and as people like Oscar Robertson and Lennie Wilkens assumed leadership of their teams as play-makers, the myth of black intellectual inferiority weakened. Wilkens was a case in point. He came into the NBA in 1960 as the second black on the St. Louis Hawks, but when he left the Hawks in 1968, after they had moved to Atlanta, the team was starting five blacks: Wilkens, Zelmo Beaty, Bill Bridges, Paul Silas, Joe Caldwell, and Lou Hudson rotated through the starting lineup. When Wilkens's playing career ended in 1975, the NBA was predominantly black. That year there were eighteen blacks in the twenty-four spots on the all-star team. In 1977 instead of speculating about black weaknesses, Americans began discussing why whites were not up to the sport, why blacks had taken over. Among blacks an element of ridicule even developed. The term "white legs" described hairy legs with little muscle tone and less spring; a "white jump shot" one launched with the feet three inches off the ground; a "white" dunk was a lay-up.

The change became a problem for pro basketball in the late 1960s and 1970s, when television audiences and season ticket holders began to dwindle. It had become a black sport watched by white fans. Basketball was different from football. Uniforms were skimpy and fans sat close to the game, able to see the sweat, watch the smiles and grimaces, smell the action. The fan distance which partially insulated football and baseball did not exist in basketball. Whites had a difficult time finding heroes. The nature of the schedule did not help. With an eighty-two game season and an endless round of play-off games, basketball players tired of the hotel-to-arena-to-airport cycle. At times in mid-season the play appeared lethargic, and sometimes it was. Players were often tired and unsure about the time zone. Drug use had also become a problem by this time. Their play only resurrected some of the traditional white beliefs that blacks did not have the competitive edge, that they didn't care as much as whites did about the game.

Basketball had changed more than the other sports. It was blacker and better and difficult for whites to accept. Some franchises made incredible mistakes trying to find a place for white players. In 1969 Joe W. Geary, general manager of the Dallas Chapparrals in the American Basketball Association, had the naivete to tell a reporter that the "team was trying as hard as possible to replace black players with whites." The New Orleans Jazz, desperate for a white superstar to boost ticket sales in the South, traded Atlanta for "Pistol" Pete Maravich, the flashy white guard from LSU, but to get Maravich, the Jazz gave up two first-round draft choices, two second-round draft choices, and two second-string players. They had given up their future for a gifted but undisciplined white man who could not, and did not, make them a winner. In the 1980s sports observers took notice when the Boston Celtics had four whites starting: Danny Ainge, Larry Bird, Bill Walton, and Kevin McHale.

The charge that blacks were not competitive was, of course, ludicrous. Sports psychologists recognized that blacks enjoyed one clear competitive edge over whites. Raised in the intensity of schoolboy basketball in the black ghettoes of the North and East, where personal status and athletic prowess were one and the same, they had few opportunities outside of sports, no chance of going to college without a scholarship, little hope of getting out of the ghetto except with a ball in their hands. In the 1983 film *Rocky III*, Apollo Creed told Rocky Balboa he needed to regain "the eye of the tiger," the insatiable lust to win the game, or in that case, the fight. Ghetto blacks had "the eye of the tiger," the willingness to suffer and sacrifice beyond the commitment of most middle-class whites, who simply had too many other alternatives to give as much to the game.

Blacks played with a desperation born of ghetto poverty. Being cut meant going home to tenement apartments, unemployment, and hopelessness.

Despite black success in professional sports, racism was hardly over. Although whites readily admitted by the early 1960s that black athletes could compete in the big leagues, there were still serious doubts about their mental competency, whether they could coach, manage, pitch, or play quarterback. The NBA did not hire a black coach until 1966, when Bill Russell took over the world champion Boston Celtics. Baseball did not have a black manager until 1975, when the Cleveland Indians hired former Baltimore slugger Frank Robinson. And by 1988 the National Football League still had never had a black head coach. Even when black superstars had achieved salary parity with whites, they complained that second-string blacks still encountered enormous discrimination—that white coaches always gave the nod to white players for bench-sitting positions, even though many second-string blacks were superior athletes. Blacks also complained that they enjoyed equality only in peripheral positions. As late as 1970 black major league baseball players had batting averages 20 points higher than whites; slugging averages 40 points higher; and earned run averages substantially lower, not so much because blacks were inherently better athletes but because club management did not keep many second-string black players. The tenth, eleventh, and twelfth spots on NBA teams were invariably reserved for whites.

The culmination to the desegregation of American sports came on March 19, 1966, before 14,253 people in the Cole Field House of the University of Maryland. Number-one-ranked Kentucky, led by collegiate Coach of the Year Adolph Rupp, was going for its fifth NCAA championship against upstart Texas Western College of El Paso. More than history was at work. Intercollegiate basketball had long been integrated in the North and West, but the South was still holding out. In 1959, Mississippi State University captured the Southeast Conference championship but refused to compete in the NCAA play-offs, despite a 24–1 record, because it would have had to play against teams with black players. In 1960 Auburn University made a similar decision. In 1961 and 1962, Mississippi State won the SEC championship, and although the players and student body wanted the team to compete in the NCAA postseason tournament, the board of regents, under intense political pressure from segregationists, refused. But that year Mississippi State and Ole Miss were the only major teams left in the country who refused to schedule games against integrated teams at home or away. When Mississippi State again won the SEC title in 1963, university president Dean Colvard allowed them to play in the NCAA tournament. Still, they had to sneak out of town to make sure segregationists didn't try to stop them.

Three years later, in 1966, Adolph Rupp and the University of Kentucky were in the NCAA finals. Rupp, faithful to his mint-julep prejudices, had refused to recruit black athletes. Kentucky was lily-white, and Rupp loved it that way. He was a racist in the tradition of southern paternalism, convinced that blacks just did not have the gumption to make it in the big time, although he would not deny their innate talent. He once remarked in a radio interview that back in Africa "the lions and tigers had caught all the slow ones." Rupp's teams were known for their discipline and control. The Texas Western "Miners" were black, the starting team composed of young men from the schoolboy basketball courts of the ghettoes: "Big Daddy" David Lattin from Houston, Bobby Joe Hill from Detroit, and Nevil Shed and the "two Willies" from New York City, Willie Worsley and Willie Cager. Texas Western beat Kentucky 72 to 65, leading all the way and dominating the game defensively.

There was an irony in the victory. The Texas Western coaching staff was all white and frequently enraged the black players by using the word "nigger" in daily language, but after the victory over Kentucky they received more than fifty thousand pieces of hate mail from whites discouraged and angry about the championship. The *New York Times* made no mention of the white-black confrontation but still described Texas Western play as "flashy" and "fancy." The Texas Western victory was the "emancipation proclamation" of southern college basketball. Two months after that victory, Vanderbilt University signed Perry Wallace, a basketball star from all-black Pearl High School in Nashville. The SEC had been integrated, and Mississippi State had no choice but to play Vanderbilt. 1966 was the last year an all-white team went to the NCAA finals. UCLA dominated the tournament for the next ten years, and Adolph Rupp began recruiting blacks early in the 1970s. An era was over.

For Art Rooney and the Pittsburgh Steelers, the National Football League trophy signified more than a championship: it was an investment.
(Credit: Mike Fabus, Pittsburgh Steelers)

# ● Work and Play

## The Business of Professional Sports

*The players can do more for themselves than any outside
representative, no matter how able that outsider may be.
By delegating someone else to negotiate for them, the
players are surrendering a privilege that has been very
valuable to them.*
—WARREN GILES

**B**lacks weren't the only people trying to make it in professional sports. Although their struggle for success had broader social
and political implications, they were no more intent on carving out a
place for themselves than the white players on the diamond and the
white owners in the field boxes. In fact, professional life wasn't that
great for whites in the late 1940s. Stan Musial, the premier hitter in
the game and superstar for the St. Louis Cardinals, earned only
$14,000 in 1946, a reasonable living but certainly not wealth. Both
white and black players, legally at least, were the chattel of the team
owners. It was an arrangement long in the making, but in 1946,
while Jackie Robinson was breaking the color line, the team owners
in professional baseball were worried.

Once World War II ended, they had confidently predicted the
return of carefree prosperity. The *ersatz* players had departed. No
longer would baseball fans be treated or subjected to such 4-F'ers as
Pete Gray, the one-armed outfielder of the 1945 St. Louis Browns.
The stars had returned—Joe DiMaggio, Ted Williams, Hank Green-
berg, Stan Musial. The fans had returned in droves, anxious to
spend part of their wartime savings on hot dogs, beer, and baseball.
The combination should have worked magic for the owners. But
problems, unexpected problems, arose.

**47**

From south of the Rio Grande came the Pasquel brothers, Alfonso and Jorge. Full of talk of high times and fortified with certified checks for large amounts, they attempted to lure big-time American ballplayers down to the new Mexican League. Restricted by the reserve clause, which insured low salaries, many players listened to the Pasquel brothers. In St. Louis the situation was particularly bad. Sam Breadon, the parsimonious owner of the Cardinals, had placed a $14,000 ceiling on salaries. Jorge Pasquel went to Stan Musial's hotel room in Florida during spring training. He put five certified $10,000 checks on the bed as up-front money and then offered Musial a five-year deal worth $195,000 to play in the Mexican League. "Stan the Man" thought about it but then declined the attractive offer. Pitchers Max Lanier and two other Cardinals accepted offers from Pasquel. So did eight members of the New York Giants, including star pitcher Sal Maglie. So did dozens of other discontented professional ballplayers.

Players who stayed at home grumbled about their inability to earn more money. Robert Francis Murphy, a Boston-born and -educated lawyer who had spent a decade in Washington working as a labor relations man, read about the sad plight of professional baseball players. He noted that many players earned less than $3,500 a year and were not paid for spring training. He learned that Jimmie Foxx, the great hitter who ended his twenty-five year career in 1945 with a .325 life-time batting average and 534 home runs, had little money to see him into retirement. The time had come, Murphy reasoned, for professional baseball players to unite.

At the time professional sports in America were undergoing profound economic changes previously experienced by most other businesses and interest groups. In the preindustrial village economy of the early to middle nineteenth century, business affairs had been primarily local, with large numbers of producers competing to supply the needs of consumers in regional and local markets. Economic events in distant places had little relevance. But the rise of national and international markets in the late nineteenth and early twentieth centuries had given the most efficient, competitive businesses new growth opportunities, and those with technological and capital advantages drove their competitors into bankruptcy. Increasingly larger market shares were controlled by fewer and fewer companies with national and then international profiles. In every major sector of the economy—automobiles, electrical appliances, steel, and transportation—big corporations took over and smaller businesses died out. Sports would not be immune from the processes of economic rationalization.

The rise of a mass, consumer culture in the twentieth century also affected sports. During the 1920s, the development of radio and movies did to vaudeville and the ethnic and regional theaters what industrialization did to small business. For the first time, Americans all across the country listened to the same programs, watched the same movies, worshipped the same heroes. Rudolph Valentino and Babe Ruth became bigger-than-life personalities with cult followings among people from diverse class and ethnic backgrounds. At the local level, theatrical groups, ethnic troupes, and city bands and orchestras came on hard times. People went to the movies or huddled around their radios to hear their stars.

Industrialization and the rise of mass culture transformed professional sports by forcing national perspectives on what had essentially been local affairs. People were rapidly acquiring broader points of view, and instead of being satisfied with local club and community teams, they wanted to know who was best, who could hit the farthest or run the fastest, which city had the finest team, who were the champions. Professional sports teams were closely identified with city boosterism and community identity, but people wanted to know how their city compared to others, and sports competition became one measure of quality. To compare the present with the past, to measure progress, Americans began making a fetish of team and individual accomplishments, maintaining elaborate records and talking incessantly about them whenever they were broken. The need for records and statistics, the development of national perspectives, competition, and heroes, demanded order—not unlike the interchangeable-parts technology of mass production or the standard railroad gauges implemented throughout the country in the nineteenth century. If sports were to measure progress and rank one region of America against another, it required rationalization: consistent rules, balanced schedules, professional refereeing, and play-offs. For most sports, that happened in the twentieth century when the barnstormers gave way to organized league play.

The highly structured professional leagues of the 1980s bear little resemblance to their early predecessors. In baseball, the National League was formed in 1876, but it played a loose schedule and allowed players to contract with any team for their services. There were some restrictions. Each team enjoyed a monopoly in its own city; the league could not issue a franchise to another local team. In 1879, the first of the reserve clauses went into effect when the National League restricted players' rights to negotiate with other teams. When the National League expelled the Cincinnati Red Stockings in 1879 for playing on Sundays and selling liquor at games, the team joined a new American Association, the first rival league to raid player rosters. The Union Association was formed in 1884 and the Players League in 1890, but both failed in their first year. The American Association went under in 1891. Ban Johnson established the American League in 1900, and it succeeded, raiding National League rosters and expanding into several eastern cities. The American League and the National League reached a truce in 1903 by establishing the first World Series, which the Boston Pilgrims (Red Sox) of the American League won in eight games over the Pittsburgh Pirates. Except for the Federal League in 1914 and 1915, the Pasquel brothers' Mexican League in 1946, and the Continental League threat, major league baseball has not faced serious competition since 1903.

Professional football started in the late nineteenth century in city club games and touring teams, but it was not until 1919 that the American Professional Football Association was established, with each of its five teams paying a $25 franchise fee. There were no set schedules, and individual teams played one another wherever and whenever it seemed profitable. After the 1920 season Joseph Carr reorganized the association into the National Football League, and it struggled until 1925, when the Chicago Bears signed University of Illinois star halfback Red Grange to a professional contract. The Bears toured the country playing games with rival teams, and professional football reached a turning point in its battle for survival. A rival American Football League was formed in 1926, but it lasted only a season, although its most successful franchise, the New York Yankees, was strong enough to be adopted by the NFL. Throughout the 1920s and 1930s, the NFL was in a state of flux, with as many as twenty-two teams playing in 1926 and only eight in 1932. Nineteen thirty-six proved to be a watershed year for the NFL. No franchises changed hands or cities; each team played the same number of games; and the amateur player draft was instituted. An All-American Conference competed with the NFL between 1946 and 1949, but it died in 1949, with three of its teams—Cleveland, Baltimore, and San Francisco—moving over to the National Football League.

J. L. Gibson established the first professional hockey team, the Portage Lakes, in 1903, and the next year the Lakes were joined by several other new professional teams to form the International Professional Hockey League. The rival National Hockey Association became the National Hockey League in 1917. It had four teams, one of them the Montreal Canadiens. For the next nine years the NHL competed in play-off contests with two regional leagues—the Pacific Coast Hockey Association and the Western Canada Hockey League—but they both dissolved in 1926. The National Hockey League then expanded to ten teams in two divisions. When World War II ended, the NHL had six surviving teams: Montreal, Toronto, New York, Boston, Chicago, and Detroit. The cultural need to determine the best team and the economic need to exploit the best sports markets brought on the rationalization of professional hockey.

Professional basketball was the last of the major sports to consolidate its league organization. By 1946, a dozen leagues competed at various times for professional dominance: the National Basketball League, the Philadelphia League, the Eastern League, the Central League, the Hudson River League, the New York State League, the Western Pennsylvania League, the Pennsylvania State League, the Inter-State League, the Metropolitan Basketball League, the American Basketball League, and the Basketball Association of America. Owners were transient, franchises economically weak, and player talent mixed. The National Basketball League was largely confined to smaller cities in the Midwest, and the Basketball Association of America, formed in 1946, had such prominent teams as the Boston Celtics, the Philadelphia Warriors, and the New York Knickerbockers. In 1948 several NBL teams, including the Minnesota Lakers and their superstar center George Mikan, jumped to the Basketball Association of America, and six more left in 1949. The National Basketball League merged with the Basketball Association of America and was renamed the National Basketball Association.

The establishment of the NBA rounded out the league structure of modern American sports. The National League, the American League, the National Football League, the National Hockey League, and the National Basketball Association had all brought order to professional sports. The best athletes in the country were finding their way into one of the clubs in one of the leagues. Balanced schedules, professional referees, consistent rules, and "world" championships changed the sports business. Professional sports functioned in a national marketplace, appealed to a nation-wide clientele, and played to the expectations of a mass culture. Modern economic forces had rationalized competition.

But in other ways, sports were unique, different from the rest of American business, defying the major organizational trends in corporate America. Not only was its pastoral setting reminiscent of the nineteenth century, but its business dimension more closely re-sembled the Robber Baron mold of the late 1800s than the corporate management of the 1950s. Although the league structure consoli-dated and stabilized during the 1940s and 1950s, and the teams tried to rationalize the labor market through antitrust exemptions and re-serve clauses, the individual club owners remained entrepreneurial autocrats, their businesses privately held and protected from public scrutiny. While other businesses were coming under the control of anonymous corporate managers—"organization men" in gray-flannel suits—eccentric, one-of-a-kind owners such as Bill Veeck, Art Rooney, Larry MacPhail, and George Halas dominated sports. Instead of faceless upper-level managers trying to please thousands of stockholders and union shop stewards, the club owners were like medieval manor lords owning their own estates, free of external in-terference, and manipulating the lives of their serf-employees. They were no less paternalistic than George Pullman, no less self-righteous than John D. Rockefeller, no less acquisitive than Andrew Carnegie.

The raid of the Pasquel brothers on the National and American Leagues in 1946 exposed the uniqueness of the sports business. In one sense, the professional sports franchises achieved a level of or-ganization unmatched in any other sector of the economy. Although consolidation and national marketing networks eventually charac-terized most industries, there was a residue of competition left be-tween the major producers, a system of oligopolies rather than mo-nopolies. When restraints on trade became too obvious or prevalent, federal legislation—the Interstate Commerce Act of 1887, the Sherman Antitrust Act of 1890, the Federal Trade Commission Act of 1913, and the Clayton Antitrust Act of 1914—was passed to restore market forces. But the sports industry by the late 1940s had become a cartel capable of all but eliminating serious competition. The National and American Leagues, the National Football League, the National Basketball Association, and the National Hockey League had strangleholds on the major sports industry.

The sports cartel in the United States rested on several powerful legal and marketing devices: the antitrust exemption; the reserve, option, and waiver clauses of personal service contracts; owner agreements not to compete; and the annual player drafts. The antitrust exemption applied specifically to professional baseball and to a lesser extent to football.

Baseball received its antitrust exemption in 1922 when the Supreme Court, in *Federal Baseball Club v. National League*, ruled that baseball was essentially an intrastate business and therefore exempt from the commerce clause of the Constitution. Justice Oliver Wendell Holmes wrote the majority opinion. The Federal League had appeared in 1914 to rival the National and American Leagues and signed a number of major leaguers to new contracts. The Philadelphia Phillies sued the Chicago franchise of the Federal League for signing catcher Bill Killifer, claiming that the Phillies had developed an "equity" in the player. In January 1915 the Federal League launched a massive antitrust suit against the National League for restraining free trade by denying them access to the player market. The suit was eventually settled out of court late in 1916, with the Federal League receiving $600,000 in return for dropping its claim. The League then folded. But Ned Hanlon and Harry Goldman, owners of the Baltimore franchise of the Federal League, then sued major league baseball, arguing that the settlement had destroyed the league and their franchise. The suit reached the Supreme Court in 1922, when baseball received its exemption from all antitrust laws, and subsequent suits over the years upheld its immunity.

Although other sports were denied any general exemption from antitrust laws, federal courts or Congress usually favored them, underwriting the basic legal mechanisms they used to limit competition. In 1966, when the National Football League and the American Football League were negotiating a merger to establish the first Super Bowl, institute a common player draft, divide television income, control expansion, and bring an end to the competitive bidding up of salaries, Congress specifically exempted them from antitrust laws. Senator Russell Long and Congressman Hale Boggs, both Democrats from Louisiana, sponsored a statutory rider to an investment credit bill giving the merger the necessary exemption. The NFL's decision to grant a new franchise to New Orleans the next year did not appear to be mere coincidence to most sports observers.

The antitrust exemption was only one dimension of the professional sports cartel; the club owners also used a variety of internal rules to eliminate competition for players' services. Reserve, option, and assignability clauses were the legal tools of the cartels. In baseball, the National League had first adopted the reserve clause in 1879, and gradually throughout the 1880s the restriction was added to most players' contracts. The reserve clause was quite simple: a portion of each contract assigns to a specific team the exclusive right to deal with him throughout his career. A player can negotiate with another team only if his own team releases him from his contract or gives permission for the negotiations. In 1887, when baseball players were being routinely sold or traded between clubs, John Montgomery Ward, a star pitcher in the National League, wrote an article in the magazine *Lippincott's* entitled "Is the Ballplayer Chattel?" He noted that like "a fugitive slave law, the reserve rule denies him a harbor or a livelihood, and carries him back, bound and shackled, to the club from which he attempted to escape. He goes where he is sent, takes what is given him, and thanks the Lord for life." By the 1920s, National Hockey League clubs were also using reserve clauses in their player contracts.

In football and basketball, option clauses were far more common than reserve clauses. Under the option system, a team has the exclusive right to retain a player's services for one year after the contract has expired. If the player is unable to sign a new contract, his salary is set at 90 percent of the previous level, and at the end of the year he is free to negotiate with any other team. Because the reserve clause essentially gave lifetime control to the club owner, the option clause was theoretically more open, but in practice both the National Football League and the National Basketball Association interpreted it very narrowly. By the 1950s both the NFL and the NBA were insisting on compensation to team owners who lost players under option clauses, and in the early 1960s the so-called "Rozelle Rule," named after NFL commissioner Pete Rozelle, guaranteed that any team signing a player who had played out his option must compensate the former team. Rozelle had the authority to determine the compensation, and it could come in the form of cash, veteran players, or future draft choices. The NBA used a similar system, and the practice substantially reduced the ability of any player to negotiate higher salaries for his services.

Professional baseball, football, basketball, and hockey also used waiver clauses in player contracts. Even when a team surrenders its exclusive control over a player, there are still strings attached preventing the player from negotiating freely with another club. Each team in the league must have the chance to purchase exclusive rights to bargain with him from the old team. Once every team has had that opportunity, there may still be limitations on the player's freedom to negotiate, especially if he has not played a minimum number of years in the league. The combined effect of reserve, option, and waiver clauses was to bind professional athletes to a single team throughout their career unless the team decided to sell or trade them.

The final monopoly tool developed by professional sports teams was the annual player draft. To maintain a balance of talent in the league, the team with the worst record during the previous year usually had the right to select first from the ranks of the most gifted amateur athletes. The drafting team had exclusive negotiating rights to the prospect, preventing any competitive bidding on salaries. The National Football League was the first to institute the annual player draft, which it put into effect in 1935, and the National Basketball Association followed suit in 1949. The National Hockey League held its first player draft in 1953, and baseball held out until 1965, when it first began drafting amateurs. Until the player drafts went into effect, various clubs tried to sign prospective stars, usually offering them bonuses and higher salaries. Along with the antitrust exemptions, reserve clauses, and option and waiver rules, the annual player draft transformed professional sports into one of the least competitive industries in the economy.

The only way to break the cartel was the establishment of rival leagues, and that is why the Pasquel brothers created such a sensation in 1946. The Mexican League did not prove to be much of a threat to major league baseball, even though the Pasquel brothers tried to throw around a lot money in 1946. They signed a few big-name stars, like New York Giants pitcher Sal Maglie and Dodger catcher Mickey Owen, but the vast majority of American ballplayers wanted to stay in the United States. The Mexican League played only a ninety-game schedule, which appealed to most players, but teams traveled by the notoriously unpredictable Mexican bus system over less than well-maintained roads, and playing conditions flirted with the dangerous. In Tampico, along the Gulf Coast, left field was traversed by railroad tracks, and games were frequently interrupted by slow-moving freight trains. At most other stadiums lighting systems for night games were poorly designed.

Americans who jumped to the Mexican League managed to anger everyone. Local Mexican players resented the high salaries paid to the "gringos," and Mexican nationalism was piqued at the influx. The federal legislature passed legislation in 1946 prohibiting any team from having rosters with more than 50 percent foreigners. The Pasquel brothers frequently reversed umpire decisions in games they were watching and transferred players from franchise to franchise at will. The quality of play varied greatly from city to city. By 1947 the movement of players to Mexico had stopped, and the league folded after its 1948 season. The threat to major league club owners was over, but they had long memories. In June 1946 baseball commissioner Albert Benjamin "Happy" Chandler imposed a five-year ban on all Americans who had abandoned 1946 contracts to play in the Mexican League, added three-year bans on anyone who had violated his reserve contract, and blacklisted any current player appearing in exhibition games with banned players.

It was an inauspicious time for the labor movement, and Robert Murphy's attempt to organize professional baseball players into a union collided head-on with owner opposition and the winds of political conservatism blowing across the land. In the 80th Congress, Republicans were enjoying their first majorities since the presidency of Herbert Hoover, and they were determined to dismantle the New Deal, particularly the labor provisions of the Wagner Act of 1935. Conservative Robert Taft of Ohio was the undisputed leader of the Senate, and he sponsored a bill to limit the growing power of national labor unions. The bill gave the president the right to obtain injunctions forcing strikers back to work for a sixty-day "cooling-off" period; prohibited contributions from union dues to political candidates; allowed states to pass "right-to-work" laws; outlawed closed shops; and required union officials to sign non-Communist affidavits. Known as the Taft-Hartley Act, the bill passed the House by a vote of 320 to 79 and the Senate by 57 to 17 early in June 1947. Harry S. Truman vetoed the measure, but Congress quickly overrode the veto on June 23, 1947.

Growing fears of Communism matched antilabor sentiments. In 1946 and 1947, the threat of Soviet expansion weighed heavily on European leaders; and Truman, wanting to promote his Truman Doctrine of aid to Greece and Turkey and the Marshall Plan to rebuild Western Europe, repeatedly talked about the dangers of world communism and how the United States would have to be vigilant in its defense of democracy at home and abroad. Fears of internal Communist subversion mounted. In March 1946 Truman signed an executive order requiring investigation of all government employees and all applicants for government jobs, and in July 1947 Congress passed the National Security Act, creating the Department of Defense, the National Security Council, and the Central Intelligence Agency. The Communist triumph in China and the Soviet detonation of an atomic bomb in 1949 intensified domestic anxieties, and in September 1950 Congress passed the Internal Security Act, forcing registration of all Communists and Communist-front organizations, prohibiting Communists from national defense work, and providing for internment of Communists during national emergencies. The Red Scare was on.

The prevailing mood of antilabor and anti-Communism in the 1940s and early 1950s doomed efforts to organize professional athletes and break the back of the league cartels in baseball, hockey, football, and basketball. Baseball occupied center stage in the dispute. It was a symbol of America, the national pastime, a perfect combination of individual prowess and team play, of power and pastoral tranquility. At a time when the Red Scare was casting aspersions on American institutions, baseball became sacrosanct, and the owners milked the public mood for all it was worth, claiming over and over again that any alteration in the antitrust exemption, reserve and option clauses, and waiver system would destroy the basic nature of the game. In April 1949 Branch Rickey of the Brooklyn Dodgers went so far as to claim that those people opposing the reserve clause and the antitrust exemption had "avowed Communist tendencies."

On April 17, 1946, Robert Murphy established the American Baseball Guild and called for a minimum salary of $6,500, impartial arbitration of salary disputes, and payment of 50 percent of a sale price to the player. He then wrote to every major leaguer and asked each one to consider joining the guild. Sportswriters, although sympathetic with poorly paid players, generally opposed the guild. They thought open salary negotiations would destroy the game. Club owners were livid. Clark Griffith, owner of the Washington Senators, argued that the guild would "be fatal to the life of baseball. . . . If the reserve clause is killed, there won't be any big leagues or little leagues."

Undaunted, Murphy decided to start his organization drive with the Pittsburgh Pirates. Pittsburgh was a strong union town, and the idea had a good deal of support among the players. William Benswanger, the chief owner of the Pirates, became personally involved in opposing the organization drive. When the club stalled on a decision to allow a vote on guild representation in July, several players called for an immediate strike. The owners allowed a vote, but Benswanger appeared in the clubhouse just before the ballot, letting each player know they could come to him individually with any of their problems. His position was not unlike that of Andrew Carnegie a half-century before, who, in anticipation of the Homestead strike, called on his workers to negotiate individually with him. The players approved going on strike by 20 to 16, but that vote fell short of the two-thirds majority they had earlier decided on. Strike talk then dissipated.

But the threat of the strike had frightened the owners, and late in the 1946 season an owners committee, headed by Leland "Larry" MacPhail of the Yankees, traveled across the country listening to player grievances. In July 1947 the committee announced a minimum salary of $5,000, a $25 per week expense account for spring training, and creation of a pension funded by owner and player contributions. After the announcement the Pirates rejected guild representation by a 15 to 3 vote, with most of the players abstaining. Robert Murphy's American Baseball Players Guild was dead.

Although the Mexican League and the Players Guild had expired, the issue of player rights had not. The five-year blacklist on

Mexican Leaguers still grated on a lot of nerves in 1947 and 1948, especially since people like Sal Maglie and Mickey Owen were not on the diamond playing for the Giants and the Dodgers. Danny Gardella attacked the blacklist. A native of the Bronx, Gardella made it onto the Giants' roster in 1944 and 1945, when so many of the top players were in the armed services. He had fairly good years, hitting .272 with 18 home runs and 71 RBIs in 1945. With the regulars coming back in 1946, Gardella signed a contract for $8,000 and a $5,000 bonus with Jorge Pasquel and joined the Vera Cruz team in the Mexican League. When Gardella tried to return home to play in 1947, he fell under Chandler's five-year ban. A sympathetic attorney, Frederic Johnson, decided to file a lawsuit on Gardella's behalf.

Johnson demanded $100,000 in damages from the National League for conspiracy in restraint of trade in taking Gardella's livelihood away. He attacked the antitrust exemption, the reserve clause, and the farm systems, which all managed to destroy an individual player's right to negotiate for the best salary. After losing at the federal district court level, Johnson took the case to the appellate courts, and early in 1949 the Second Circuit Appellate Federal Court in New York's Southern District agreed to hear the case. The case was scheduled for November 1949. But in June, rather than risk an adverse federal court ruling, Happy Chandler lifted the ban and extended amnesty to all Mexican League players. Gardella settled out of court, with the National League paying him $60,000 in damages. He split the settlement with Johnson. For the owners the settlement prevented any unwanted test of the antitrust exemption.

• • •

During the 1950s and early 1960s, the American economy was marking time, recovering from the inflationary binges of the Korean War and building up to the stagflation disaster which began to appear late in the 1960s. Economic growth, powered by a defense budget totaling 50 percent of annual government spending, was steady, unemployment was low, and prices were stable. The Taft-Hartley Act of 1947 had imposed certain restraints on union activity, but Republican hopes of returning to a pre–New Deal world where labor suffered at the capricious whims of management were hopelessly naive. Prosperity is usually an asset for labor unions; management fears the threat of lost profits, and workers enjoy choices and alternatives. In 1955 the American Federation of Labor and the Congress of Industrial Organizations ended their twenty-year estrangement and forged the AFL-CIO, the largest union in the country. By that time the major industries in the United States had all been organized.

But labor did not make any extraordinary gains during the 1950s and early 1960s either. These were tranquil years, almost a calm before the storm, between Korea and Vietnam, and most Americans were content to leave things alone. The smokestack industries of the North and East were darkening the skies with steady increases in production, while the farms of the South and West were burying the world in wheat, rice, corn, and cotton. The United States was coasting along, and few people, particularly those with any influence, had major complaints about the status quo. A mood of cultural conservatism, broken only by the rise of rock and roll and the first desegregation encounters, blanketed the country. Most people preferred things the way they were.

In sports, management tried to consolidate its power, and labor made some feeble attempts at organizing, but neither gained much ground. The fundamental economic and legal relationship between owners and players, locked in place since World War II, remained intact throughout the 1950s and early 1960s. Television was a case in point. In 1949 there were fifty-nine minor leagues and a season attendance of 42 million people. By 1953, there were only thirty-eight leagues, and attendance had dropped to only 21 million. Television was one of the culprits, and in 1951 the major league owners prohibited National and American League broadcasts into minor league areas on the day of a minor league game. The Justice Department quickly informed the owners they would probably be found guilty of restraint of broadcast trade, and they backed down. But in 1953, federal courts upheld the right of the National Football League, and other professional sports franchises, to black out television broadcasts in home cities to protect the gate.

Baseball and football also tried, with only mixed results, to expand their legal immunities in the 1950s and early 1960s. In 1951 Brooklyn Congressman Emanuel Celler, chairman of the House Sub-Committee on Anti-Trust, opened hearings into organized baseball with the intention of either overturning the antitrust exemption or giving it legislative authority. Celler, an avid baseball fan and enthusiastic supporter of the Brooklyn Dodgers, favored the latter, and he invited a string of former players and club owners to testify in favor of the antitrust exemption and the reserve clause. Democratic Senator Edwin Johnson of Colorado, also president of the Class A Western League, was as enthusiastic as Celler in support of the owners. But in its May 1952 report, the Celler committee decided on the status quo, agreeing that the judicial antitrust protection ought to stand—"to protect the integrity of the game"—but recommending no congressional action on the matter at all. Celler reconvened the committee in 1957 when he heard that Walter O'Malley was going to move his beloved Dodgers out to Los Angeles. After those hearings Celler sponsored legislation placing all professional sports teams, including baseball, under existing antitrust regulations, but the measure never passed.

The National Football League tried unsuccessfully during the 1950s to secure the same antitrust exemption baseball had enjoyed since 1922. That protection seemed especially important in 1957 when the Supreme Court ruled in favor of William Radovich, whom the NFL had blacklisted after he refused to sign a contract with the team drafting him out of college. The court ruled that the NFL was subject to antitrust regulations. Emanuel Celler's subcommittee heard that year from a number of witnesses, with NFL commissioner Bert Bell and Chicago Bear owner and coach George Halas calling for specific congressional exemption from the antitrust laws. They failed to secure the protection afforded to baseball, but four years later Congress gave the NFL a specific antitrust exemption when the league negotiated a new television contract. Unlike earlier contracts, with each team keeping the revenues from its own local market, the 1961 NFL agreement provided for a pooling of gross revenues between teams, which allowed the clubs in smaller media markets to benefit more from the television bonanza. In 1961 Congress generously exempted the pooling arrangement from antitrust laws.

But the management and labor issues in American sports during the 1950s and early 1960s were not simply reflections of the external economic and social environment. Football, hockey, baseball, and basketball had internal rhythms of their own which affected management decision-making and labor organization. Compared to the major leagues in baseball and the National Basketball Association, the National Football League was a model of harmony and co-operation. Rather than succumbing to their competitive urges, as far as their pocketbooks were concerned, team owners created a benign political and economic atmosphere in which the survival of all the teams was as important as the success of any individual franchise.

During the 1920s and 1930s, when success was problematic at best, the original owners sensed that survival for the league was going to be a group phenomenon, and for social reasons they were able to implement that point of view. The dominant figures in the National Football League—Tim Mara of the New York Giants, George Halas of the Chicago Bears, Art Rooney of the Pittsburgh Steelers, and the Washington Redskins syndicate of George Marshall, Vincent Bendix, Jay O'Brien, and M. Dorland Doyle—were devout Roman Catholics. The immigrant Catholic culture of the National Football League owners set them apart from the rest of the professional sports world.

Immigrant Catholic culture contradicted Anglo-American values on several levels. While much of American history had celebrated individualism and created a political system sensitive to individual aspirations, immigrant Catholics had invested all of their energies into the parish, parochial school, and church—into the community and its corporate view of society. The individual was not necessarily more important than the group, and the politics of the NFL reflected its internal solidarity. The NFL was the first professional sport to install an amateur player draft; that 1936 agreement saved league members from the bickering and salary bonuses baseball endured until the creation of its draft in 1965. To maintain a good level of competition within the league, the NFL decided in 1961 to pool all television revenues, a move which allowed teams in the smaller markets, like the Green Bay Packers or the St. Louis Cardinals, to enjoy financial parity with media-gifted teams like the Los Angeles Rams or the New York Giants.

Immigrant Catholic culture had worshipped land and place, homes and neighborhoods. They were "urban villagers" who preferred stability to mobility, and in the 1940s and 1950s, before the mass flight to the suburbs, their neighborhoods enjoyed a tenacious sense of identity. National Football league franchises, after the financially dark days of the 1920s and 1930s and before the expansion times of the 1960s and 1970s, reflected that preference for home. Except for the shift of the Cleveland Rams to Los Angeles in 1946, and the wanderings of the unsuccessful New York Yanks franchise from Boston to New York to Dallas to Baltimore in the late 1940s and early 1950s, the NFL teams stayed put. At a time when baseball and basketball were stricken by franchise flights, professional football maintained a sense of place.

Finally, while Anglo-American culture constantly praised the virtues of democracy, immigrant Catholicism offered instead a belief in the social efficacy of hierarchy and authority. They were willing to admit that adhering to the decisions of a strong, benevolent tyrant might be a more successful way of ordering society than following the whims of the majority. The National Football League ran itself according to an authoritarian model rather than a democratic one. While team owners in baseball and basketball virtually controlled league affairs and dominated league commissioners, the NFL has been content with only two commissioners—Bert Bell and Pete Rozelle—over a forty-year period. Bell and Rozelle both administered league business with an iron hand, one provided by the willingness of owners to defer to their decisions. The fact that NFL player salaries in the 1980s were far behind those of basketball, baseball, and hockey players was simply a function of the internal unity of the football cartel.

Pete Rozelle was the pivotal figure in the success of the National Football League. During the difficult times of the 1930s and 1940s, NFL owners had formed a united front out of religious and cultural loyalties, but in the 1960s, 1970s, and 1980s that unity was maintained more by the personality of Pete Rozelle than because of any cultural heritage, particularly after expansion brought new owners into the cartel. Rozelle knew that the future of the National Football League was in television revenues, and he also knew that to sustain viewing audiences, fans would have to be given evenly matched contests each week. Rozelle was convinced that without some formal way of sharing television revenues, the teams in the major media markets would be able to buy talent that teams in smaller cities could never afford. In 1976, Rozelle testified before the House Select Subcommittee on Professional Sports and said:

> The NFL operates with the highest degree of profit-sharing of any
> professional sport. . . . The NFL, for example, after direct game ex-

penses, splits the gate receipts of each game on a sixty-forty basis—sixty percent to the home team and forty percent to the visiting team. . . . Every NFL club is thus economically dependent on the successful home business operations of every other NFL club. NFL clubs also pool and divide equally all regular-season and post-season game television receipts.

Ed Garvey, executive director of the NFL Players' Association, called the arrangement "socialism for management."

Given the solidarity of the National Football League owners and the stability of the franchises, the players had a difficult time organizing and bargaining with management. Although the National Football League Players' Association was established in 1956, and was primarily concerned with insurance benefits and creation of a pension fund, it made little headway against commissioners Bert Bell and Peter Rozelle. Part of the weakness of the players was an inability to identify themselves as workers instead of professionals. Creighton Miller, legal counsel to the NFLPA during the 1950s, refused even to call the association a union, and the owners would not bargain in good faith. Although the players made some progress in improving their insurance benefits and establishing a pension fund, they did not achieve a collective bargaining agreement with the league until 1968.

Organizing professional hockey players was a different matter. After his ill-fated experiment with the American Baseball Players' Guild in 1946, Robert Murphy had set his sights on the National Hockey League, but he had come away astounded at the conservative authoritarianism of most players. During the 1950s nearly 90 percent of the men playing in the National Hockey League were Canadians—farm boys from the prairies of Saskatchewan and Alberta, lumberjacks from the forests of Ontario, fishermen from the Maritime Provinces, and French Canadians from Quebec. The farmers, lumberjacks, and fishermen were notoriously independent people, suspicious of any institutions out to restrict them. French Canadians were similarly conservative, but for different reasons. Burdened for centuries by the yoke of Anglo Protestantism, the French Canadians had hidden behind their language and religion, deferring to the church on all social, economic, and political questions. They were also strongly antiunion. Unlike other Catholic immigrants to the United States, the French Canadians were rock-ribbed Republicans, the backbone of the GOP consensus in Maine, Vermont, and New Hampshire. Employers regularly used them as strikebreakers in the New England mill towns against the Irish-dominated unions. To say the least, the French Canadians were hard to organize.

The structure of the National Hockey League also militated against successful labor organization. The NHL drew most of its players from the ranks of the minor league Junior A teams, and Canadian kids often left high school to enter the minors. High school diplomas and college educations had a low priority for most of them. Young, impressionable, and politically naive, they tended to be deferential to management and easily controlled. Appeals for group unity usually fell on deaf ears. Hockey players as a group were also reverential about the sport. They wanted to play about as much as they wanted to breathe; anything keeping them off the ice—strikes, boycotts, hold-outs—was anathema to them.

Labor organization in hockey also came up against the tightest monopoly in professional sports—the James Norris–Arthur Wirtz conglomerate. Wirtz, a 1922 graduate of the University of Michigan, parlayed a little bit of cash and a lot of business acumen into a Chicago business empire of rental housing, liquor distributorships, banks, radio stations, and movie theaters. He teamed up with James Norris, a wealthy Chicago businessman, in 1933 to purchase the six-year-old Olympia Arena in Detroit for $250,000 and the Detroit Red Wing hockey franchise for $100,000. The two bought the 17,000-seat Chicago Stadium in 1935 for $300,000 and the Chicago Black Hawk hockey franchise in 1946. Eventually, Wirtz and Norris also bought a 40 percent interest in Madison Square Garden and what amounted to control of the New York Rangers. Along with promoter Conn Smythe, who owned the Toronto Maple Leafs and the Maple Leaf Garden, they ran the NHL like a fiefdom. Norris died in 1952, and his son, Jim, Jr., inherited the family assets and Wirtz partnership. By that time both Wirtz and Norris were implicated in the organized crime debate raging in America during the early 1950s. Through their International Boxing Club, they promoted fights at Madison Square Garden, the Polo Grounds, and Yankee Stadium, but they also kept company with Frankie Carbo, an underworld figure eventually sentenced to twenty-five years in prison for extortion. Jim

Norris, Jr., and Art Wirtz kept out of trouble, even though their reputations were tarnished. It didn't matter much to them. They were rich and kept the National Hockey League small and exclusive, with only six teams—the Boston Bruins, the Chicago Black Hawks, the Detroit Red Wings, the Montreal Canadiens, the New York Rangers, and the Toronto Maple Leafs.

Norris, Wirtz, and Smythe had no qualms about limiting salaries or regularly trading players between teams. By 1957 the minimum salary was only $7,000 for a seventy-game schedule. Smythe understood the game and the crowds, and his Maple Leafs gained a reputation for scrappy violence on the ice. In reply to critics of the violence, Smythe sarcastically remarked, "Yes, we've got to stamp out this sort of thing—or people are going to keep on buying tickets."

There was little the players could do, even if they had wanted to. In 1956, NHL president Clarence Campbell, at the urging of Wirtz and Norris, signed a ten-game television contract with CBS, but none of the money went for player salaries or pensions. This irritated some players, but they did nothing about it until 1957, when Campbell negotiated a twenty-one game contract with CBS. At that point, several players, led by "Terrible" Ted Lindsay, formed the National Hockey League Players Association, demanded a share of the television revenues, and filed an antitrust suit against the NHL. Their suit came in the midst of the Celler committee hearings on sports. Rather than invite an investigation, Norris and Wirtz agreed to make payments to a player pension fund, and the union dropped the lawsuit. Satisfied with that "victory," and convinced that the NHL was essentially fair in its treatment of them, players backed away from the union, and the players' association disappeared for the next decade. Hockey players were just too conservative, and management was too self-contained, for any sustained confrontation in the 1950s between labor and the owners.

In sharp contrast to the cultural harmony prevailing among NFL owners and the NHL empire presided over by Arthur Wirtz and Jim Norris, the major leagues in baseball and the NBA were business free-for-alls bedeviled by bitter internecine warfare and franchise shifting. Although labor relations in basketball were not nearly as neolithic as in hockey, they still lagged behind baseball and football. The National Basketball Players Association, guided single-handedly by Harvard-trained attorney Larry Fleisher, was not founded until 1961, compared to the creation of the NFL Players Association in 1956, the Major League Baseball Players Association in 1954, and the NHL Players Association in 1957. The last of the four major sports to consolidate its league structure, professional basketball was still a marginal operation in the 1950s. Few teams actually turned a profit, and the competitive atmosphere among the owners was so great that they did not even permit any sharing of gate receipts with visiting teams—a practice good for teams in New York and Philadelphia but bad for those in Waterloo and Sheboygan. Between 1950 and 1960, the Pittsburgh Ironmen, Toronto Huskies, Providence Steamrollers, St. Louis Bombers, Sheboygan Redskins, Waterloo Hawks, Anderson Packers, Denver Nuggets, and Indianapolis Olympians all went under. Arenas were often small, attendance was limited, and management was weak. By 1954 the NBA had declined to eight franchises. During the 1956–57 season the Fort Wayne Pistons moved to Detroit and the Rochester Royals to Cincinnati. The Syracuse Nationals were then the smallest city in the league. The Philadelphia Warriors moved to San Francisco in 1962, at the same time that the Minneapolis Lakers were going to Los Angeles. In 1963 Syracuse moved to Philadelphia.

Weak enterprises are poor targets for labor organizations, and the NBA in the 1950s was no exception. But the ethnic factor also worked on basketball players, though not like the ethnoreligious conservatism of French Canadian hockey players. Throughout American history, racial animosities between workers have proven to be organized labor's greatest handicap. The American Federation of Labor excluded blacks for half a century, and employers regularly brought in unemployed blacks as strikebreakers. Nothing so dramatic happened in the NBA, but as blacks became increasingly important in the league during the 1950s, a racial wedge worked against player unity, and not until the early 1960s, when blacks began to dominate league play, did players enjoy the unity a successful labor movement required.

Although baseball had the advantages of longevity and commercial stability, the internal relationship between team owners resembled a dog fight more than the business harmony prevailing in the National Football League. While the NFL and NHL owners had agreed to pool television revenues by 1961 in order to maintain a competitive balance in the league, baseball and basketball teams had preferred to let the free market prevail, leaving the teams in major cities in a much better economic position. And unlike the NBA, the NFL, and the NHL, baseball owners had refused to install an amateur player draft until 1965, nearly thirty years after the National Football League had done so. Instead, they had competed among themselves to sign the best talent, a practice good for the players but hardly in keeping with the cartel-like business practices sports executives preferred.

Although franchise shifting was not nearly as pronounced in baseball as it was in basketball, it was far more common than in football and hockey, primarily because the club owners were not nearly as inclined to cooperate with one another. In 1950, there were eight teams each in the American League and the National League, and during the 1950s and 1960s six of the sixteen clubs switched cities. The Boston Braves were first to go, when owner Lou Perini moved the club to Milwaukee in 1953. The franchise had lost a good deal of money between 1920 and 1950, and Perini anticipated larger television revenues in Milwaukee. He was right. The Braves drew 1.8 million fans in Milwaukee their first year, and their success triggered a rash of franchise shifts. In 1954, the American League approved the shift of the St. Louis Browns, whose attendance had averaged only 250,000 a year, to Baltimore, where they became the Baltimore Orioles. The next year the Philadelphia Athletics, long the property of the Connie Mack family, moved to Kansas City. In 1961, the Washington Senators abandoned the nation's capital for greener pastures in Minneapolis–St. Paul, and in 1964 the Braves moved again, to Atlanta, to take advantage of a lucrative television contract. The Kansas City Athletics then moved to Oakland.

The franchise shift which raised the most protest, exposed owner greed, and served as a beacon for the American sports future was Walter O'Malley's decision in 1957 to move the Brooklyn Dodgers to Los Angeles. O'Malley, once described as having "a face even Dale Carnegie would want to punch," was a driven businessman intent on profits and prestige. In the early 1950s, no baseball franchise was as closely associated with a city as the Dodgers were with Brooklyn—both of them proud, ethnically diverse, and scrappy. The team was also one of the most successful franchises in the National League, regularly drawing more than a million fans and enjoying the most lucrative television contract in baseball.

But O'Malley wasn't satisfied. With only 35,000 seats, Ebbets Field did not have the potential for future growth; its parking facilities were far too limited; and the surrounding neighborhood was rapidly deteriorating. He was also worried about the success of Lou Perini and the Braves in Milwaukee, where their gates were exceeding the Dodger totals. O'Malley suspected that the Braves would soon be outbidding the Dodgers for amateur talent because of the revenues they were taking in at County Stadium. He tried to negotiate for a new stadium somewhere in Brooklyn, but New York Park Commissioner Robert Moses didn't like the idea of using public funds to subsidize private professional sports teams. So instead O'Malley cast his gaze on Los Angeles, a city which had been actively soliciting a professional franchise since 1941. In 1956 Mayor Norris Poulson made O'Malley an offer he couldn't refuse—more than 300 acres at Chavez Ravine, a vacant area close to downtown and crossed on three sides by new freeways, with the city providing $5 million worth of earth moving and freeway access roads to the new stadium. It was an extraordinarily good deal for O'Malley; Chavez Ravine was appraised at $18 million.

Three problems stood in O'Malley's way: the Los Angeles Angels, a Chicago Cub franchise in the Pacific Coast League; prohibitive travel costs for teams traveling to Los Angeles; and the feelings of two million Brooklynites. Phil Wrigley solved the first problem. Convinced that the future of baseball depended on expansion to the West Coast, Wrigley sold the Los Angeles Angels and Wrigley Field to O'Malley for $3.25 million. O'Malley then traded Wrigley Field for Chavez Ravine with the city of Los Angeles. To cut down on travel costs, O'Malley convinced Horace Stoneham, the owner of the New York Giants, to move his franchise out to San Francisco. Stoneham was tired of the ancient Polo Grounds for the same reason O'Malley disliked Ebbets Field. He needed the Dodger rivalry to attract fans to the Polo Grounds; without the "Bums" he worried about the collapse of his own franchise. So at the invitation of the city of San Francisco, Stoneham took Willie Mays and the New York Giants out to San Francisco. As for the feelings of the Brooklyn fans, O'Malley simply said the hell with them and moved the team in 1958. Dodger attendance climbed steadily, and by the 1980s they were regularly drawing more than three million people a season.

Against owners as cavalier about other people's feelings as Walter O'Malley, the players had an uphill battle during the 1950s and early 1960s trying to organize. The collapse of Robert Murphy's American Baseball Players' Guild in 1946 had discouraged the players, as had the antiunion sentiments of the time. By the early 1950s, however, they were angered again, this time by Commissioner Ford Frick's refusal to disclose any details about the status of the pension fund. In November 1953, the Supreme Court had once again upheld baseball's antitrust exemption, and in December the players formed the Major League Baseball Players' Association, with legendary pitcher Bob Feller as president. The owners were predictably apoplectic, one of them even accusing the players of "trying to shoot Santa Claus," but they met with the association and agreed to an increase in the minimum salary to $6,000 a year and dedication of 60 percent of World Series and All-Star Game television revenues to the pension fund. But in those early years the players said nothing about the antitrust exemption or the reserve clause, failed to pay their dues consistently enough to support the MLBPA financially, and studiously avoided referring to themselves as a labor union.

• • •

Although the 1950s and early 1960s saw very little change in collective bargaining between players and owners, there had still been real financial progress in the four major sports. Between 1950 and 1960 the median income of professional athletes increased more than 130 percent, compared to only 77 percent for other workers. Television revenues were the major reason for the pay raises; however, the owners, when faced with concerted player opposition or the threat of legal or court action, had usually responded in at least a minimal way. Both owners and players still basically accepted the antitrust exemptions and the reserve clauses as the natural order of things. Both sides were usually willing to fine-tune some of their outstanding differences, but neither of them really questioned the legitimacy of the cartel arrangement in professional sports.

But the organization of the players' associations in professional sports as well as the franchise shifts, especially the move by the profitable Dodgers to Los Angeles, were signs of the future. By the early 1960s, times were changing. The status quo values of the 1950s gave way to activism and rebellion among young people, blacks,

Hispanics, and women. The steadily growing momentum of the civil rights movement and the controversy surrounding the war in Vietnam changed the mood of America, inspiring skepticism about tradition and basic institutions. At the same time, the economic decline of the Northeast, the rise of the Sunbelt, and the triumph of television provided new growth opportunities for professional sports. The combination of new social attitudes and new economic opportunities would revolutionize the place of sports in American society. An era was coming to an end, and nobody more clearly represented the past than Art Rooney of the Pittsburgh Steelers. He loved the team, stayed with them through good times and bad, and viewed the franchise as a family demanding and deserving friendship, support, and loyalty. Born in Coulterville, Pennsylvania, and raised in Pittsburgh by a working-class family, Rooney was a devout Roman Catholic blessed with a special sense of place and community. He was a gifted swimmer and boxer, loved sports and competition, and had a penchant for the ponies, with enough skill as a handicapper to win a fortune at the racetracks. Rooney purchased the Steelers for $2,500 in 1933. Long after he had accumulated a personal fortune, he still lived in a three-story house across the street from his childhood home. He loved the neighborhood and stayed there even after urban blight set in.

For fifty years Rooney watched every Steeler game, at home or on the road, suffering through the decades of doormat status in the NFL and then exulting with the heroics of Terry Bradshaw, Franco Harris, Lynn Swann, and "Mean Joe" Greene and the championships of the 1970s. By that time Rooney was a sports dinosaur living in tune with the rhythms of an earlier era. He cared about his players as people, worried about their problems and their families, wanted to give them the best. Amidst the controversies and franchise shifts of the 1970s and 1980s, Rooney remarked that he "never thought of moving the club, or selling the club. None of us ever looked to get out. We were all in the game because it was our life, something we truly loved. When you love something, you don't just walk away from it. . . . Pittsburgh is my home. The Pittsburgh Steelers are my team." But Rooney was one of the old guard, a traditionalist. The new businessmen entering professional sports did not have such loyalties.

Winning wasn't enough. Some pros like boxer Jake LaMotta found they could earn more by agreeing to lose. (Credit: University of Notre Dame)

# • Scandal Time

*I must say I'm getting a little tired of all this deemphasis
business. Do they want us to deemphasize a player's
ability? Or deemphasize the interest of the spectators?
Or shall we deemphasize the winning of a ball game? I
think it's time we deemphasized the deemphasis.*
—ADOLF RUPP

The lure of fame, power, and money—the trinity of professional sports—seduced amateur athletes as well as professionals. After 1945, because of economic consolidation, urbanization, and the Cold War, sports had increasingly become the mirror in which Americans interpreted their own culture and expressed their values. The power struggles of international Olympic politics, racial integration, and professional commercialism had pushed sports past mere recreation and diversion. Sports became a larger-than-life business, a guaranteed way to achieve success and recognition—for individuals, cities, and institutions. At the amateur level of American colleges, the ideals of gentlemanly competition and sportsmanship gave way to victory, gate receipts, national rankings, and championships. The drive to win and be number one exposed the darker side of human nature and sport. Schools big and small experienced the same problems.

•  •  •

Clair Bee was a study in contradictions. Born among the strip miners of West Virginia, he worked his way toward New York City in search of learning. He believed in hard work and education. He held graduate degrees in four different subjects, and he wrote scores of books and articles. He wrote a series of novels for adolescent boys which featured a clean-cut, All-American scholar-athlete named

**73**

Chip Hilton. Chip was the Protestant work ethic incarnate. A vision of Bee's ideal boy, Chip played three sports, excelled in them all, and still found time to be a perfect son, a great friend, and an A-plus student.

In 1931 the president of Long Island University, a small private college located in an industrial section of Brooklyn, hired Bee to coach football and baseball for the school. The board of directors at LIU believed that a successful athletic program would stimulate student morale, increase the university's enrollment, and help compensate for classes which convened in factory buildings, lofts, and a rented hall above a bowling alley. Bee began immediately to build LIU into a sports power. He expected his players to be disciplined, and he carefully instructed them on the intricacies of their positions. Above all else, he wanted to win games, even if the morals and ethics of Chip Hilton had to be shelved temporarily. One of his former players remembered: "Breathing and winning had the same importance to Clair Bee. The day before a football game, Bee would go to a coal mining town in Pennsylvania and recruit players to represent LIU." Another former player recalled that Bee used similar tactics to win baseball games: "There was one day in 1935 when Bee desperately needed a pitcher for a game against Princeton . . . Bee came up with a guy named Mike DiVito, who happened to be enrolled in NYU at the time. DiVito was at NYU on a baseball scholarship but was temporarily ineligible because of low grades. DiVito pitched and won the Princeton game for the Blackbirds."

In 1932 Bee added basketball to his list of coaching duties. During the next twenty years he turned LIU into a national basketball power. At first LIU played home games in a match-box gym rented from the Brooklyn College of Pharmacy. The Druggist's Den, however, was not large enough to contain Bee's ambitions. Aided by shady recruiting tactics, he soon fielded a team of national caliber, and Madison Square Garden, the Mecca of college basketball, became the Blackbirds' unofficial home court. For Bee and his team, the larger Garden audiences were far more impersonal than the loyal fans that crowded into the Druggist's Den to watch the Blackbirds: "Now the boys were exposed to the hard, brassy atmosphere of show business. They looked around the jammed arena and all they saw was the Broadway crown. Their own schoolmates were in the peanut gallery, temporarily out of sight and mind. They were surrounded by a sea of strange faces peering at them as though they were livestock exhibits."

As the years passed, basketball became LIU's greatest source of revenue and national prestige. Between 1933 and 1951 few, if any, teams won as many games as the Blackbirds. LIU's teams blended speed and power with a disciplined style of play. As great as the teams were, however, by the 1940s in one area they were surprisingly weak. The Blackbirds consistently failed to cover the point spread against vastly inferior opponents. Sure they won, but they won by six points in games they were picked to win by ten, three points in games which they were favored by five. By 1950 there were rumors that various city schools were shaving points for gamblers. CCNY, NYU, St. John's, and Manhattan were all suspect. At LIU talk had gone far beyond the rumor stage. It was simply accepted as a fact that LIU was shaving points. By the 1950–51 season several bookmakers refused to take bets on LIU games. On the street, such evidence of a fix amounted to a smoking gun.

The arrests started during the cold early months of 1951. Six LIU players admitted that they had taken money to shave points. They were joined by seven players from CCNY, two from Manhattan, and one from NYU. The timely intervention of an influential lawyer kept the police away from St. John's, but the point-shaving scandal spread to the Midwest, encompassing such national powers as Kentucky, Bradley, and Toledo.

When Bee heard the news about Eddie Gard, the first LIU player to be arrested, he was "very disappointed." But, he claimed, "the rest of my boys are innocent. I swear it on the heads of my children." His confidence was unwarranted. Other LIU players soon joined Gard at police headquarters, including Sherman White, who had just been named as the *Sporting News'* Player of the Year in college basketball. Within one week LIU had suspended the guilty players and dropped its entire intercollegiate sports programs.

Afterward in a *Saturday Evening Post* article, Bee admitted: "Confidence in college basketball is shattered and the fault is partly mine. I was a 'win-em-all' coach who helped to create the emotional climate that led to the worst scandal in the history of sports." As Bee indicated, the problem was one of misplaced priorities. College basketball had become a very profitable war waged between universities, and the players were the soldiers. "We were playing basketball for money and some boys followed the college's example." Too late Bee learned that winning was not everything. "I know (now) that having a losing team is better than having no team at all. Anything is infinitely better than waiting beside a telephone at four o'clock in the morning while kids in a police station are signing confessions that will brand them as long as they live."

The basketball scandals of 1951 brought into the open the problems—the deep corruption—of intercollegiate athletics. It was not a new story. Forged transcripts, special treatment for players, illegal payments, slush funds, and the like had been around for a half century. Nor would the scandals lead to any large-scale reforms. The abuses which led to the scandals of 1951 would continue to plague college sports. Unlike professional sports, neither the government nor the leaders of college athletics have shown any inclination to clean up the sordid situation. The result has been that nothing has changed except the names of the accused.

• • •

The political mood of the 1950s cast a long shadow. Shocked as Americans were by the revelations that the Russians had an atomic bomb and that the Communists had China, an uneasy but expectant quiet spread across the nation. As yet in the early 1950s it was without form, just a vague feeling that America was losing its postwar grip on the rest of the world, that important events were occurring in a haphazard manner. Though often unarticulated, it was a feeling that was nevertheless unnerving, and many thoughtful Americans longed to awake and find that their uneasiness was only a nightmare. Most frightening of all, there was simply no way to predict what would happen next.

The activities of restless youth took on sinister new meanings. As the father in *Bye, Bye Birdie,* a comic parody of a very serious time, asked, "What's the matter with kids today?" This was particularly true in the world of sports. It was commonly believed that organized sports were good for young men, that they taught such socially useful virtues as hard work, team play, discipline, delayed gratification, and sacrifice for the good of the whole. By the late 1940s, however, it had become apparent that sports also offered lessons in greed, ruthlessness, brutality, and dishonesty.

Corruption surfaced first in professional sports. Boxing had never had a clean reputation, but it reached a low point in the late 1940s and 1950s. In 1947 heavyweight champion Joe Louis retired, and through a complicated process the promotional power in the sport passed from Mike Jacobs, who had promoted Louis's fights, to millionaire sportsman James Norris, Jr. Norris, in turn, shared his newly won power with several other men, most prominently John Paul "Frankie" Carbo, a leading underworld figure who had been arrested and imprisoned on charges that ranged from vagrancy and felonious assaults to grand larceny, robbery, and murder. Carbo dressed conservatively, abhorred the daylight, and was almost universally feared. Before joining Norris, his last major trial had taken place in 1940. In a brief biography of Carbo presented in 1960 to the Subcommittee on Antitrust and Monopoly of the Committee of Judiciary of the United States Senate, headed by Senator Estes Kefauver, New York City detective Frank Marrone said:

> On Thanksgiving Day in 1939, Harry Shachter, alias Harry Greenberg also known as "Big Greeney," a member of Murder, Inc., was assassinated outside his home in Hollywood, California. . . . Al Tannenbaum, a member of Murder, Inc., . . . testified that Carbo fired five bullets into Shachter, and that "Bugsy" Siegel drove the getaway car. This trial resulted in a hung jury and Abe "Kid Twist" Reles, a witness who was to testify against Carbo in the second trial, fell or was pushed from a hotel window in Coney Island. Carbo was not retried for this homicide.

Norris's International Boxing Club controlled almost 90 percent of all championship fights, and according to Barney Nagler, Carbo was "the Rasputin behind the Norris boxing empire." Boxing's integrity, a phrase which has been a near non sequiter in the best of times, was almost totally sacrificed. If a fighter hoped to battle for the championship, he had to deal with Carbo. For example, Jake La Motta, an outstanding middleweight contender, was told that if he hoped to get a title shot against champion Marcel Cerdan, he first had to lose a bout against Billy Fox, a boxer managed by Carbo's close associate Frank "Blinky" Palermo. La Motta agreed. On November 14, 1947, La Motta and Fox put on a shameless exhibition. After the first round, La Motta allowed Fox to pummel him around the ring, but Fox was unable to hurt La Motta. Proud of his reputation for taking a punch, La Motta refused to go down. He was willing to compromise his integrity on a purely business deal, but not his reputation. In the fourth round the referee stopped the fight. The bout was clearly fixed, a detail which La Motta later confirmed under oath. Several years after the bout La Motta signed an exclusive service contract with the IBC and was matched against Cerdan for the title. La Motta won and became champion.

No one knows how many other fights were fixed. But Billy Fox's career offers several telling suggestions. When Fox fought La Motta he had already won 50 of 51 fights, all by knockouts. At least that's what the record books indicated. In truth, some of his fights were mythical, others were fixed. In 1956 Fox said that life with Palermo was full of surprises. "The first funny thing happened when I fought his Larry Kellum, who I had already beat under his own name. This time he called himself Andy Holland." In another fight Fox was tired and losing going into the late rounds. Palermo told him, "Throw a lot of punches. Throw a lot of punches." Fox recalled, "It's funny, I think I remember, I *think* I remember Blinky in the other guy's corner . . . before the 10th round started. I threw a lot, but I didn't think I had any power in my punches. I was surprised when he went down." When Fox questioned Palermo about fights on his record that he had never had, Blinky told the boxer that he added them for the sake of publicity. Looking over his record, Fox commented, "There was Jimmy Davenport. I don't remember him. Billy Smith, he's in here twice. I don't remember him either. Who's this Kid Wolf? Johnny Furia, Wesley Hayes, I never heard of those guys."

Fox's career ended sadly. Behind Carbo and his associates' activities, there is another quite human story. Fox cared about his career and the La Motta fix hurt him deeply. "I still feel hurt. It affected my whole life. Made me feel despondent, downhearted, disgusted. . . . Why couldn't he have done it to a guy who didn't give a damn." After his "victory" over La Motta, Fox's career took a sharp turn downward. He had lost respect for himself. "I used to brush my teeth twice a day, not only in the morning but in the night, too. Was a time where, I think it was three weeks, I didn't brush my teeth at all. Just didn't feel like doing anything, the way I felt." He started to smoke, lost the will to train, and spent what little money he had saved. By 1956 Fox had found his way to a boxer's retirement home—a state mental hospital.

Fox's case was not unusual. Most of the fighters controlled by Carbo's cronies ended their careers penniless. Ike Williams, the great lightweight champion, was forced to take on Palermo as a manager if he hoped to get any fights. In 1948 Williams fought championship matches against Beau Jack and Jesse Flores. Palermo kept the entire purses from both fights. Bitter about the affair, Williams recalled: "The commission doesn't care, they don't care. I fought those two fights for nothing, and paid taxes on them!"

Norris's and Carbo's primary enemy was their own success. They controlled too much of the fight industry, deciding who would fight for the championship and who would battle in the lucrative television matches. They had forged a classic monopoly. In 1952 the Justice Department initiated an antitrust suit against the IBC. In 1957 Federal Judge Sylvester Ryan ruled that the IBC was in restraint of trade and ordered "divestiture, dissolution, and divorcement." Two years later the IBC officially disbanded, and the legal framework of the monopoly collapsed.

Carbo, of course, exerted his influence behind the scenes in an illegal manner. Although his wife was on the IBC payroll, he was not a legal member of the organization. Judge Ryan's ruling did not actually limit Carbo's power. By the later 1950s, however, Carbo had more serious problems of his own. In 1959 Carbo was convicted of operating as an undercover manager without a license. He was sentenced to two years in prison. During the next year Carbo was also indicted, tried, and ultimately convicted for income tax evasion and conspiring to violate interstate commerce by extortion. For the second offense, Carbo was given another twenty-five years.

Few people knew how extensively organized crime controlled boxing. And when the corruption was exposed, even fewer people were surprised. It had always been a low-life sport populated by seedy characters, and rumors of fixed fights were as frequent as Friday night bouts. During the 1950s, 32 percent of boxers and 12 percent of managers had criminal records. By the early 1950s, however, athletic corruption had spread to the supposedly wholesome sports. Some of the greatest basketball players in America's universities and colleges were involved, and this scandal upset many people. University leaders charged with the task of instilling ethics and morality in American youth were directly involved.

In the years after World War II, Americans became increasingly concerned with the country's rising juvenile delinquency rates. They saw an answer to their problem in sports. "Organized sport is one of our best weapons against juvenile delinquency," commented J. Edgar Hoover in 1947. He essentially divided youths into two categories—those who played sports and those who did not. The first group channeled their skills and energy into football, basketball, and baseball; they competed for championship trophies. The second group turned to crime for excitement and competed for "wrist watches, bracelets and automobiles that belong to other people." Sports could save America, Hoover believed. But, he warned, "we can have no patience with any evil practices trying to establish roots in our sports, because clean sports mean too much to the country."

Certainly by 1950 sports were identified as a national resource. They developed the minds and bodies of young boys and girls, and they strengthened the health of the nation. No athletes were viewed as more virtuous than the college All-Americans. They formed a natural aristocracy based not on birth, wealth, race, or religion, but on ability. Visions of Gilbert Patten and Frank Merriwell, two fictional All-Americans, continued to dominate American thinking about college athletes. They were heroes who were modest in victory, gracious in defeat (or would have been gracious if they had been defeated), and at all times fair and honest. Before 1950 the periodic college recruiting scandals failed to erase this myth. Then came 1951.

The first scandal of that year involved basketball. Most of America was football country, but in New York City college basketball was king. New York made college basketball. Before the 1930s basketball was primarily a sport to condition young boys and girls, and it was mostly played in physical education classes. Compared to football, it seemed to be a "sissy" sport, and outside of a few areas it did not generate much spectator interest. Then in 1931 Ned Irish, a young reporter, convinced mayor Jimmy Walker that college basketball could be used to raise money for the city's unemployed. On December 31, 1931, Madison Square Garden held the first of its famous triple-headers between six New York City colleges. It was a remarkable success, as were the triple-headers held during the next two years. In 1934 Irish started renting the Garden and putting on basketball shows to raise money for himself. College basketball became a passion in the City. As Charles Rosen commented in *Scandals of '51,*

"The Garden became synonymous with quality, big-time, big-pressure college basketball. Every schoolboy in the country dreamed about playing there."

As college basketball was growing in popularity in New York City, another rage swept the country. In the early 1940s Charles K. McNeil, a former math teacher in a Connecticut prep school, opened a bookmaking operation in Chicago. Looking for a way to attract customers and make gambling more interesting, he introduced a revolutionary form a betting which he called "wholesaling odds." Instead of using the traditional system of odds—4 to 1 that North Carolina would beat Kentucky, or 5 to 2 that Notre Dame would defeat Navy—McNeil rated each team and then estimated how many points the favored team would win by. Gamblers bet then not on the odds but on the point spread. In a basketball game, if UCLA was favored to defeat Kentucky by 5 points but won by only 4 points, anyone who bet on Kentucky won. UCLA would have to win by 6 points for its supporters to win their bets. This form of handicapping quickly spread across the country. As one ex-bookie noted, "The point spread was the greatest discovery since the zipper."

In sports, however, the point spread created real problems. A team could win and lose at the same time. It could defeat its opponent but fail to cover the point spread. It was in this gray area that college players and professional gamblers found common ground. A player could agree to "shave points" off the point spread but not to actually throw the game. In return the gamblers would reward the obliging player. In college basketball, which was steadily becoming big business for the universities, shaving points became a business proposition for the players.

During the 1940s rumors of point shaving surfaced as often as unwanted friends. In 1945 a game between Brooklyn College and Akron was cancelled because of reports that Brooklyn players had agreed to fix the contest. The players later confirmed the report. New York City schools—CCNY, NYU, Columbia, St. John's, Brooklyn, Manhattan, LIU—were particularly suspect. By the mid-1940s the great Kansas coach Forrest "Phog" Allen was clearly worried about the reputation of his sport. A scandal was ripening, he warned, and it was going to "stink to high heaven."

In mid-February 1951 the scandal broke. The College of the City of New York, the Cinderella team from the 1949–50 season, was one of the first schools to feel the humiliation of exposure. Many people considered CCNY to be the elite school in New York City. Located in the middle of Harlem and spread over several streets, it was a pure cement urban university. It had no ivy walls, no Ivy tradition, and no tuition. Students needed a high average to get into CCNY and the willingness to work hard to stay there. As Charles Rosen noted, "In the later 1940s, CCNY was nothing less than the world's third largest university and it had a reputation to match. A City College grad could get a job anywhere in New York."

CCNY also had a proud basketball tradition. Nat Holman, a great coach by everyone's standards, especially his own, guided the team. Born on the Lower East Side into a Russian immigrant family, Holman had been one of the premiere basketball players of his day; he was the star of the original Celtics during the 1920s. In most ways, he was a cold, incredibly self-centered man. But he knew how to play, coach, and teach basketball. During the 1930s and early 1940s, he made CCNY one of the best basketball schools in the country. Although he had trouble remembering his players' names, he knew how to win basketball games.

When academic and basketball standards collided at CCNY, a compromise course was usually discovered. During the late 1940s Floyd Layne, whose high school average was below CCNY standards but whose basketball credentials were beyond question, was admitted as a "special student." His high school teammate, a gifted player named Ed Warner, graduated 827th in a class of 942. But Warner, too, gained admission to CCNY as a "special student." Finally Alvin "Fats" Roth, another New York high school standout whose grades did not warrant admission to CCNY, was admitted to the school. His high school records were changed so that he could meet CCNY's standards for "special students." As one of Holman's players remembered, "Forging transcripts was a widely accepted practice at City. . . . It was no big deal. . . . All Nat wanted was ballplayers. He didn't care how he got them."

In 1950 CCNY accomplished what no team before or since had done. They won both the National Invitation Tournament and the NCAA championship. And they won with only one experienced player. Holman started one senior and four sophomores—Layne, Warner, Roth, and Ed Roman. During the two tournaments they handed legendary Adolph Rupp of Kentucky his worst defeat ever and twice beat number one ranked Bradley. And they did it all while shaving points. In his history of college basketball, Neil D. Isaacs put this last detail in the proper prospective: "In a sense, abstract if not cynical, this argues that they were even more skillful than their record indicates."

CCNY was as deep in point shavers as basketball talent. At one time or another, all five of the CCNY starters and the two top reserves were guilty of shaving points. Had it not been so serious, it might have been humorous. At times the players worked at cross-purposes. Early in the 1950–51 season, CCNY played Brigham Young in the Garden. At the behest of Salvatore Sollazzo, the gambler who controlled most of CCNY's point shavers, Warner and Layne agreed to attempt to exceed the point spread. However, Roman and Roth had "suspiciously poor games," and CCNY won by only two points.

By the Christmas holidays, bookies and sports columnists were suspicious. And CCNY was not the only suspect team. LIU, Manhattan, NYU, St. John's—they all seemed to be playing more games than just basketball. Not only the quantity but the quality of point shaving was improving. Sherman White, LIU's best player and leading shaver, recalled, "We seemed able to control the game much better. We could now shave as close as we wanted without blowing the game. I guess we were getting to be better dumpers." When the arrests started LIU was undefeated.

What was bound to happen started in early January 1951. Junius Kellogg, the first black to play basketball for Manhattan College, reported a bribe attempt to the Bronx district attorney. This led to the arrest of two Manhattan players for point shaving. For a few weeks it was a big story. There was plenty of talk about ungrateful Judases and pieces of silver. The *Chicago Tribune* blamed the affair on the New Deal, and the *Daily Worker* said it was the fault of Wall Street, bankers, and greedy politicians. A number of editorials asked the general question, "What's the matter with the kids, today?" The answers were mostly vague and irrelevant, and after a week the story lost its news appeal.

Frank Hogan, the Manhattan district attorney, was not about to let the story die. Starting in mid-February there were more arrests—many more. Before the arrests ended, more than thirty players from seven schools were hauled into police headquarters.

The best players from the best City schools admitted that they had shaved points for money. It could—and probably should—have been worse. A devout Catholic, Hogan showed little inclination to go after players at the local Catholic universities. In fact, in several cases he chose to overlook—or at least not to press—damning evidence that implicated St. John's players.

Since the February arrests featured only New York City players, the press and much of the public reached a simple conclusion. Cities bred corruption. It was a familiar refrain, as old as America itself. Reporters transformed Madison Square Garden into a den of iniquity, characterizing it as an immoral melting pot stewing with dishonest gamblers and greedy black and Jewish basketball players. Anti-Semitism and racism ran riot through journalists' stories. Like the Garden, the Jewish Catskill Mountain resorts were singled out for criticism. Many of the best college basketball players "worked" in the Catskill resorts during the summer. Their jobs consisted mainly of playing basketball for a resort team. It was there in the Borscht Circuit, claimed reporters, that Jewish gamblers corrupted the athletes.

Midwestern reporters and coaches raised the loudest antiurban, anti-Semitic cry. Phog Allen, the respected Kansas coach, claimed: "Out here in the Midwest these scandalous conditions, of course, do not exist. But in the East, the boys, particularly those who participate in the resort hotel leagues during the summer months, are thrown into an environment which cannot help but breed the evil which more and more is coming to light." Adolph Rupp, the legendary Kentucky coach, agreed: "Gamblers couldn't get at my boys with a ten-foot pole." In short, Midwesterners noted a clear difference between the ethnically diverse urban players and the wholesome, generally WASPish Midwestern players.

At the end of July 1951, new reports ended midwestern smugness. Toledo and Bradley players were arrested and confessed that they too were guilty of shaving points. During the 1949–50 season, Bradley had been the best team in the Midwest; CCNY defeated Bradley in both the NIT and NCAA finals. And like CCNY, seven players on the team were point shavers, including the star guard Gene Melchiorre. But the biggest blow to the Midwest was yet to come.

Throughout the spring and summer, Kentucky's Adolph Rupp

had maintained that his program was clean. But as the scandals spilled over into the Midwest, Rupp became less critical of the guilty players. For the coach, such relative silence was unusual. As Rupp once admitted, "I'll say anything for a column." He loved to see his name in print as much as he enjoyed taking credit for Kentucky's wins. Rupp was not modest about his team's success. "It's good coaching," he readily admitted. And during the late 1940s there was no more successful college basketball program. Kentucky won the NCAA championship in 1948 and 1949, and five of its players were selected to represent the United States on the 1948 Olympic basketball team. In Kentucky and across the country, Ralph Beard, Alex Groza, and Bill Spivey were recognized All-Americans.

In the fall, the Kentucky greats joined the other confessed point shavers. Investigators also showed that Rupp had illegally paid his players after the New Orleans Sugar Bowl tournament. Rupp, however, considered the $50 payments small change. Although the Kentucky program and players were punished, Rupp was not about to alter his win-at-any-cost attitude. As one school after another reassessed their sports programs, Rupp refused to be hypocritical: "I must say I'm getting a little tired of all this deemphasis business. Do they want us to deemphasize a player's athletic ability? . . . I think it's time we deemphasized the deemphasis."

The scandals ended with Kentucky. Undoubtedly District Attorney Hogan could have pressed forward and exposed other schools, but he chose not to. In truth, the point had been made. Enough schools, coaches, and especially players had suffered. Although few of the players ever went to prison, most suffered deeply because of their involvement. The best players—White, Warner, Layne, Roman, Roth, Beard, Groza, Spivey—were barred from the NBA. Those who wanted to continue to play basketball—and many of them did—eventually joined the semi-pro Eastern Basketball League, where for about $50 a game they displayed their great talent before small crowds in dingy arenas. For many of the players, the scandals ruined their lives. Some dropped out of sight, others turned to drugs, and many lived with a haunting sense of guilt. Ralph Beard remembered that he worked on the road for fifteen years after the scandals. "Sometimes I worked from eight in the morning until ten-thirty at night. But I thought about the scandals all the time."

America was also traumatized by the ordeal. Discovering that college athletes had been paid to throw games was akin to learning that Davy Crockett had been paid to lose at the Alamo. It smacked of the un-American during a time when that was the last thing a person wanted to be. In 1950 Senator Herman Welker of Idaho, a man who loved sports as much as he hated "Red Rats," proudly boasted, "I never saw a ballplayer who was a Communist." A year later such a remark could not be made as assuredly. If a ballplayer would sell out his teammates, could he be beyond the grasp of Communism? Many Americans were not sure. Indeed, numerous editorialists were quick to link the scandals with America's Cold War problems. McCarthyism, the Korean War, and Senator Estes Kefauver's investigations made irrational reactions seem normal.

As Hogan was extending his investigations into the Midwest, another sports scandal muscled its way onto the front pages of American newspapers. And this one was even more shocking. It involved academic cheating, not point shaving, and it was limited to only one school—the United States Military Academy at West Point. In August 1951, West Point authorities dismissed ninety cadets for violation of the school's honor code. Half of the guilty cadets were football players. Their offense was termed "cribbing," which entailed learning the details of an exam before one actually took it. As Gene Filipski, one of the dismissed athletes, explained, "If you want to rationalize, cribbing as compared to outright cheating in the classroom is like shaving points in basketball compared to downright throwing the game . . . there are shades of difference. And you're going against human nature by putting temptation in front of a group of fellows in the form of, say, a chemistry test that your friends took yesterday and you're to take today."

As was the case with the basketball scandals, the ninety cadets who were dismissed probably represented a small portion of those who were actually cribbing. For example, Filipski estimated that at least 50 percent of the 450 cadets in the 1951 graduating class were cribbers, and not one of them was thrown out of West Point. Cribbing, however, was particularly widespread among Col. Earl "Red" Blaik's football players. Faced with the demands of academics, football, and honor, most of the athletes chose to emphasize football over their studies and their personal honor. Football, the cribbers maintained, represented "the honor of the Academy," and they

worked hard—practiced long hours to the point of "unbelievable fa-
tigue," said Blaik—to uphold the school's honor on the gridiron.
Harold Loehlein, honor cadet, captain-elect of the 1951 football
team, and president of the First Class, stated the players' position:
"Sure, I cribbed at times, but a lot of the boys thought it was justified
because we gave a lot of time to the football team. In some cases,
friendship comes above the honor system." Although he did not attack the honor system, Coach Blaik defended the guilty players, one
of whom was his son. "I know them to be men of excellent character," Blaik told reporters.

The three-man board that investigated the episode disagreed.
They felt that the morality of the country would be endangered if
they allowed any dishonorable men to be graduated by West Point.
The code was sacrosanct. It had been set up in 1817 by Sylvanus
Thayer, the "Father of West Point," and given its final shape by
Douglas MacArthur during the 1920s. It was, according to Dwight
Eisenhower, "akin to the virtue of (a cadet's) mother or sister." Defending the code in an editorial in *Newsweek,* retired General Carl
Spaatz criticized "the athletic clique" whose "distorted sense of
values led them to assume that football and the maintenance of a
winning team was the ultimate objective of their service at the Academy." Spaatz considered any change in the code "unthinkable," but
he urged a reevaluation of the role of football at West Point.

The week that Army superintendent Major General Frederick
A. Irving announced the dismissals, 67 American soldiers were
killed fighting in Korea. That lifted the total to 13,407, with another
10,624 missing. Thus, any scandal that questioned the honor of West
Point became a hot political topic. Senator Harry F. Byrd of Virginia
was outraged by the cribbing: "These acts have struck a blow at the
morals of the youth of the country which will last for a long time." 
Arkansas' Senator J. William Fulbright called for the suspension of
football at West Point. President Harry Truman announced that he
had ordered an investigation of the athletic programs at both service
academies. For several months editorialists worried about the implications of the scandal. What was wrong with America's youth?
What had happened to America's sense of mission? Was morality a
relative concept? "Make sure to choose the harder right instead of
the easier wrong," said the "Cadet Prayer of West Point." Had college sports made a mockery of such noble words?

The most important result of the scandals of 1951 was that after all of the righteous indignation subsided, very little changed. There were no significant attempts to correct the abuses in intercollegiate athletics. Several schools deemphasized their sports programs, a few more suffered minor punishments, and most of the ones located west of the Hudson River decided to stay away from Madison Square Garden. But there was no attempt to eliminate athletic slush funds or curtail illegal payments to players, forged transcripts, and other forms of special treatment for athletes.

In fact, the struggle for athletic dominance intensified. The NCAA encouraged this trend through its actions. In 1948 the NCAA had recognized the right of schools to give scholarships and jobs to athletes, but under the "sanity code" the NCAA insisted that all aid had to be based on demonstratable financial need. The object was to help young men with athletic ability to get a college education, not to simply reward athletes for being athletes. It was a fine distinction, but a real one nonetheless. In 1952 the NCAA removed even that distinction. It repealed the sanity code and allowed colleges to award scholarships based only on athletic talent. Increasingly, the word "student" in the phrase "student athlete" became a meaningless modifier.

Illegal recruiting similarly intensified. The fight for the best athletic talent reached shocking proportions. Wilt Chamberlain, the greatest high school basketball "product" of the 1950s, was recruited by over 200 colleges and universities—77 "major" schools and 128 "minor" schools. He started visiting colleges during his sophomore year in high school, and he finally decided to attend Kansas, coached by sanctimonious Phog Allen. The decision aroused the interest of the NCAA, the FBI, the IRS, and thousands of journalists. Why would a black from the streets of Philadelphia want to relocate to the prairies of Kansas? Rumors had it that wealthy Kansas alums had agreed to pay Chamberlain $30,000 after his Kansas career ended. The stories were false. By his own estimation, Chamberlain had probably been paid "less than $20,000" by the time he left Kansas after his sophomore year. And that was far less than he had been offered by other schools. Rationalizing his decision to accept the illegal payments, Chamberlain noted, "With me playing basketball, Kansas University, the city of Lawrence, the state of Kansas, and all these alums get richer. People bought tickets to see me play, and they ate meals and bought clothes and rented motels while they were there. . . . Why should I let them exploit me, without reaping a little of the profit myself? I figured it was a fair trade."

Connie Hawkins went to Iowa for the same reason Chamberlain went to Kansas. One of the best high school basketball players in the country, he wasn't even sure what went on inside a college. "I thought college must be kind of a big Boys High (his high school), but with girls and a better basketball team," he remembered. Recruiters offered Hawkins everything and then promised him more. Lou Carnesecca, then freshman coach and chief recruiter for St. John's, said to Hawkins's high school coach, "Look Mickey, we want Hawkins badly. But I'm not going to bother you. You just collect the offers. When you get them all, pick out the best one and show it to me. Then we'll top it, no matter what." In the end, Hawkins chose Iowa for simple but compelling reasons: "They seemed like nice people, and they offered me the most money."

Soon it was 1951 all over again. William H. Breezley in his perceptive discussion of the 1961 scandal commented: "The athlete's general feeling was that he had been hired to play basketball. The prevailing feeling on the part of gamblers was that if the athlete could be hired to play the game, then he could be hired to play it not quite so well." Once again, the gamblers were right. Generally speaking, they were good at their jobs. Art Hicks, one of Seton Hall's point shavers, gave credit where credit was due: "One thing you never hear about the gamblers is how good they were at what they did. They were experts at human nature. . . . They catch you at just the right time, when you're vulnerable. They can look at a kid's game and see there ain't no love there. They can tell when a kid don't respect his coach. They knew that blacks at certain schools had no social life. Whatever the problem, they knew how to exploit it." By 1957 rumors were once again circulating that gamblers were exploiting the problems.

Jimmy Breslin, a reporter with good sources among New York gamblers, was not surprised when police exposed another basketball scandal. Between 1957 and 1961 he heard a series of reports that games across the country were being fixed. In 1957 he wrote an article for *Sport* in which he detailed the signs. High-pressure recruiting and big-money gambling created the right conditions for a scandal. It was, he suggested, only a matter of time.

In March 1961 District Attorney Hogan announced that he had uncovered another point-shaving scandal. One investigator reported, "Just wait until it all comes out; it'll make 1951 look like peanuts." Of course, as in 1951, the full extent of the corruption probably never has been uncovered. Officially, the 1951 scandal involved 7 schools, 33 players, and 49 fixed games played in 23 cities and 19 states. Officially, in 1961 Hogan's list included 22 colleges, 37 players, and 44 fixed games. But a great deal of evidence was simply ignored. For example, Hogan had evidence that Jack Molinas, one of the central figures in the scandal, had made deals with more than 50 players from 23 schools.

The public exposure of the point-shaving scandal began after Hogan arrested Aaron Wagman and Joseph Hacken, two New York gamblers and fixers. Once again, players from the City schools were the most deeply involved. Players from NYU, Brooklyn College, and Columbia admitted that they had rigged games. And unlike the 1951 scandal, players at Catholic St. John's were drawn into the affair. But the scandal quickly moved south, from St. Joseph's and La Salle to North Carolina, Tennessee, and Mississippi State. In truth, probably the reason that New York City schools and players were featured so prominently in both the 1951 and 1961 scandals was the result of Hogan investigations. Had Hogan started his work in Philadelphia, Chicago, or any other major basketball city the scandals might have involved a different cast of characters.

Once again, Americans wondered why. Certainly greed was a factor, but the players pointed to other reasons. Art Hicks, the star of an outstanding Seton Hall team, spoke about the latent racism in college sports. A black, he was recruited to Seton Hall to play basketball, and this was his only tie to the school. It was a typical scenario. During the late 1940s and 1950s Catholic schools freely recruited blacks to play on their basketball teams, which were bringing them national attention. Chuck Cooper, the first black to play in the NBA, and Sihugo Green played for Duquesne; Walter Dukes for Seton Hall; Maurice Stokes for St. Francis of Pennsylvania; Bill Russell and K. C. Jones for San Francisco. They were out of place—Protestant blacks in overwhelmingly white Catholic colleges. Cheered on the court, many had trouble adjusting off the court. Hicks remembered his moment of truth. He overheard one of his white teammates say, "Tomorrow we got an easy game, so we won't be giving the ball to the niggers." Alienation made the decision to shave points easier.

So did the desperation of poverty. Raymond Poprocky was a blond-haired guard for NYU. With work he might have played in the NBA. But in 1960 he was in economic trouble. His father had recently died, his wife had to quit her job because she was pregnant, and besides carrying sixteen credits in school and playing basketball, he worked a regular shift in a fruit cannery. He knew it was wrong to shave points, but said he would do it again in the same circumstances. "Not because I'd want to, but because I'd be forced to. It was better than robbing a grocery store."

There was plenty of blame to go around. The case of North Carolina State was illustrative. Four Wolfpack players—Stan Niewierowski and Anton Muehlbauer, Jr., of Brooklyn, Terry Litchfield of Louisville, and Dan Gallagher of Kentucky—admitted they had accepted money to shave points in eleven games. A few southern journalists blamed the characters of the New York products. Even Wolfpack coach Everett Case remarked: "Maybe the ethical sense of New York boys is all screwed up, I don't know, but North Carolina boys would certainly be loyal." Other reporters questioned the school's coaches and administrators, who often placed a winning sports program above their educational charge. One editorialist noted, "The sense of values that needs looking into is that of a university which recruits young men not because they are good students, but because they are good basketball players." Secretary of Commerce Luther Hodges, a former governor of North Carolina, had some sage advice for North Carolina State: "Quit buying teams."

Public reaction to the scandals of 1961 was less pronounced than in 1951. By 1961 cheating in any form had lost its ability to shock the public. In late 1959 Charles Van Doren, the clean-cut quiz show genius, admitted that his *21* show victories had been fixed. The scandal rocked the television industry. In May 1960 leading rock-and-roll disc jockey Alan Freed was indicted, along with seven others, for accepting payola from record companies. The ensuing trial exposed the seamy side of the music industry. Indeed, as Bill Lee of the *Hartford Courant* noted, "Cheating seems almost to have become the fashion of the day, criminally phoney television quizzes, rigged contests, dishonest disc jockeys, bribery in the highest places, wide-

92 •  **Winning Is the Only Thing**

spread tax dodging, and downright cheating." The 1961 basketball scandal was simply a thread in the fabric of the time.

Just as the 1961 scandal did not cause much public outrage, so too, it did not lead to any significant reform in intercollegiate athletics. In 1929 the Carnegie Foundation for the Advancement of Teaching released its study of college athletics. Entitled *American College Athletics,* the three-and-one-half-year study chronicled the commercialism and hypocrisy of college sports. It contained evidence of grade tampering, slush funds, illegal payments, and alumni abuses. Far from building character, big-time college sports impaired the "ethical and moral standards of schoolboys through the commercialization of athletics." The report called for widespread reform. No real reform followed. The abuses remained then—and beyond. In fact, during the entire twentieth century the major change in intercollegiate athletics has been the dollar amounts earned by the schools and paid to the players.

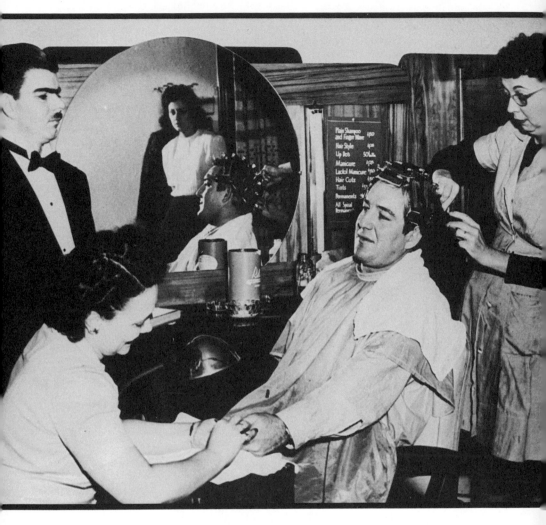

Pro wrestler Gorgeous George's prettified toughman routine made for high entertainment and box office sales.

(Credit: University of Notre Dame)

# • Television, Sports, and Mass Culture

*You can't give it away and sell it at the same time.*
—JACK "DOC" KEARNS

Although global politics, racial integration, and the lure of money and fame brought sports into the public spotlight after World War II, it was technology which made it the new cultural currency of America. The revolution which television brought to popular culture in the 1950s and 1960s was unprecedented. Regional dialects, local heroes, community drama societies, and small-town theaters disappeared, parochial culture giving way to the cowboy shows, sitcoms, soap operas, and game shows of a new Atlantic-to-Pacific popular culture, the whole country sharing programs and celebrities. Among the most glamorous of the new heroes were the new superstars of sports. But television did not just elevate a new set of demigods; it also changed the nature of sports.

During the mid-1950s there had been a main-event match on television nearly every night. Red Skelton, another staple during the early years of the tube, even joked about the love affair between television and boxing. "The Monday fight, scheduled for a Tuesday this Wednesday, has been postponed till Thursday and rescheduled for Friday this Saturday because Sunday's a holiday," Skelton told his viewers. Those were the good times. And now they were ending. In July 1960, the National Broadcasting Company (NBC) cancelled the "Friday Night Fights," the longest-running sports program on television. It was also the last boxing show on the air. Explaining—or rather, announcing—the position of NBC, an executive of the network said, "Anything we broadcast is our responsibility, and we felt we had adequate reasons not to continue the fights."

The reason was simple enough. Ratings were down and had been down for several years. The sponsor of the "Friday Night Fights," the Gillette Safety Razor Company, was unconcerned by the ratings. The men who purchased Gillette products liked the fights, and the company was saddened by NBC's decision. A spokesman for the company noted, "The audiences have been very loyal to us and to boxing and we don't like to deprive them of fights in the future." Nor was Madison Square Garden, which put on the matches, happy with the decision. Television revenues had outstripped live gate revenues during the preceding decade, and the loss of the money meant the end of weekly boxing at the Garden. This in turn translated into less money for boxers, managers, promoters, matchmakers, referees, seconds, cut men—the entire boxing community. But the decision was NBC's to make. And the "Gillette Cavalcade of Sports" gave way to a series entitled "Moment of Fear" and described by one Brooklyn woman as "a worse program than most of the fights."

The first Friday after the cancellation there was a deafening silence in most of the bars across the country. Willie Pep, who in 1944 had defeated Chalky Wright in the first televised boxing match, lamented the emptiness in his own bar. "No fights, no fights! Sixteen years we've had fights on television almost every Friday night, but not tonight. Well my television won't be turned on. . . . The TV can just sit there and look at the people who are not looking at it." Another tavern keeper mourned the death of the Friday night community of strangers. "Many traveling people used to come in on Friday just for the fights. They used to strike up friendships and sit around for a while. Tonight they came in, drank a beer and left."

One group of boxing fans rejoiced at NBC's decision. They blamed television for the decline in the beloved sport. Television, they claimed, had killed the small local clubs where boxers were nourished and slowly initiated into their profession. Who wanted to pay to see club fighters when he could watch champions for free on television? "You can't give it away and sell it at the same time," said boxing manager Doc Kearns. Critics of television added that it encouraged boxers to take on big fights before they were ready. "Television ruined my boy," an unemployed manager griped. Former heavyweight champion Jack Dempsey spoke for the antitelevision legions: "Now we should see the return of something like normal in boxing. Now fighters will have to be brought along slowly, on their merits, in small clubs. And people will begin going back to the boxing arenas in person. In the long run this will help boxing very much."

Boxing was not the only sport between 1945 and 1960 to experience a rocky affair with television. Baseball, wrestling, football, and roller derby also had problems dealing with the new medium. Spokesmen in all these sports compared television to some sort of electronic Bluebeard which systematically killed all of its brides. In truth, television moguls were only partly to blame. They were often greedy, but baseball team owners and boxing promoters were just as greedy. But the problem was even more complex. During the period American leisure patterns changed. Families moved to the rapidly expanding suburbs, spent more time at home, and ventured into the cities less and less. Bars became less subcommunities in and by themselves and more simply establishments for getting drunk. As result, attendance at sporting events plummeted, and television became the scapegoat for impersonal demographic trends.

• • •

Sports on television started as a novelty. On May 17, 1939, NBC televised a baseball game between Columbia and Princeton played at Baker Field in New York. If not quite a technical disaster, it was certainly far short of a success. NBC employed only one camera, located near the third-base line. Any ball hit out of the infield might as well have gone into orbit so far as television viewers were concerned. A *New York Times* reporter remarked that the players looked like "white flies" and that the "ball was seldom seen except on bunts and other infield plays." Television viewers were not satisfied. Gone were the green grass, the bright sun, the fresh air, and the blue skies. The freedom of the outdoors—the very essence of the game—was lost. When it was over, no prophets sang the praise of the new medium.

But experiments continued. NBC used two cameras to record a double-header between the Brooklyn Dodgers and Cincinnati Reds. The results were a little better. Boxing and wrestling matches, because of the fewer people and smaller playing area, proved easier to televise. Before the end of 1940, television producers experimented with televising football, tennis, hockey, and basketball, as well as baseball, boxing, and wrestling. But by the end of 1940, America was moving toward the turmoil that had already enveloped most of the rest of the world. During World War II television forgot about sports, and Americans forgot about television.

At the war's end, conditions in the United States were ideal for the takeoff of the television industry. Electronics companies, freed from the need to produce war materiel, were willing to gamble on a new electronic product. Americans, who had been denied consumer goods during the war, were also ready for a small gamble on a harmless diversion. And manufacturers of all kinds began searching for new methods to advertise their goods. Television suited the needs of America's secular trinity—producers, consumers, and advertisers. As Eric Barnouw noted in *Tube of Plenty*, the acceptance of television came with "surprising suddenness."

Although the Federal Communications Commission (FCC) readily licensed new television stations, the industry confronted serious programming obstacles. When television buyers turned on their sets they expected to see something more than test patterns on their seven-inch, twelve-inch, and fourteen-inch screens. To satisfy this entirely reasonable expectation, television moguls had to replace test patterns with programs. But what made for satisfying television viewing? One of radio's virtues was that it forced listeners to use their imaginations. Evil villains and beautiful heroines came without faces. The listener had to supply the proper visage and imagine the countless details of every scene. Television had to replace individual imaginations. It was a difficult task.

Given this production problem and hundreds of hours of air time to fill, television producers looked for other, easier alternatives. Televising sports provided an answer. An athletic contest came with its own heroes and villains, its own sets and props and plots. It supplied action and suspense and drama. It was a world onto itself, a universe that overflowed with "the thrill of victory and the agony of defeat." And, most important of all, each contest took time, each was more interesting than a test pattern to watch.

It was love at first sight. Television was the insatiable suitor, sports the eager, obliging partner. Media critics recognized the rightness of the pair. In June 1946 NBC telecast the Joe Louis–Billy Conn rematch for the heavyweight championship. Their first fight had been a classic. This one, as so often happens, fell below expectations. But as a television event it was a magnificent success. Afterward, a *Washington Post* columnist wrote, "Television looks good for a 1000-year run."

During the next fifteen years, the love affair between television and sports ran hot and cold. Each alternately praised and condemned the other. The men who controlled sports hungered for the dollars that television moguls passed out. In return, television producers regarded sports as a program. If the ratings were good—fine. If not—cancel the program. Altruism was a word never spoken, a concept never imagined. Between 1945 and 1960, television began to change the structure and tempo of sports. It dramatically affected boxing, baseball, and football, as well as influencing wrestling and Roller Derby.

Television did not damage wrestling and Roller Derby. Although both activities laid claim to being sports, neither had any real integrity to destroy. Professional wrestling as practiced in 1945 had no pristine past. And Roller Derby had no past at all. Both were entertainment forms more than competitive sports and had more in common with theater and dance than with boxing and baseball. Some critics contended that they were morality plays, staged conflicts between good and evil. Others asserted that they provided good, mindless fun. But no one seriously confused them with "real" sports. Television, however, never said it was in the "real" sports business. Its *raison d'etre* was simply to entertain.

The history of wrestling stretches far back into antiquity. Ajax and Ulysses wrestled. So did Hercules and Antaeus. The history of professional wrestling in the United States is not so heroic, but even it had brief moments in the sun. William Muldoon, a Greco-Roman wrestler, acquired considerable fame and prestige during the 1870s and 1880s. America regarded him as an equal to the classical wrestlers in bodily form and strength. Other famous wrestlers followed Muldoon. George Hackenschmidt, Frank Gotch, Joe Strecher, and Strangler Lewis were widely regarded as athletes. But by the mid-1930s legitimate professional wrestling had its back on the mat.

During World War II a new form of professional wrestling emerged. Eschewing any pretense of legitimacy, it strove for pure entertainment. The pioneer of this dramatic genre of wrestling was George Wagner, whose *nom de guerre* was Gorgeous George. A farm boy from Nebraska, Wagner had tried to play it straight, and he had failed. After ten lean years, he decided to take a gamble. He had noticed that the "freaks, baboons and foreigners" who passed themselves off as wrestlers gained the public's curiosity. Since the novelty wrestlers were poor wrestlers, they soon faded into obscurity. "What if," Wagner asked himself, "a guy had a flair for showmanship *and could also wrestle*—would he go over?"

In 1943 Gorgeous George was born. The lean, brown-haired Wagner let his hair grow, dyed it platinum blond, and worked it into a tight marcel. He adopted props and physical mannerisms to accent his hairstyle. Before he climbed into the ring, he sent in his valet. During his career he was serviced by valets named Tommy, Hunter, Friday, Hugo, James, and Jeffries. Armed with an ornate atomizer, the valet would spray a fine, sweet-smelling cleansing mist on the canvas, ropes, and, stealthily, on George's opponent. This accomplished, the valet spread a mink in George's corner. Then, to the sound of "Pomp and Circumstance" George would swish regally toward the ring. Clad in a robe of red satin with a white ermine collar said to be worth between $1,500 and $3,000— which nevertheless resembled a dowdy housewife's robe—George was ready to wrestle. All in all, he was a splendid non sequiter.

Gorgeous George and television seemed to be made for each other. Announcers never tired of describing George's gorgeous costumes. They reported that he had eighty-eight satin outfits and that he wore an ermine jockstrap. He had gold-plated and sequined Georgie pins for his hair and a monogrammed towel. Only the lack of color television limited the effect of his presence. Ringside announcers had to list the colors: "He's going to be in chartreuse tonight, folks! Correction, it'll be cherry red."

Of course, lovers of "true" sports decried George's behavior. Dan Parker criticized his "pseudo-pswish." After watching George wrestle, Arthur Daley, sports columnist for the *New York Times*, was even more incensed. In his column "Sports of the Times," Daley wrote, "If Gorgeous George has not killed wrestling in New York for good and all, the sport is hardy enough to survive a direct hit by an atomic bomb. It was a most insufferable and obnoxious performance. . . . "

Wrestling did not die in New York. In fact, during the late 1940s and early 1950s George and wrestling experienced something of a renaissance throughout the country. It was the triumph and fault of television. Wrestling grew with the industry. In 1946 there were only seven thousand sets in America. By 1950 there were five million. Between 1949 and 1952 an average of a quarter million sets were sold every month. And the pace never slackened during the 1950s. For a time, Gorgeous George and like-minded athlete-entertainers found unlimited opportunities to display their unusual talents.

Wrestling soon became too big of a business to be left to wrestlers. Ex-boxers got into the act. Jack Dempsey, Primo Carnera, and "Two-Ton" Tony Galento turned to wrestling for a living. Midgets and women also entered the field. Women in particular found rich opportunities. The best of the "muscle molls" made $50,000 or more each year. Billy Wolfe, who controlled women's wrestling during the early 1950s, freely discussed the reasons for his sport's growth: "There's no doubt that television has made a difference. We're now screening applicants for looks and glamour as well as ability. . . . Amazons are on the way out. . . . I'm given orders no girl is to enter the ring without make-up and carefully made up coiffure."

Wolfe waxed rapturously about the new breed of female wrestlers. He said Gloria Barattini, for example, was "a charming Baltimore belle," an heiress to a $200,000 fortune who had studied voice at the Peabody Conservatory of Music. Other less financially involved observers had slightly different opinions of the female wrestlers—new breed and old. William Manchester in *The Glory and the Dream* probably came closer to the reality of the female wrestlers: "great hulking earth bitches with breasts like half-loaded gunnysacks and pubic hair dangling down their thighs. They always seemed to have cut themselves shaving." But "muscular beauties" or "earth bitches," they held the attention of television viewers. Just as Gorgeous George owed part of his success to America's fascination with homosexuality, female wrestlers capitalized on male daydreams of lesbianism and erotic masochism.

Wrestling was not the only quasi-sport whose popularity depended upon television. Roller Derby was almost as much a creation of television as the latter-day "Battle of the Network Stars." Roller Derby was the brainchild of Leo A. Seltzer, a Chicago entrepreneur who staged dance-marathon contests during the Depression. In 1935 he invented Roller Derby, rounded up a few roller skaters, and toured the country with his new sport. In some ways the sport was like the Depression itself: it involved roller skaters madly moving in circles, waiting, it seemed, to be knocked down. Like marathon dancing, success was as much a matter of remaining on one's feet as actually winning the contest. The sport was not an immediate success. Remembering those early days, John Lardner commented that "Mr. Seltzer was satisfied with a stampede of 300 or 400 people, at any wide place in the road. He did not care how many of them wore shoes."

Television lifted Roller Derby from its wandering obscurity. Writing in 1949, Lardner noted that "in the age of so-called video, [Seltzer] measures his clients by the millions. The incidence of shoes among them is getting higher." For a time, Roller Derby even threatened to replace wrestling as television's darling quasi-sport. Like wrestling, it too had women athletes who swore, punched, and scratched with savage abandon. "The girls in this sport are tougher than the boys," said Seltzer. A particular television favorite was Marjorie Clair "Toughie" Brashun. Renowned for her body checks and grudge matches, she was a regular on television and in the penalty box.

Only by television's generous lexicon could Roller Derby be defined as a sport. As Lardner wrote, if Roller Derby was a sport, then so were defenestration (pushing people out of windows), extravasation (blood-letting), and lapidation (stoning people to death). But critics of Roller Derby and television missed the point. Television was in the business of entertainment, which by its own definition was morally neutral. For a time, Roller Derby entertained television viewers. Whether it was a sport or not was not even an issue. When viewers lost interest—which they did in late 1951—Roller Derby left the air and returned to its former obscurity.

The novelty of wrestling and Roller Derby wore off in a few years. The action was so stylized and predictable that one match blended into the next and they all looked like reruns of the previous week's contests. Boxing, baseball, and football had more staying power and therefore developed stronger relations with television. The relationship, however, came with strings. Television moguls paid well, but they had high expectations. They demanded that competitive sports be more than just competitive: they also had to be entertaining. As a result, the traditional nature of boxing, baseball, and football changed to satisfy the new medium.

During the late 1940s and 1950s, boxing forged the strongest ties with television. It was the ideal sport. The action involved only two men in a small area. Easy and inexpensive to televise, boxing also had an undeniable attraction for sponsors. It was a manly sport, just as razor blades, beer, automobiles, and cigarettes were manly products. Madison Avenue executives praised the advertising virtues of boxing: "Boxing sells itself and our products, who could ask for more."

For a decade, boxing was the most popular show on television. National networks televised it during prime time almost every night. In 1954, for example, ABC televised matches every Monday night from the Eastern Parkway Arena in Brooklyn, and Dumont aired its own fights from St. Nicholas Arena on the opposite station; CBS televised a bout every Wednesday; NBC aired a Madison Square Garden match every Friday; and ABC televised another fight every Saturday. Those, of course, were only the nationally televised bouts. Weekly local fight shows were broadcast from Los Angeles, Montreal, Detroit, Mexico City, Hollywood, San Francisco, Philadelphia, and a dozen or more smaller cities. It was a boxing junkie's heaven.

At first, everyone connected with television and boxing appeared pleased by the symbiosis. It was a boon for boxing promoters. Harry Markson, director of boxing at Madison Square Garden, estimated that the Gillette Safety Razor Company paid the Garden $15 million between 1944 and 1964 to sponsor the Friday (and later Saturday) night fights. In 1944 Gillette paid the Garden $25,000 for the right to sponsor the weekly fights for a year. With time the price went up. After 1953 the Garden received $24,000 a week from Gillette. When ABC finally cancelled "The Friday Night Fights" in 1964, Markson still praised the sponsor: "Let me say this. Gillette has been great to work with. . . . Never a squawk. Never a regret. A wonderful sponsor."

On their end, television executives and sponsors were equally satisfied. Production costs for televising a fight were low and returns, measured by the ratings, were remarkably high. During the mid-1950s the cost of staging the average nationally televised fight was about $50,000. By comparison, a variety show or a situation comedy cost twice as much. For this relatively small investment, sponsors were rewarded with the best ratings on television. In 1953, for example, the Rocky Marciano–Jersey Joe Walcott rematch captured 68.7 percent of the viewing audience, and the Chuck Davey–Kid Gavilan fight scored a 67.9 rating. As one Madison Avenue executive remarked, "We not only get a bigger audience for less money than the big razzle-dazzle shows, but we get what practically amounts to a captive audience. A fight has to be a real smeller for anybody to tune it out."

The major question for television executives was exactly what constitutes a "smeller." To maintain their high rating, they attempted to devise a deodorant formula which guarded against the smeller. In the process, they began to alter the form, rhythm, and tempo of professional boxing.

To a large degree, the medium and the audience created new standards for judging whether a fight was good or bad. Because of technical limitations, television reduced the experience of watching a boxing match. It failed to capture much of the nuance and subtle violence of the sport. The thin, red trickle of blood and the red and blue color of a pummeled body were lost to the television viewer watching a black and white set. Nor could television capture the force of a stiff jab or cross. In addition, most people who became television boxing viewers lacked a frame of reference for watching a fight. Few had ever sat at ringside and witnessed the power and awesome brutality of professional boxing. Fewer still understood the slow process by which a fighter feels out and sets up his opponent. Consequently, their demand for frantic action was greater than that of an experienced fight fan.

A "smeller," then, came to be defined by television executives and viewers alike as a fight between two subtle, careful craftsmen. Soon a new type of main-eventer emerged—the TV boxers. They followed a pattern. Most were over 147 pounds; television fight fans especially favored middleweights and heavyweights. Technically, they fought at a faster tempo and favored wild hooks and haymakers to more controlled jabs and crosses. They were not necessarily more effective or better boxers, but they were more active fighters.

Hurricane Jackson, who started fighting professionally in the early 1950s, while still in his teens, exemplified the style of the TV boxer. Of course, the term *boxer* fails totally to describe his style of combat. Hurricane was a nonstop puncher. He did not hit particularly hard or connect particularly often, but he threw hundreds of punches from dozens of angles each round. In 1954 boxing writer Frank Graham called him "the human buzz-saw," and around Stillman's Gym in New York City he was known simply as "the Animal." Both names were appropriate. In fact, he learned his fighting style from different animals. Talking about his double uppercut, Hurricane noted, "I saw a kangaroo in a zoo once and he gives me the idea." Although he was never a first-rate fighter, he was very popular on television.

Had Jackson been white, his popularity would have been limitless. Television executives and audiences were particularly drawn to handsome white boxers. During the 1950s a series of white boxers with very little talent gained popularity on television. They were billed as middle-class heroes, fighters who were also well-rounded, well-educated citizens. Roland LaStarza captured the public's imagination in the late 1940s and early 1950s. Reporters more frequently discussed Roland's "two years at CCNY" and his politeness than his ability as a boxer. According to a 1949 article, LaStarza didn't drink or smoke, attended church regularly, and was working hard to learn how to become mean in the ring. Sportswriter Lewis Burton worried about Roland: "He needs more deep-down villainy, and there's a question whether it can be acquired, since he is a good-natured, disciplined product of a well-ordered home."

In truth, LaStarza was a capable boxer who proved to be a worthy opponent for Rocky Marciano in their two fights. Other of the white TV boxers were not so talented. Television made the career of Chuck Davey, a handsome white boxer who had spent at least some time on the campus of Michigan State University. During the early 1950s promoters matched Davey against a series of hand-picked, pugilisticly toothless journeyman. Davey's star rose steadily, and he was the darling of television fight fans. Then in 1953 matchmakers pitted him against the great Cuban welterweight Kid Gavilan for the title. Gavilan utterly dominated the fight and knocked out Davey in the tenth round. For Davey it was the end of a career. As a promoter Chris Dundee remembered, "One bad fight on TV would kill a guy. Because everybody—I mean everybody—could see it."

Slowly over the years the demands of television, which boxing promoters anxiously tried to satisfy, changed boxing. Craftsmanship suffered as fighters were brought along too rapidly and encouraged to learn to slug rather than box. "Today's fighter," wrote Charles Einstein in *Harper's* in 1956, "is primarily a slugger. The boxer, the hitter, the combination man is gone. The sponsor does not want him. The sponsor wants a man who'll sell his product, somebody popular and colorful."

By putting a premium on slugging, television increased the level of brutality in boxing. Since television as a medium tended to soften the violent nature of boxing, few viewers realized how much punishment fighters were actually absorbing. Veteran boxing referee Arthur Donovan emphasized this problem after watching and scoring the 1953 Rocky Marciano–Roland LaStarza fight on television. Donovan had no doubt that Marciano was winning the fight when referee Ruby Goldstein stopped the fight in the eleventh round. Yet he could not judge how much punishment LaStarza absorbed: "I couldn't tell how badly LaStarza was hurt, or whether he was hurt at all, because the camera wasn't powerful enough to show the details of his facial expressions. When a fighter is hurt it shows first in his face." Surprised when the bout was stopped, Donovan said to himself, "Ruby's getting squeamish in his old age." Only later did he learn that in fact LaStarza had been badly beaten and hurt during the brutal fight.

Television further destroyed craftsmanship by undercutting the process through which novice fighters learned their craft. Until the late 1960s, few professional boxers learned to fight as amateurs. If an amateur fighter showed any promise he was encouraged to immediately turn professional. Once a professional, his real education began in the hundreds of neighborhood boxing clubs throughout the country. Before he ever fought a main event bout in a major arena, he had to prove himself and learn his trade in the dingy clubs. To take an extreme example, the great light heavyweight Archie Moore fought close to 200 fights over a sixteen-year period before he received a title match.

If club fighters were not seasoned professionals, few spectators seemed to care. It was cheap entertainment, often less expensive than attending a professional baseball game. And true club patrons enjoyed the chance to predict which fighters would advance beyond the club level and which would remain "ham-and-eggers" for the rest of their careers. Said one club fan, "Hell, I saw Louis take out Lee Ramage in Chicago. Sure he was raw—like a green onion. But I could tell that someday he'd be as sweet as they come."

By bringing main event fights for free into every home and bar that had a television set, TV destroyed the club system. With television broadcasting fights on Monday, Wednesday, Friday, and Saturday, the club promoters were forced to compete or get out of the business. And since they did not have the money to compete, their options were further limited.

The big fight arenas suffered as well. Although television provided a new source of revenue, it dramatically reduced live gate revenues. In 1943, for example, thirty-three Madison Square Garden fights drew 406,681 fans who paid $2,062,046 for tickets. Ten years later, in 1953, thirty Garden fights attracted 152,928 spectators who paid $629,775. That same year television executives paid Madison Square Garden $1,768,000 to broadcast their fights. Although the live gate and television revenues for 1953 modestly exceeded the live gate revenues of 1943, the concession business at the Garden fell off precipitously.

By the late 1950s the long-running romance between television and boxing had become stale. The high ratings of the early years were but memories. The new numbers were ominous. In 1952, 31 percent of the available audience watched boxing matches. By 1959 that figure was down to 10.6 percent. One by one, the nationally televised weekly fights were dropped for low ratings. By 1960 only NBC's "Friday Night Fights" remained, and that summer NBC too dropped boxing. Overexposure and better prime-time programming had ended boxing's long run on the tube.

The Gillette Safety Razor Company briefly revived televised boxing during the early 1960s. In return for all Gillette's uncommitted advertising dollars ($8.5 million), ABC agreed to pick up Gillette's "Friday Night Fights." But ABC was not very enthusiastic about the sport. The early 1960s was a bad period for boxing. In 1960 the Kefauver Committee hearings had showed the seedy underside of the sport. In 1962 Emile Griffith killed Benny "Kid" Paret in a nationally televised fight. Then in 1964 NBC aired a hard-hitting and self-righteous exposé about boxing's multifarious problems. In addition to showing sad scenes of former champions Maxie Rosenbloom and Beau Jack selling neckties and shining shoes, and brutal footage of the death of Paret, it detailed boxing's underworld connections. In short, boxing's wagon was gaining momentum on a downhill slope. Two days before Christmas in 1963, ABC jumped off. A network spokesman announced, "We have no plans to continue our weekly boxing show next season." True to its word, it didn't. After helping to change the structure of boxing, television finally abandoned the sport. Of course, the separation would not be permanent.

• • •

Baseball faced different sorts of problems in its dealings with television. Many were simply technological. Early television was not sophisticated enough to capture the complexity of team games. Television was particularly unequipped to convey the experience of a baseball game to its viewers. As Benjamin G. Rader observed in *In Its Own Image*, "The essence of baseball involved an acute awareness of the entire playing area. The baseball fan not only enjoyed the isolated instances of action—the pitch, hit, catch, or throw; he also wanted to see the runner leading off base, the signals of the third-base coach, and the positions taken by the fielders. . . . Only the fan in the stands, not the television viewer, could command all these perspectives."

Technological limitations distorted the nature of baseball. Watched live at the ballpark, baseball is a game of constant movement, sometimes as dramatic as a line-drive homerun or, more often, as subtle as a base runner taking a walking lead. Early television robbed the sport of much of its motion. By focusing on the duel between pitcher and batter, television glorified the dramatic action at the expense of the subtle action. Watching baseball on television became analogous to watching a series of random Shakespeare soliloquies. Roy Eisenhart summed up the experience quite well: "People can't learn to watch baseball that way; they're just learning to watch television."

The baseball experience, however, was not as important to the owners of professional baseball clubs as their own financial experience. They were a hard-headed lot, not given to philosophic and aesthetic speculations. Roone Arledge, who as head of sports programming for ABC got to know the owners rather well, aptly remarked, "The baseball team owners are just a loose confederation of carny operators and robber barons, with a small sprinkling of enlightened statesmen thrown in."

Greed motivated and characterized the early attitude of baseball club owners toward television. As so often in the history of professional baseball, it was each man for himself, regardless of the cost to the game. Starting in 1946, when Yankee head Larry MacPhail sold television broadcast rights for that season to the DuMont network for $75,000, owners began to negotiate and sign their own individual contracts with local television stations. It was quite an individual process; no real consideration was given to negotiating a national network deal and sharing the revenue.

The result, predictably enough, was that the rich teams located in the large television markets got richer, and in baseball, the richest teams usually win the most games. The New York Yankees in particular benefited from lucrative television contracts. It was an advantage they hardly needed.

Televised games also took their toll at the gate. During the late 1940s baseball attendance soared. Record seasons became the norm for major and minor leagues alike. Then starting in the early 1950s, attendance rapidly dropped off. Major league baseball attendance fell a full third between 1948 and 1956. Several teams attempted to offset the decline by moving to greener markets; others simply got used to playing before near empty houses. As one player from the era remembers, "I was only up for one season, and I guess I was pretty bad. But fortunately nobody showed up at the games to witness my career."

The reasons for the attendance drop-off were complex. People moving to the mushrooming suburbs discovered new pastimes—boating, golf, tennis, and barbecuing to name a few. As whites and federal funding migrated from the cities, urban centers started their slow decay. Suburbanites considered the inner city, still the home of most professional baseball teams, to be unsafe and unsavory, hardly the place to take the wife and kids. It was easier and safer and cheaper to drive into the country for a picnic. As for baseball, there was always Little League and softball.

Critics tended to overlook the complex reason for the slump and to blame television. To be sure, television did contribute to the attendance decline. Cleveland's gate admittances fell off dramatically after it signed a generous television deal. Between 1948 and

1956 the decline exceeded 67 percent. Brance Rickey was especially opposed to television. Not only did television hurt the live gate, Rickey said, but it promised to kill the minors and thus create a future player talent shortage. He called for owners to regulate the medium. The owners ignored Rickey.

Certainly the minor leagues faced difficult times during the 1950s and 1960s. In 1949 over 49 million people attended minor league games. That figure fell to 15 million in 1957 and 10 million in 1969. As Rickey suspected, television had helped to produce "major league fans out of minor league fans." But new entertainment alternatives, ranging from better television programming to the increasing popularity of participant sports, also undercut the minor leagues.

Unlike baseball club owners, who found television to be a double-edged sword, the leaders of professional football owed much of the growth and popularity of their sport to the electronic medium. The early years of professional football were hardly glorious. It was the red-headed bastard of the college game, often played by hard-bitten, potbellied coal miners and steelworkers before few spectators. It wasn't a money sport, and it wasn't a glamour sport. The owners of the major teams were in the game, it seems, for the love of the game. They were men like Art Rooney, owner of the Pittsburgh Steelers. Rooney, noted Roy Blount, Jr., in *About Three Bricks Shy of a Load*, ran the Steelers "the way you might run a good, rowdy, but respectable saloon."

Gambling on television came easy for owners who did not have to risk anything. Led by Bert Bell, an able commissioner, and unified among themselves, the team owners worked together for the good of the sport and the entire National Football League. The owners functioned as a single economic cartel. Unlike owners of professional baseball teams, they decided to negotiate a single television package and split the revenues equally. In addition, as Benjamin G. Rader wrote, they sought "the blackout of home games [and] the blackout of other NFL games in the home city when a team was playing at home." All and all, it was the NFL's parody of Karl Marx.

Cautiously, slowly, and frugally, television began to court the NFL during the 1950s. Television executives didn't expect much, but they were surprised. Again unlike baseball, football proved to be a good television sport. The ball was big and easily seen even on small television screens, and simply following the path or flight of the ball supplied action and enjoyment. Commercials did not seem obtrusive, and the short pauses between plays allowed time for second guessing and added an extra element of suspense to the game.

The 1958 championship game between the Baltimore Colts and the New York Giants dramatically demonstrated the major commercial possibilities of professional football. Before the game, commented Dave Klein in *The Game of Their Lives*, the players were "working men, tradesmen, glamorous only when compared with the miners and factory workers who were their fathers and brothers." After the game—that memorable 23–17 sudden-death Colt victory—the players were legends, genuine folk heroes. Unitas, Huff, Gifford, Marchetti, Ameche, Berry, Grier, Robustelli, Rote, Moore—television introduced these men to a nation of television viewers who watched their heroics on that cold December Sunday. It was the consummation of a sport and an autumn Sunday ritual.

By 1960 television was firmly part of the sporting scene. It brought good and bad. It allowed millions of people to see professional contests that otherwise they would not have seen. It allowed farm kids in Nebraska to watch Unitas march his team toward that final score. It permitted Oklahoma ranchhands to watch their native son Mickey Mantle bat for the Yankees. It brought the tense atmosphere of a championship fight into the homes of Americans across the country.

At the same time, television often overexposed and changed the structure of sports. This was not the fault of the television networks. Executives were rightly concerned with their own survival and advancement of their own companies. They were part of a commercial entertainment business. Their job was to buy, produce, and televise entertaining programs. It was not their duty or responsiblity to safeguard the special character, structure, and rituals of the sports world. The minor leagues were not their problem, nor was the fact that fighters rushed too quickly into big-money bouts. They simply paid for the right to televise. Baseball team owners, boxing promoters, managers, and coaches might have attempted to protect the interests of their sports. But with the exception of professional football team owners, they really did not. And by 1960, the temptations and problems were only beginning.

**ABC Sports made "Monday Night Football" an American institution and sports anchors like Frank Gifford, Al Michaels, and Don Dierdorf became household names.**

(Credit: Mary Ann Carter)

# • The Roone Revolution

*What we set out to do was to get the audience involved emotionally. If they didn't give a damn about the game, they still might enjoy the program.*
—ROONE ARLEDGE

**T**he real revolution in sports television came in the 1960s and 1970s, and the moving force behind the change was Roone Arledge, head of sports programming at ABC. A multifaceted man, Arledge had a curious relationship with Richard Nixon. Their first meeting took place in the fall of 1969 during the Texas-Arkansas football game that decided the national championship. Arledge planned to fly to Hawaii that weekend in order to save—or at least attempt to save—his shaky marriage. At the last moment Nixon, a great college football fan, decided to attend the game, and Arledge felt he should produce the contest personally. It cost Arledge his marriage, but as he later remembered, if there had been an assassination, he wanted to cover it. The game was played, Nixon wasn't assassinated, and Texas won. When the contest ended, President Nixon visited both dressing rooms, dispensing the usual clichés. His talk to the Arkansas players moved rapidly from clichés to heartfelt emotions. Arledge recalled, "Nixon began discussing defeat in the most intensely personal terms. It was extremely moving, since, as we all realized, he was actually talking about himself."

Four days later, Arledge met Nixon again, this time for a talk at the president's suite in the Waldorf Towers in New York City. It was not the most relaxed atmosphere: "The room was empty; just an American flag, the Presidential flag, and one man: the President of the United States." Nixon tried to put the television sports executive at ease. For a half hour they talked about sports—Arledge's business. Eventually Roone attempted to move the topic away from sports toward his other interests—music, theater, the problems of America's cities. Each time Nixon brought the conversation back to sports. Finally Arledge realized that Nixon "wasn't trying to put me at ease, he was trying to impress me with his knowledge of sports trivia. While he was rattling off the times of quarter-milers in the 1936 Olympics, I remember saying to myself, I can't believe it. The President of the United States is trying to impress *me*."

There was a third meeting, and it was the strangest of all. Nixon agreed to appear on ABC's "Wide World of Sports" and be interviewed by former New York Giants football great Frank Gifford. During a break in taping, the president took Arledge aside for another chat. He explained that when Gifford was a Giant and he was living in New York, he often attended Giff's parties. "I know Frank Gifford," Nixon boasted. "He remembers me." Arledge was amazed: "Here was the President of the United States trying to impress people, first, because he remembered some Olympic records, and second, because he knew Frank Gifford. And because Frank Gifford knew *him*!"

An odd set of events, certainly. But not totally beyond belief. In fact, the Richard Nixon who loved to talk about sports was in part a Roone Arledge creation. Probably the most important single individual in modern sports, Arledge not only changed the manner in which athletic events were watched and understood, but he also dramatically increased interest in sports. In a complex society, divided along economic, social, and racial lines and often sadly impersonal, sports became a currency which all races and classes dealt in. Rich and poor, black and white, young and old—if they could communicate on no other level, they could always talk about sports. They all had television sets, they watched the same sporting events, they were familiar with the same sports heroes, and they all had opinions about what they saw and what they liked. And a man like Nixon, a president who was oddly uncomfortable around most people, used sports to avoid real social interactions. It was an escape— or perhaps benefit—he shared with millions of other Americans who were influenced by the Roone Revolution.

In 1960 Roone Pinckney Arledge did not look like a revolutionary. Slightly pudgy, heavily freckled, and red-haired, Arledge resembled an Irish version of the Pillsbury doughboy. Nor did his earlier career denote a revolutionary nature. Born in Forest Hills, raised in upper-middle-class affluence on Long Island, and educated at Columbia University, Arledge's background prepared him for the New York business world. During the late 1950s he produced Shari Lewis' puppet show "Hi, Mom." He won an Emmy Award for his work, and his future with NBC seemed bright. In 1960 the 29-year-old Arledge moved to ABC. About a month before the 1960–61 football season, he gave Tom Moore and Ed Sherick, the network's programming and sports directors, a revolutionary document. It contained a bold new plan for covering football games. He recommended the use of directional and remote microphones, the use of hand-held and "isolated" cameras, the employment of split screen, and other technical innovations. In addition, he called for a more dynamic halftime show, replacing marching-band performances with in-depth analysis and highlights from the first two quarters. In essence, Arledge wanted to bring the sporting experience into America's living rooms. He believed sports and athletes should be examined "up close and personal." The Roone Revolution had begun.

Impressed by Arledge's plan, Moore and Sherick made Roone producer of ABC's college football programs, thereby giving him an electronic pulpit from which he could preach his new philosophy. Behind his every move rested a central belief: the marriage of sports and innovative entertainment techniques would produce higher ratings. Arledge was convinced that he could use sports to entertain people who were not really sports fans. Through hype and technology he could create a large new audience for ABC's sports programming.

In addition, Arledge had near-perfect program judgment. It was his "principal genius," noted former senior vice-president of ABC Sports Jim Spence. As Spence observed in *Up Close and Personal,* Arledge "had an almost infallible sense of such critical factors as how long segments should last, what interviews should be aired, the sequence of presentation for various segments in order to build audience attention, and particularly about the importance of the human element in sports. He realized early on that the *people* participating in the events were the essence of sports."

Arledge's first task was to improve televised college football. As Arledge saw it, his job became "taking the fan to the game, not the game to the fan." The idea was simple and revolutionary, and to execute it Arledge and his staff employed sophisticated technology. He wanted the viewer sitting in his living room to see, hear, and experience the game as if he were actually in the football stadium. Before Arledge, television executives had been content simply to bring the viewer the game. Using three or four situated cameras they were able to document the game. For those who loved football, it was enough, but it was not very attractive for the casual viewer.

Arledge, of course, coveted that casual viewer, the person with one eye on the screen and one hand on the dial. Discussing his philosophy in 1966, Arledge wrote: "What we set out to do was to get the audience involved emotionally. If they didn't give a damn about the game, they still might enjoy the program." To do this Arledge used more cameras. He put cameras on cranes and blimps and helicopters to provide a better view of the stadium, the campus, and the town. His technicians developed hand-held cameras for close-ups. In the stadium he employed seven cameras, three just for capturing the environment. "We asked ourselves: If you were sitting in the stadium, what would you be looking at? The coach on the sideline, the substitute quarterback warming up, the pretty girl in the next section. So our cameras wandered as your eyes would."

Often what Arledge decided would interest his mostly male viewers were young and beautiful women. One of Arledge's most successful directors, Andy Sidaris, became famous in the industry for his "T and A shots." Commenting on his specialty, Sidaris noted, "I'd rather see a great-looking body than a touchdown anytime. You can see thousands of touchdowns every weekend, but a great-looking woman is something to behold." Sidaris's philosophy, like Arledge's, emphasized entertainment, even titillation, over sport. The game was only one part of the sporting experience.

Arledge also brought the sounds of football to the television viewer. Before Arledge, producers would hang a mike out the window to get the sound of the crowd. Normally the television viewer would hear a damp, muffled roar, similar to hearing the sea from a half mile away. Occasionally a few sharp, clear expletives might break the solemnity of the announcers' voices. Arledge's technicians developed the rifle-mike to pinpoint sound. Now the viewer could hear the clash of shoulder pads and helmets, the bark of a quarterback calling signals, and the thump of a well-struck punt.

Analysis and play-by-play announcing were not immune to

the genius of Arledge and his technicians. The instant replay was one of Arledge's innovations. In 1960 he asked ABC engineer Bob Trachinger "if it would be possible to replay something in slow motion so you could tell if a guy was safe or out or stepped out of bounds." Trachinger designed the device. Arledge remembered using the instant replay during the 1960 Boston College-Syracuse game: "That was a terrific game and, at one point, Jack Concannon, a sophomore quarterback, was trapped in the pocket but ended up running 70 yards for a touchdown. Six or eight people had a shot of him and we replayed the whole thing in slow motion with Paul Christman analyzing the entire play as it unfolded. Nobody had ever seen anything like that before and the impact was unbelievable. That moment changed television sports forever."

From the very beginning Arledge's approach to sports was successful. As he suspected, he could satisfy sports fans and still entertain casual viewers. His college football broadcasts featured heretofore unseen angles both of football players and cheerleaders. For ABC, which in 1960 was running a distant third in the ratings race, Arledge's innovations meant better ratings, higher rates for advertising, and corporate growth. Before long ABC replaced NBC as the leader in sports programming. By the 1970s ABC was the top-rated network. Arledge played a considerable role in ABC's rise, and between 1960 and 1975 his salary rose from $10,000 to approximately $1 million a year.

For Arledge, college football was only the beginning. If sports programming was to have a significant impact on the television industry, he needed important events to televise twelve months a year. Aggressively, sometimes ruthlessly, Arledge went after the television rights for major sports events. "When it comes to acquiring rights," an executive at another network remarked, "the man is totally unscrupulous. A jackal. He'd rip my heart out for a shot at the World Series." Arledge was less dramatic, but as usual perfectly correct: "If you don't have the rights, you can't do the show." Over the years Arledge's list of acquisitions would put most conglomerates to shame. In addition to college and professional football and professional baseball, Arledge and ABC have acquired the rights for major golf tournaments, horse races, summer and winter Olympics, All-Star games, and a host of other events.

Arledge's impact upon American sports and entertainment

can be seen in several of the sports shows he launched. "Wide World of Sports" was an idea he inherited from Ed Scherick but gave his own distinctive stamp. He oversaw every aspect of its production and even wrote "the thrill of victory, the agony of defeat" opening. In April 1961, after a difficult search for sponsors, "Wide World of Sports" made its debut. It fit perfectly into Arledge's definition of sports as entertainment. The program allowed ABC film crews to roam around the world and televise what they thought was interesting, even if it were only tangentially involved in athletics. The production emphasis was concerned as much with the location and personalities as with the sporting event.

Most importantly "Wide World of Sports" allowed Arledge to control time, the crucial element for programming. The shows did not have to be televised live and were not contained by seasonal schedules. It realized Arledge's vision of "a year-around sports show that could fill the void [between sports seasons] and not have to worry about blackouts." In addition, prerecorded shows could be edited to increase suspense and eliminate dead time. A three-hour downhill skiing event could be edited into two 8-minute segments; an all-day mountain climb could be fit into a half-hour slot. "Wide World of Sports" was, in short, tailored to the average viewer's attention span. "In sports they aren't that familiar with, or in events that aren't important," Arledge noted, "people do enjoy the knowledge that something different will be coming every ten minutes."

To keep "something different coming" continually, "Wide World of Sports" used the broadest possible definition of what constituted sporting activity. Between 1960 and 1966 Arledge presented eighty-seven different sports, ranging from international track and field meets and world championship boxing contests to demolition derbies and an Eiffel Tower climb. And he used sophisticated technology to make each event as interesting—as entertaining—as possible.

Of course, critics carped. Sports purists claimed that "sports" was the least important word in the "Wide World of Sports" title. Programs containing the demolition derby contests particularly drew hostile comments. Again, however, the critics misunderstood Arledge's job. He was in a commercial entertainment business. His duty was to produce shows that attracted high audience ratings, not rave critical reviews. By the 1970s the demolition derby drew up to

25 million viewers to "Wide World of Sports." That number pleased ABC executives and "Wide World of Sports" sponsors.

As far as Arledge was concerned, if an event was visually exciting and had colorful personalities it would "work" on "Wide World of Sports." And if a little creative editing could improve the excitement and color, so much the better. For example, during the Le Mans automobile race there was a major accident in a section of the course where ABC had no cameras to record the wreck. Viewing and editing the film footage back in New York, producer Robert Riger sensed that the "missing crash robbed the story of some of its excitement and drama." To correct this problem, he put several miniature cars into a flowerpot, set them on fire, and filmed the result. He then edited the footage into his Le Mans coverage, where, according to Jim Spence, "it looked pretty good." Again, it was bad, even dishonest, sports coverage but good entertainment.

As a good business executive, Arledge gave the people what they wanted, or at least what they would have wanted if they knew it existed. Arledge used the same business acumen to find and to acquire broadcast rights for little-known events. "Wide World of Sports," for example, introduced the Acapulco cliff divers to the American audiences. Arledge negotiated personally with the head of the Acapulco divers' union. The senior diver told Arledge that the going rate for a special was $100,000. As Arledge recalled the episode, "We told him the price was a little out of line, and that he'd have to reduce it some or we'd forget about it. 'I'll talk to the boys,' he said. A few minutes later he returned. 'We'll take $10 a dive,' he said. He held us to it. He made us pay for all three dives."

Just as "Wide World of Sports" broadened the definition of sport, it also created sports heroes out of marginally athletic individuals. A case in point was the "athletic career" of Robert Craig "Evel" Knievel. Beginning in 1967, he appeared sixteen times on "Wide World of Sports." His motorcycle stunts became sports pseudo-events. Millions of people watched Knievel not to witness the "thrill of victory" but on the chance of seeing the ultimate "agony of defeat." Knievel didn't die for ratings, but he came close on several occasions. In 1967 he broke his back and his pelvis when he attempted to jump the fountains in front of Caesar's Palace in Las Vegas. It was a spectacular crash, and "Wide World of Sports" showed it and other Knievel failures repeatedly in painful slow motion. Knievel might have been bad sports, but he was great television, and as such an Arledge success.

"Wide World of Sports" is the longest-running sports show ever televised, and like most successful series, it has produced a number of spinoffs. Oftentimes the spinoffs have had less to do with sports than the parent show. "The American Sportsman" teamed announcer Curt Gowdy with a series of celebrity "sportsmen." Together they went after wild animals and untamed fish. The show had all the attraction of "Wide World of Sports": famous personalities, exotic locations, and prerecorded, easily edited events. It could be used to fill empty weekend programming, and if it had to be delayed or even cancelled for a week, there was no real problem. In short, it was, from a business point of view, perfect television sports.

A second successful spinoff of "Wide World of Sports" was "The Superstars." Again, Arledge employed the same formula. Major athletic personalities were pitted against each other in such events as tennis, bowling, swimming, rowing, running, golf, bicycling, and an obstacle course race. The events or the rules of the events were subject to yearly change. "The Superstars" became a huge success, and it fathered its own spinoffs. True it was a "trash sport," an ersatz sport created and packaged by television, but it was also successful television programming. It showed that the viewing audience was as intrigued by incompetence and failure as by success. Like Evel Knievel's grand failures, the memories of Joe Frazier and Johnny Unitas floundering in a swimming pool lingered longer in the public mind than Lynn Swan's graceful speed.

By 1970 Arledge was ready for his next bold move. Encouraged by the commissioner of the National Football League, Pete Rozelle, Arledge decided to invade prime time with "Monday Night Football." If it was not an entirely new game, success would certainly be measured by different standards. On Sunday afternoon, any NFL game that attracted 20 million viewers gave cause for network celebration. The same number during prime time would lead to cancellation. Success during prime time entailed an audience of between 40 to 50 million. To reach that level, Arledge had to attract a wide variety of viewers. The casual viewer suddenly became far more important than the dedicated football fan. And sport took a back seat to entertainment.

How to attract the new viewers? One way was to use more and better technology. Arledge employed a two-unit production team. Chet Forte coordinated play-by-play, and Don Ohlmeyer handled isolated coverage. ABC used more cameras, more technicians, and more videotape than had ever been used before in a football game. The result was tantamount to a perfectly filmed and produced documentary. Every aspect of the game was filmed, and the best footage was rerun, discussed, and analyzed. The result was to make the game larger than life, to give each contest an epic quality. The use of sophisticated technology made even an average game seem exciting.

Technology, however, had always been a staple of an Arledge telecast. The team of announcers he chose for "Monday Night Football" made the show. His casting was designed to create an entertaining balance of humor, controversy, and tension. Instead of two men in the broadcast booth, Arledge employed three. He chose Keith Jackson to do the play-by-play. Jackson's role was clearly defined. As Howard Cosell wrote in *Cosell by Cosell:* "It was impressed on [Jackson] time and again that he was to think of himself as a public-address announcer, slipping in and out, factually, accurately, with the vital information—who made the tackle, who threw the ball, who caught the ball, how many yards were gained, what down it was."

Arledge picked Don Meredith for his country charm and humor. A former Dallas Cowboy quarterback, Meredith knew the game and looked good on camera. This was his advantage, for Arledge intended Meredith to be the darling of Middle America. Meredith was, in short, cast to play the untutored hayseed from Mount Vernon, Texas, come to the big city to talk on TV.

Howard Cosell rounded out the team. Cosell had been with ABC since 1956, when his radio show "Sports Focus" became the summer replacement for "Kukla, Fran, and Ollie." In 1961 he was put on the ABC-TV New York nightly news. The show that brought national attention to Cosell, however, was "Wide World of Sports." Cosell regularly covered boxing for the show, and his outspoken support of Muhammad Ali drew strong critical reactions. "Get that nigger-loving Jew bastard off the air," ran a typical letter to ABC. Cosell's brash, conceited, obnoxious style bothered viewers, but it did not make them turn the dial to another station. In fact, "Wide

World of Sports" telecasts featuring Cosell scored high ratings. Cosell was and would remain for several decades "good TV."

For "Monday Night Football" Arledge cast Cosell as the man
America loves to hate. Cosell was supposed to irritate, to get under
people's skin, to arouse controversy. ABC research predicted that
the majority of viewers of "Monday Night Football" would come
from the young-adult population, people, noted Cosell in *Like It Is,*
"who had been growing up in swiftly changing, severely trying,
turbulent, even tormented times. Such people would not be likely
. . . to be responsive to a studiedly serious transmission of a football
contest placed in the context of an event solemn enough to be orig-
inating from St. Patrick's Cathedral." What they wanted was ir-
reverence, humor, and controversy. It was Cosell's and Meredith's
job to give it to them. From the first, then, "Monday Night Football"
was a television casting success. It is easier to compare it with CBS's
"All in the Family" than with any other sports telecast.

Reactions to the show were predictably strong. Cosell's performance drew hate mail and death threats. On several occasions, FBI
agents filled the broadcast booth. As Arledge had hoped, Cosell had
touched a nerve. Meredith's irreverent humor also attracted attention and viewers. When he said, "There's got to be more to life than
what's going on down there," he captured the essence of ABC's attitude toward prime-time football. "Monday Night Football" treated
the sport like the game it was. To Arledge football was entertainment, not a religion. And successful entertainment was a matter of
good casting.

Arledge altered the cast for the second season. He replaced
Keith Jackson with former New York Giant star Frank Gifford. Like
Meredith, Gifford was a handsome, articulate ex-player who was
popular with Middle America. Even more important, ABC research
indicated that Gifford was the most popular sportscaster in New
York City, the nation's largest market. Promptly hired, Gifford was
given more freedom than Jackson had enjoyed. Now Arledge had a
near-perfect cast—Cosell, Meredith, and Gifford. Ratings shot up.
By the time Cosell left the show in 1983, "Monday Night Football"
had become the longest-running prime-time hit on television, out-
lasting such blockbusters as "I Love Lucy," "M*A*S*H," "Rhoda,"
and "All in the Family."

In his most recent book, *I Never Played the Game*, Cosell modestly claims, "Who the hell made *Monday Night Football* unlike any other sports program on the air? If you want the plain truth, I did." He notes that his ability of "humanizing the players" and entertainingly communicating to a large prime-time audience insured the show's success. Actually, Cosell simply filled a role in a cast. Arledge made "Monday Night Football." He demonstrated how sports could become successful prime-time entertainment.

Just as Arledge "created" prime-time football, he changed the way Americans saw the Olympic Games. Before ABC acquired the rights to televise the Games in 1968, no major network had attempted any sort of comprehensive coverage of the Olympics. In 1964, for example, NBC's coverage of the Tokyo Olympics was minimal. Because of the time difference, NBC covered the Games with fifteen-minute shows televised late at night. Most Americans found it easier to follow the Olympics in their newspapers than on their televisions.

Arledge rightly saw the entertainment possibilities of the Olympics. And he knew how to negotiate for the rights. He promised the host city what it wanted—publicity and exposure. As "Wide World of Sports" had demonstrated, part of Arledge's formula was extensive coverage of the exotic places where sports were played. ABC's coverage of alpine skiing had provided great tourist publicity for such towns as Garmisch, St. Moritz, and Innsbruck. Arledge used this approach to win the rights to televise the 1968 Winter Olympics in Grenoble, France. After the conclusion of the negotiations, a French committeeman told Arledge, "I must tell you that NBC was here, too, and told us about the very impressive list of events they carry. In this connection, there is one question I would like to ask you. What are all these Bowel Games they have the best of?" The committeeman felt such contests were of questionable taste. It was a case of athletic culture shock. Garmisch the French understood. Roses and oranges were only flowers and fruit.

Heroic technology and extended coverage best describes ABC and Arledge's approach to the televising of the Olympic Games. Arledge sent a 250-man crew to cover the Grenoble Games, and he beamed the result home via the Early Bird satellite. Over the years the numbers of Arledge's army steadily escalated. At the 1972 summer Games in Munich, Arledge's team exceeded 330 men and women. As the number of technicians increased, so did the hours of coverage. ABC squeezed 27 hours of television from the Grenoble Games. Eight years later, in Innsbruck, ABC extended its coverage to 43½ hours. The increased technology and coverage returned handsome dividends. The reviews and ratings were tremendous. Both winter and summer Games became prime-time successes.

By the mid-1970s ABC executives had found a way to capitalize on their Olympic telecasts. Instead of selling all of the commercial time to outside sponsors, they decided to hold back large blocs to promote their own television shows. This tactic worked especially well during the 1976 summer Games. While the other networks were televising summer reruns, ABC ran over a hundred hours of Olympic coverage from Montreal. In addition, the network devoted hundreds of commercial minutes to their forthcoming fall lineup of shows. As a result, in the fall of 1976 ABC passed CBS in the Nielsen ratings for all shows.

By the mid-1970s Arledge's string of uninterrupted successes had made him one of the top executives in the industry. Few challenges remained for him in the field of televised sports. In 1975 he decided to attempt a bold move. In "Saturday Night Live with Howard Cosell," Arledge tried to parlay Cosell's success on a prime-time sports show into even greater triumph on a prime-time variety show. Cosell believed fully in the idea. Since the start of "Monday Night Football" Cosell had become a genuine telecelebrity. Millions of Americans tuned in to hear what new outrageous things Howard would say. As David Halberstam noted in "The Mouth that Roared," Cosell "became the issue: What would Howard do? Whom would be assault? Would he self-destruct? Would someone finally turn on him? He became in the process what television wants more than anything else, an event." "A legend in his own mind," Johnny Carson called him, and indeed he was. Cosell assured Arledge that the planned variety show would be a success. "I have a lot of due bills out," Cosell announced. It was Howard's gentle way of assuring everyone that he could bring in the real talent.

Howard said he was only telling it like it is. But as Jimmy Cannon commented, "Can a man who wears a hairpiece and changes his name be trusted to tell it like it is?" Cosell's influence was not up to his vision. Perhaps some indication of the pull he believed he exerted came when he proposed to John Lennon that the Beatles reunite on "Saturday Night Live with Howard Cosell." NBC's "Saturday Night Live" had made the same proposal to George Harrison as a joke. Cosell was quite serious. Lennon listened to Cosell's idea and then politely declined the offer.

"Saturday Night Live with Howard Cosell" was an unqualified failure. In *I Never Played the Game*, Cosell blamed Arledge: "As soon as Arledge realized the show was doomed, he quit on me. He became remote and inaccessible. Chaos set in." Arledge blamed the show's time slot: "At eight o'clock Saturday night, none of the people Howard appeals to are home—the audience consists mostly of children and old people. . . . There is ample evidence that even if Elizabeth Taylor did a strip tease at eight P.M. Saturday on ABC, it wouldn't get more than a 15 percent share." In truth the show's real problem was the premise that celebrity status is transferable. Famous athletes and sports personalities are rarely able to achieve equal success in other areas of the entertainment industry.

The ill-fated show, however, did not hurt either Cosell's or Arledge's careers. Inside the insular sports world, Cosell was still a celebrity. As for Arledge, in 1977 he began his move out of sports, a slow process that would take eight years. In that year he became president of ABC News. Although he also remained president of ABC Sports, he devoted most of his energy to the news division.

• • •

ABC's spectacular rise forced the other networks to reevaluate their coverage of sports. Ousted by ABC from its first place in the Nielsen ratings, CBS was particularly swift to respond. Head of CBS Sports Robert Wussler and CBS chairman of the board William Paley decided that they had to beat ABC at their own game—Olympic coverage. Although CBS had long taken a cavalier attitude toward sports coverage, its chief executives were now determined to win the rights to televise the 1980 Moscow Games.

Suddenly the Russians had something American capitalism very much wanted. More than a touch of humor and irony colored the courting of the Kremlin apparatchiks by the leading executives of CBS and ABC. For a few months Mouton Rothschild and vodka mixed agreeably. Both ABC and CBS programming took a new attitude toward the Soviet Union. As Benjamin Rader described the search for détente, "ABC's morning show *A.M. America*, presented a week of reports on life in the Soviet Union. 'We made Moscow look like Cypress Gardens without the water skiers,' admitted one embarrassed ABC man. CBS followed with a prime-time bomb in 1976 featuring a shivering Mary Tyler Moore standing on a street corner in Moscow where she hosted a show about the Bolshoi Ballet."

The Russian negotiators adapted well to the free enterprise mode of television. ABC, CBS, and late-arriving NBC bid against each other. In the end, NBC won the battle, agreeing to pay the Soviet Union $85 million for television rights to the Olympics. Of course, the eventual United States boycott of the Moscow Games cost NBC dearly.

The Moscow Olympic battle was the first engagement of an eight-year war between the three major networks over the control of television sports. NBC and CBS had taken note of ABC's spectacular rise. Clearly, network executives reasoned, outstanding sports programming was essential to their corporate growth. Not only did sports programming please the affiliates, but it also provided a solid platform for launching the network's fall season. Good sports promoted good ratings, and the sum total of both equalled increased corporate profits.

Such reasoning inevitably created a highly competitive atmosphere. The big-time sports industry became a sellers market, a fact that the men who controlled that industry quickly realized. Giving little consideration to the future problem of overexposure, they sold television executives all the programming the networks desired. Of course, the price was high. Pete Rozelle, commissioner of the NFL, was probably the best—and the greediest—negotiator. After becoming commissioner in 1960, this former public relations man demonstrated his ability to negotiate with network executives. In 1964 CBS agreed to pay $14 million a year for the rights to televise professional football. At the time, owners considered that amount to be staggering. In 1966 CBS raised its annual payments to $18.5 million. By the 1970s such numbers would provide only laughter at the negotiating table. Starting in 1970 Rozelle allowed all three networks to televise professional games. In 1977 the networks agreed to pay the NFL $656 million over a four-year period. In 1982 the networks upped the amount to $2 billion over five years. In 1985 each team in the NFL received $65 million from the television package. As Arthur Rooney, Jr., had said years before, "Pete Rozelle is a gift from the hand of Providence."

College football and professional baseball and basketball similarly profited from the networks' increased interest in sports. In 1970 the National Basketball Association received $1 million from television revenues; by 1986 that amount had been raised to over $40 million. During roughly the same period (1970–85) professional baseball's annual television revenues rose from under $20 million to $160 million. Finally, college football's revenues made the phrase "amateur sport" seem somehow empty. In 1977 the NCAA signed a four-year deal with ABC for $120 million. In 1981 the NCAA agreed to allow CBS and the Turner Broadcasting System as well as ABC to televise games. The new price was $74.3 million per year.

By the late 1970s and the early 1980s the networks seemed sports mad. With the exception of hockey, all the major professional and amateur sports profited. Behind Sugar Ray Leonard, its new hero, boxing made a strong comeback on television. Ruled by two separate organizations—the World Boxing Association and World Boxing Council—the sport offered television networks almost weekly championship fights. Television coverage of tennis and college basketball also increased dramatically. Aided by new cable stations and such all-sports networks as Entertainment and Sports Programming Network (ESPN), Americans watched more sports on television than ever before.

The major networks even turned to trash sports to augment their sports programming. Once again Arledge and ABC led the way. In 1973 "The Superstars" made its debut. The show was rooted more in vindictiveness than in imaginative programming, but it captured considerable viewer interest. In part, the NBA was responsible for the show. Between 1965 and 1973 ABC televised NBA games on Sundays. Although the ratings were never great, it captured enough of an audience to satisfy Arledge. Then in what Arledge considered a breach of faith, the NBA dumped ABC for CBS. Arguing unsuccessfully against the switch, Boston Celtics coach Red Auerbach warned, "You don't really think a man like Roone Arledge is going to take this lying down, do you?" Arledge didn't. Furious and feeling betrayed, he moved to destroy the NBA on television. He put a Sunday version of "Wide World of Sports" opposite the NBA games, publicizing the show as if it were the jewel of ABC Sports. The show was a great success. Its ratings quickly moved past those of professional basketball. During that season, Arledge filled one Sunday show with a program called "The Superstars." It was so successful that Arledge expanded the single program into a series of programs the following year. Roone had his revenge and television had a new concept in sports.

The success of "The Superstars" encouraged the networks to create their own athletic contests. Out of "The Superstars" emerged several sequels. "The Women Superstars" gave the show more sex appeal. "The World Superstars" added a touch of the exotic. "The Superteams" pitted teams from different sports against each other. Using essentially the same themes created by ABC, NBC and CBS aired their own trash sports—"US Against the World," "Dynamic Duos," "The Challenge of the Sexes," and "Celebrity Challenge of the Sexes."

Soon anything went. There were buffalo-chip-throwing contests and Bazooka Bubble Gum blowing contests. Championships were staged to discover who was the strongest man and who was the strongest bartender. The most popular contests, however, featured women in tank-top bathing suits. Particularly anxious to display the best features of their performers, the networks joined together in "Battle of the Network Stars." Although men as well as women competed, the real "stars" were the physically blessed women in form-fitting bathing suits. The show's format provided ample opportunity to allow the bathing suits to be saturated with water. Often the difference between "Battle of the Network Stars" and a wet T-shirt contest amounted to the difference between a tank top and a T-shirt. "Saturday Night Live"'s parody of the show, "Battle of the T and A's," certainly provided a more accurate name for the friendly network championship.

Mercifully, by the early 1980s the Golden Age of trash sports had passed. More important, by that time there were signs that the Golden Age of television sports might also be ending. The industry was changing in fundamental ways. Communication satellites and the end of the legal restriction on cable television allowed local "superstations" and cable networks to compete head-to-head with the major networks. Ted Turner's WTBS in Atlanta epitomized the aggressive mood of the superstations. WTBS televised professional baseball and basketball and college basketball, and it charged its sponsors less than the major networks did for similar programming. ESPN and USA, the two major sports cable networks, similarly offered sponsors outstanding sports programming for less money. By the mid-1980s the three major networks faced a real crisis.

Increasingly traditional sports sponsors began moving their advertising dollars into other areas. For years Madison Avenue had talked about the sports package, which included sponsors from the beer, shaving cream, life insurance, and automobile industries. Advertising experts believed that most of the selling done on prime time was to women. They regarded sports programming as the last place where advertisers could reach men, and they believed that the male still decided what kind of beer he would drink, shaving cream he would use, car he would drive, and life insurance he would purchase. Since ultimately the advertisers paid most of the bills for televised sports, any change in their thinking and spending would send shock waves throughout the television and sports industries.

The first tremors were felt in the late 1970s. In December 1979, General Motors decided to pull out of CBS's NBA package. The decision—based largely on poor ratings for the NBA and the desire to move into college basketball, which attracted a younger, more affluent viewer—staggered CBS Sports and the NBA. After several hastily arranged conferences, Subaru joined the package, "delighted," wrote David Halberstam in *The Breaks of the Game*, "to sell Japanese products by means of American sports." But Subaru paid far less than the going $18,000 for a thirty-second spot.

By the mid-1980s the tremors were registering high on the Richter scale. They affected every major sport. In part, it was a result of a change in family pruchasing patterns. Car-buying decisions, for example, are made more and more by women. Thus advertisers can reach their target audiences more efficiently on "Murder, She Wrote" or "Dallas." In addition, beer-drinking men can be reached much more cheaply on such cable networks as MTV. In 1980 the Miller Brewing Company spent 95 percent of its advertising dollars on televised sports; by 1985 that figure had dropped to 70 percent. A Miller spokesman noted: "Sports programming used to be a bargain compared with prime-time. Now it's as expensive or more. With that, other types of programming become just as important. We are using MTV, late-night shows like David Letterman, and some comedy programming to reach our target audience."

Television networks found themselves caught between rising costs for television rights and falling advertising prices. In 1985 the major networks lost $45 million on the NFL. Although all three networks have been hurt, ABC has suffered the most. In 1984 Olympic coverage helped ABC Sports to achieve a record $70 million profit. In 1985 ABC Sports lost between $30 and $50 million. William Taaffe for *Sports Illustrated* dubbed it "a $100 million-plus Wrong Way Corrigan."

Although the full effect of the earthquake is not yet known, the major networks are starting to assess the damages and beginning their clean-up. ABC has made the most dramatic move. In 1985 Capital City Communications, a media conglomerate, bought ABC for $3.7 billion. Howard Cosell called it "a friendly takeover by the smaller company." Not everyone at ABC, particularly the Sports division, believed the takeover was so benign. One of Cap City's first major moves after the takeover was to replace Roone Arledge in Sports with Dennis Swanson, a no-nonsense, bottom-line ex-Marine. Swanson immediately let it be known that ABC Sports' free-spending days had ended. With Arledge as boss, ABC Sports had taken on an expensive country club air: "Six-block limo rides to executive lunches, hotel suites on the road, helicopters at event sites, and lavish parties were part of the fun," wrote Taaffe. Swanson is not cut from Arledge cloth. Said one insider of Cap City, "Their idea of a good party is pretzels, potato chips, and sodas from the machine in the hallway."

Less subtly, NBC and CBS have moved along the same path as the new ABC. Undoubtedly in the future, professional and college sports executives will not be able to extract as much money from the networks for sports rights. The signs are clear. NBC purchased the rights for the 1988 Seoul Summer Olympics for an unexpectedly low $300 million; ABC cancelled the award-winning, money-losing "SportsBeat" and perhaps gave Cosell reason to rethink his "friendly takeover" thesis; CBS dropped its coverage of the Belmont Stakes, and ABC decided not to renew its contract with the Gator Bowl. The end result might well mean less sports for less money on the major networks. Looking into the future, CBS's sports head Peter Lund commented: "The impact hasn't been felt yet, at least not entirely, by the leagues. The reason is that the [new] baseball and football contracts haven't come up yet. That's where the rubber is going to meet the road—where there is either a leveling off or a diminution in the rights paid to those leagues."

Perhaps the free-spending era ended with ABC's acquisition of the 1988 Winter Olympics in Calgary, Canada. After a brutal bidding war, ABC "won" the rights at a cost of $309 million, an increase of $217.5 million, or 337 percent, over the cost of the 1984 Winter Olympics in Sarajevo, Yugoslavia. From the first, ABC realized that they had bid too high, that pride or vanity or competitiveness had overcome common sense. In fact, the network lost over $50 million on the event. Mae West said that "too much of a good thing is wonderful," but by 1989 the major networks were beginning to reevaluate her sage advice, at least regarding televised sports.

The Roone Revolution, then, is nearing its end, or at least network competition for sports is slackening. But sports will never be the same as they were before Arledge. Nor will television's coverage of sports return to the flat days before Arledge took over ABC Sports. More than any other person, Arledge changed the economic and aesthetic foundations of sports.

As the front office increased ticket sales and profits, league headliners like Dodger Sandy Koufax commanded higher and higher salaries. (Credit: UPI/ Bettmann Newsphotos)

# • The New Rules of the Game

*I think that in this great democracy we live in, if a man wants to take his property somewhere else and can do it legally, then I could not stop him.*
—WILLIAM D. ECKERT, on the 1966 move of the Milwaukee Braves to Atlanta

*After twelve years of being in the major leagues, I do not feel I am a piece of property to be bought and sold irrespective of my wishes.*
—CURT FLOOD

The revolution in sports television also had a dramatic effect on the economic leverage of the players. Under the impact of huge television contracts in the 1970s and 1980s, player salaries sky-rocketed. But the revenue bonanza to owners was not an unmixed blessing. In modern America, sports and film superstars had become the new celebrated rich. In the 1890s Andrew Carnegie and John D. Rockefeller, along with other entrepreneurial business giants, had enjoyed the celebrity status Americans give to the very rich. But when corporate consolidation made business leaders anonymous in the twentieth century, the country needed new symbols of the Horatio Alger rags-to-riches dream, and athletes and actors assumed that role. The viewing public did not really resent the spectacular salaries athletes began commanding; such wealth to a select few was an old story in the United States. What the public resented was any interruption in programming, any limitations on their living room "spectating." Dependent on television contracts for most of their revenues, owners could not afford such interruptions, and

**133**

when players recognized that vulnerability, the power of player unions rose dramatically. The wave of the future first appeared in Los Angeles in 1966.

Baseball hadn't seen anything like it for fifty years, not since Ty Cobb tried to do it to the Detroit Tigers in 1913. Late in February 1966, the sports headlines of the *Los Angeles Times* and the *Herald Examiner* announced that Dodger pitchers Sandy Koufax and Don Drysdale had refused to sign their contracts for the year. Worse still, at least as far as an enraged Dodger owner Walter O'Malley was concerned, they had hired an agent, J. William Hayes, to negotiate for them, and they had joined forces, demanding a joint contract paying them $1 million for a three-year period. Sportswriters and team owners throughout the country were extremely critical of Koufax and Drysdale, but the two pitchers were in an excellent bargaining position. The Dodgers had won National League pennants in 1955, 1956, 1958, 1963, and 1965, with World Series victories in 1956, 1963, and 1965. But by the 1960s, the power hitting of Duke Snider and Carl Furillo had given way to speed, defense, and pitching. Shortstop Maury Wills would get a bunt single, steal second, advance to third on a Junior Gilliam hit or infield out, and then score on a Willie Davis single, a Frank Howard sacrifice fly, or a Tommy Davis fielder's choice. Ahead 1 to 0, the players then waited nine innings for Koufax or Drysdale to shut out the opponent.

Sandy Koufax was a quiet, shy, and decent man who had started out in Brooklyn as a left-handed fireballer with no control. There were times when a Koufax fastball, which hitters described as an aspirin riding the cone of a rocket, went over the catcher's head, the umpire's head, and hit the backstop on the fly. Hitters cheated in the batter's box, giving themselves just an extra inch or two from the plate. Sandy's windup was tight, his eyes peering just over his right shoulder, the left hand coming from behind his left leg and then almost straight over the head, the fast ball hurtling toward the plate at 100 miles per hour, the curve ball dropping like it was falling off a table. Under the tutelage of pitching coaches Preacher Roe and Don Newcombe, however, Koufax gradually got control of the fastball, and by the early 1960s he was leading the majors in wins, shutouts, and strikeouts.

Don Drysdale was a taller, more powerful man, skilled enough as a batter for manager Walter Alston to use him frequently as a pinch hitter. He had a little less speed than Koufax, and a little more control, but his windup and delivery were a bit unorthodox and un-settling, his body undulating in slinky fashion into a three-quarter or even sidearm pitch, the ball racing in from outside to inside on right-handed hitters. Drysdale had a temper too, and opponents angered him at their own peril.

Together in 1966 Drysdale and Koufax were the franchise, and as spring training dragged through March, O'Malley's resolve never to speak to J. William Hayes weakened. Over the years O'Malley and his general manager, Buzzy Bavasi, had tried to use Koufax and Drysdale against each other in salary negotiations, promising them decent raises in alternate years. Both players were sick of it. Willie Mays was getting a $100,000 salary up in San Francisco, and they wanted the same. In mid-March, with opening day just three weeks off, Koufax and Drysdale announced their retirements, and Hayes offered them lucrative roles in a television movie. In the meantime they were both throwing a hundred or so pitches a day to keep in shape. O'Malley surrendered at the end of March. Hayes got $130,000 for Koufax and $115,000 for Drysdale in 1966.

Although the Koufax-Drysdale holdout was the most cele-brated player-management dispute of 1966, a far more important drama had opened quietly in Florida and Arizona, where Marvin Miller, the new head of the Major League Baseball Players' Associa-tion, was visiting spring training camps drumming up support for player unity in dealing with management. Except for some minor adjustments, the essential relationship between players and owners had not really changed in fifty years. Basketball, hockey, football, and baseball all had players' associations by 1966, but the organiza-tions were dormant, either poorly funded through sporadic, volun-tary player contributions or dominated by the league owners.

Lured by the prospects of rich television contracts, the Mil-waukee Braves had moved to Atlanta in 1966, abandoning a city which had been very good to them during the previous fourteen years. The shift of the franchise generated a good deal of criticism, and in defending his decision to do nothing about the move, base-ball commissioner William Eckert remarked: "I think that in this great democracy we live in, if a man wants to take his property somewhere else and can do it legally, then I could not stop him."

By the early 1960s professional athletes were feeling the same way about their services. Koufax justified his holdout with Drysdale on simple grounds: "The goal was to convince them that they would have to approach us not as indentured servants but as coequal partners to a contract, with as much dignity and bargaining power as themselves." Marvin Miller wanted to do for all ballplayers what Hayes had done for Koufax and Drysdale. Robin Roberts and Jim Bunning, both well-known pitchers, had negotiated with Miller after he was recommended to them by a labor relations professor at the Wharton School of the University of Pennsylvania. After twenty years as a federal arbiter and negotiator for the United Steelworkers of America, Miller was ready for a change; he agreed to become the full-time head of the Major League Baseball Players' Association.

Ambitious but soft-spoken, afflicted with a minor birth defect in his right arm, Miller's calm demeanor belied a ferociously tenacious personality. His father, a worker in the New York garment district, had been a dedicated, lifelong member of the Amalgamated Clothing Workers and a vigorous supporter of workers' rights and unionism. The elder Miller was also the contrary sort, growing up in Brooklyn but rooting for the crosstown New York Giants. Marvin Miller saw that the players were in an enviable position: "I never before have seen a group of people who are so irreplaceable in relation to their work." Strikebreakers would never do, not and satisfy the quality of play fans expected. Back in 1912 Ty Cobb, tired of being heckled by an irate fan, went into the stands and beat the guy up. American League president Ban Johnson suspended Cobb for ten days; Cobb's Tiger teammates went on strike. For the Saturday Tiger-Athletic game at Shibe Park in Philadelphia, Tiger manager Hugh Jennings fielded a team of college players, semi-pros, and sandlotters. It was a farce. The Tigers lost 24 to 2 and hundreds of fans stormed the ticket office demanding refunds. In 1966 Marvin Miller was right: ballplayers were irreplaceable.

Miller opened a full-time office for the Major League Baseball Players' Association (MLBPA) on Park Avenue in New York City and stunned the owners when he secured an overwhelming vote of support from the players—489 to 136—with most of the opposition coming from coaches, managers, and trainers eligible to vote. By the end of 1966 every major league player but one had joined the association and paid the $344 annual dues. The owners had expected the players to be as sporadic in paying their dues as they had been in earlier years, but the opposite had happened. Miller got the league owners to agree to trade the All-Star and World Series radio-TV revenues in favor of an annual payment of $4.2 million to the pension fund. Times were changing.

The stable 1950s had become the turbulent 1960s, in sports as well as in America. The Vietnam War and the civil rights movement changed the way most Americans viewed their own institutions. Popular resistance to the war began to mount in 1965 after President Lyndon B. Johnson had initiated massive bombing of North and South Vietnam and deployed tens of thousands of regular ground troops into the conflict. The antiwar movement had its original center on college campuses, but by 1966 and 1967 the resistance had spread out from there to middle America. The image of the United States as the moral leader of the world, nurtured throughout World War II and the Cold War, was being undermined by the foreign policy disaster in Vietnam.

More important than the Vietnam War, however, was the civil rights movement, at least in terms of the growing militancy among professional athletes. It had all begun back in 1955 in Montgomery, Alabama, when Rosa Parks, tired after a long day of work, refused to give up her seat on a city bus to a white man. She set off a chain reaction, with blacks refusing in droves to use city buses and the Montgomery city transportation system moving perilously close to bankruptcy. Under the leadership of a young minister, Martin Luther King, Jr., Montgomery blacks demanded an end to segregation on the buses and more black bus drivers. The boycotts spread to other cities.

That was only the beginning. On February 1, 1960, black students from the Negro Agricultural and Technical College at Greensboro, North Carolina, sat down at the lunch counters in several department stores and demanded service. When denied service, they refused to leave and inaugurated the "sit-in" movement. In May 1961 the Congress of Racial Equality organized black and white "freedom riders" to go into the South to test compliance with federal court orders to integrate interstate transportation. In 1962 and 1963, King took his crusade to Birmingham, Alabama, demanding equal employment opportunities, integration of public facilities, and enforcement of court-ordered desegregation rulings. City police attacked the demonstrators with tear gas, billy clubs, and dogs while fifty million Americans watched on television. In August 1963 King brought more than 250,000 people together on the steps of the Lincoln Memorial in Washington, D.C., where he gave his "I Have a Dream" speech and electrified the nation. After the assassination of President John F. Kennedy, Lyndon Johnson pushed the Civil Rights Act of 1964 through a reluctant Congress, ending segregation in public facilities.

The civil rights movement had a direct impact on the situation of professional athletes. Although they were certainly well-paid, at least by the standards of most poor black workers in the South, the reserve and option clauses, the amateur player draft, the baseball antitrust exemption, and federal tax regulations relegated them, legally at least, to the level of chattel—prosperous slaves to be bought, sold, and traded at the whim of team owners. Such a morally dubious legal situation could not survive long in a political atmosphere loaded with talk of freedom, equality, and liberation.

By 1966 the salary expectations of professional athletes had been magnified by the rivalry between the National Football League and the upstart American Football League. In 1965, David A. "Sonny" Werblin, owner of the American Football League's New York Jets franchise, signed Joe Willie Namath, star quarterback from the University of Alabama, for the unheard-of salary of $400,000. The news spread through the country and the ranks of professional sports like a prairie fire. The new American Football League, blessed with a $34 million television contract with NBC, had brought competition to professional football, and the AFL and NFL found themselves in the middle of an escalating bidding war for graduating college seniors.

The AFL was the brainchild of Lamar Hunt, an SMU graduate and heir to the billion-dollar fortune of his tight-fisted father H. L. Hunt. An avid football fan, Lamar Hunt wanted to bring a pro franchise to Dallas. A business rival of his in Dallas, Clint Murchison, Jr., wanted to do the same. Throughout the 1950s they both tried to purchase the defunct Dallas Texans, the San Francisco Forty-Niners, the Washington Redskins, and finally the Chicago Cardinals, but some hitch always interfered. Angry and frustrated, Hunt announced the creation of the new American Football League in 1959, with franchises in Houston, Dallas, New York, Boston, Denver, Los Angeles, Oakland, and Buffalo. The recruitment war was on.

The establishment of new franchises and rival leagues was long overdue by 1959, when Hunt made the wager even his gambler father questioned. The American economy, like the society it produced, was rapidly changing. Technology, demographic change, economic development, and federal tax laws all provided new investment opportunities in sports. Technology was partly responsible. Throughout the first half of the twentieth century, professional sports competition had been confined to the Northeast and Midwest because of travel restraints. Only football, with its weekly schedule, had the ability to spread out across the country, which explains the move of the Cleveland Rams to Los Angeles in 1946. For hockey, baseball, and basketball, with their daily or near-daily schedules, cross-country travel was impossible until the appearance of commercial jet travel in the mid-1950s. It opened the West Coast up to baseball, hockey, and basketball.

Television, however, was even more important than Boeing 707s. During the 1950s television supplanted radio, magazines, newspapers, and movies as the primary vehicle of American information and entertainment. But advertising revenues depended on Nielsen ratings and market shares; advertisers paid more for each commercial minute when larger audiences were watching. With no professional football, baseball, hockey, or basketball teams in the South and West, national sports broadcasts in those areas attracted only marginal audiences. The minor league Los Angeles Angels, playing out of Wrigley Field, enjoyed attendance and television ratings in the 1950s comparable to that of many major league teams. Major cities of the South and West were far more likely to participate in national sports broadcasts if one of their own teams was competing, and market shares would be larger. So the economics of television finance created a new pressure for expansion franchises.

Television revenues did the same. Between 1952 and 1971, total television revenues in professional baseball increased from $5.4 million to $40.7 million, and in basketball, from $130,000 to $5.5 million. Broadcasts rights in football went from $4.9 million in 1960 to nearly $50 million in 1970. Then the revolution really began, especially in football and baseball. By the 1980s, television contract rights exceeded $1 billion for baseball (including contracts with the networks for national broadcasts and with local stations) and $500 million for football. Television money accounted for more than 40 percent of all baseball revenues and more than 50 percent of football revenues. By the 1970s few professional teams could have survived without broadcast revenues. Television revenues had become a critical element in the financial success of a franchise. In 1963, the Milwaukee Braves negotiated a $500,000 contract for local television rights, the highest total since they had moved to Milwaukee from Boston in 1952. Atlanta offered them a guaranteed $1.2 million, and they moved. Charley Finley moved the Kansas City Athletics to Oakland in 1968, and his television contract increased from $98,000 to $705,000.

Federal tax laws also created investment opportunities in professional sports, attracting new money and intensifying the pressure for new leagues and new franchises. To stimulate business investment, federal tax regulations by the late 1950s provided for accelerated depreciation of real assets. For most professional sports teams, particularly those which did not own their own stadiums, the primary business asset was the players and a small amount of equipment. It was possible for team owners to argue that in real economic terms, even a couple of players constituted "the franchise," and that loss of those players would substantially reduce the value of team property. A professional basketball team renting use of a city arena, for example, could justifiably claim that of the $10 million net worth of the franchise, players constituted $9 million in assets. Since the average playing life of each team member was only three years, and tax laws allowed for an annualized depreciation of that "property," the franchise owners enjoyed a yearly tax deduction of $3 million. If the owner was in a 70 percent tax bracket, the savings amounted to $2.1 million on a $10 million investment—a 21 percent return on capital. Few other investments were as lucrative. Although the Tax Reform Act of 1986 reduced tax rates on higher incomes and eliminated many deductions for "passive" business activities, sports franchises still retained many of their lucrative tax advantages.

By the late 1950s and early 1960s a series of economic and demographic changes were also appearing, and during the 1970s they accelerated. The professional sports complex was confined to the Midwest and Northeast, but the economy of the "Rustbelt" was beginning to deteriorate. The factories, smelters, furnaces, and mines of the Northeast had all been constructed before the turn of the century, and by 1960 new technology abroad was making them less competitive. Blue-collar jobs as a percentage of total employment declined year after year, replaced by white-collar, service, and professional positions. The cities of the Rustbelt, plagued by congestion, pollution, unemployment, urban blight, and cold winters, went into a long-term decline. People and companies took off for the South and West.

Southern and western cities were ready for the influx. Ever since Reconstruction northern investors had looked enviously at the investment potential of the South: a warm climate and long growing season, cheap labor, and abundant natural resources. But the instability of southern race relations had scared them off, until the 1960s at least. By then millions of southern blacks had migrated to northern cities, and the civil rights movement was changing southern customs. Fed by incoming northerners, a number of southern cities leaped past places like Detroit and Cleveland in size. Memphis and New Orleans became major port cities draining the Mississippi Valley; the Houston-Dallas-San Antonio triangle grew in size and power on the back of the oil industry; Atlanta became the commercial and retail center of the Southeast; and Miami, Orlando, Tampa, and Jacksonville rose to prominence because of retirement and recreation money and middle-class Cuban immigration. The South was ready by the 1960s for professional sports.

So was the West. Politically independent but traditionally beneficiaries of federal largesse—in the form of grants for railroad construction, water development, and public-domain grazing in the nineteenth century—the western states did equally well in federal grants after World War II, this time for aerospace, weapons development, and military bases. California was an economic gold mine—a leading producer of oil, natural gas, citrus, and cotton in the world. The West Coast's port facilities—San Diego, Long Beach–Los Angeles, San Francisco–Oakland, and Seattle–Vancouver—were the best in the world and tied the region to the booming Asian economies in Japan, South Korea, Taiwan, and Singapore. This was the "Pacific Slope" economy, prospering in the 1960s and 1970s.

Acquiring a professional sports team became critically important to the expanding cities of the South and West. Sports franchises serve as labels proving that cities have achieved a certain status. The media recognition alone provides volumes of advertising that money cannot buy. The success of the 1984 summer Olympic Games, for example, gave Los Angeles a global exposure it could have received in no other way, and on a lesser scale a professional sports franchise provided the same benefits. So just as team owners were ready to move out of the Northeast, the cities of the South and West were anxiously prepared to court them.

The deal Irving, Texas, made with Clint Murchison and the Dallas Cowboys was a perfect illustration. In order to get the Cowboys as their team, Irving officials agreed to finance the construction of a new stadium with the issue of $25 million in thirty-year bonds. Management of the stadium during the life of those bonds was left exclusively in the hands of the Texas Stadium Corporation, a Cowboy subsidiary. The building contract for constructing the stadium went to the J. W. Bateson Company, a corporation owned by Murchison. The concession contract was the exclusive property of the Cebe Corporation, another Murchison subsidiary. Liquor rights went to the Cowboys' Stadium Club, and the insurance contract was awarded to Kenneth Murchison Company.

Under the impact of television, federal tax codes, and the expanding economies of the South and West, the business of professional sports—in terms of league structure, ownership, and labor relations—underwent profound changes. Lamar Hunt's American Football League limped along after 1960, many of the franchises just a step ahead of bankruptcy. But the presence of the AFL forced the National Football League into expansion or facing the loss of valuable television markets. When Hunt got his own AFL franchise, the Dallas Texans, the NFL awarded Clint Murchison a rival franchise—the Dallas Cowboys. Hunt eventually relocated his franchise to Kansas City. Desperate to bring the salary wars to an end, the two leagues merged in 1966 into the National Football League, divided into the National Conference and the American Conference. The Super Bowl decided the world champion. The congressional legislation exempting the merger from federal antitrust laws was sponsored by Congressman Hale Boggs and Senator Russell Long, both Democrats from Louisiana, and the next year the NFL awarded New Orleans a new football franchise. Tampa, Florida, and Seattle later received expansion NFL franchises as well. The AFL-NFL merger brought about shared television revenues and a common amateur player draft, ending for a time the salary wars.

The creation of the American Football League inspired a young entrepreneur, UCLA graduate Gary Davidson, to take advantage of the new demand for sports franchises. In 1967, just thirty-three years old, Davidson founded the American Basketball Association. At the time, he was worth only $50,000. Back in 1961, Abe Saperstein, the owner of the Harlem Globetrotters, had founded the American Basketball League with eight franchises, but the rival league lasted only one season. The ABL gave Connie Hawkins, who was blacklisted from the NBA because of some nebulous gambling charges, a chance to show the world his talent, but the league simply did not have the financial backing to survive. But Davidson, by requiring up-front payments from franchise purchases, made sure that only well-heeled investers got into his ABA. Davidson brought Hawkins back into the game, where he starred for the Pittsburgh Pipers, and signed such top NBA talent as Rick Barry, Billy Cunningham, and Joe Caldwell. He also got former Minneapolis Laker center George Mikan to serve as the ABA commissioner. The American Basketball Association survived for nine years, although a good number of franchises went under: the Anaheim Amigos, the Houston Mavericks, the Miami Floridians, the Minnesota Pipers, the New Orleans Bucks, the Oakland Oaks, the Pittsburgh Condors. In 1976 the NBA, tired of the salary-bidding wars, absorbed the ABA's four strongest franchises through a merger.

Davidson had made a personal fortune off the American Basketball Association, and he decided to expand into professional football and hockey. In 1974 he formed the World Football League. Although the new league folded in 1975, it enriched Davidson and a number of players. He sold franchises to twelve investors for $600,000 up front each; all but eliminated the option clause from player contracts; and managed to sign such NFL stars as Larry Csonka, Jim Kiick, Paul Warfield, Calvin Hill, Daryle Lamonica, and Kenny Stabler. But the WFL failed to secure a television contract and went under in 1975.

The collapse of the WFL, however, did not deter Gary Davidson, and in 1971 he turned to hockey, forming the World Hockey Association. After a generation with only six teams, the National Hockey League expanded to twelve teams in 1966, and Davidson saw still more opportunity for expansion. In 1972 the WHL took to the ice with twelve teams and in the greatest coup possible signed

Chicago Black Hawk superstar Bobby Hull to a $2.75 million, ten-year contract. Hull played with the Winnipeg Jets. The legendary Gordie Howe signed with the Houston franchise. Still, the WHL was at best a marginal operation. By 1979 there were only six viable franchises left, and negotiations to merge with the NHL were completed. The National Hockey League accepted four WHL teams: the Edmonton Oilers, the Quebec Nordiques, the Winnipeg Jets, and the New England Whalers.

The last of the new leagues, the United States Football League, launched its first season in the spring of 1983 with its championship game in July. Heisman Trophy winner Herschel Walker of the University of Georgia signed a $3.9 million, three-year contract with the New Jersey Generals; SMU halfback Craig James went to the Washington franchise for $700,000 a year; and BYU quarterback Steve Young signed an incredible $40 million, long-term contract with the Los Angeles Express. Despite initial success in securing high-quality players, the USFL was floundering by 1984, and in 1985 agreed to switch to a fall schedule in 1986. Its hopes of merging with the NFL were slim indeed by that time; television contracts were disappointing and too many franchise owners simply did not have the resources, even with the tax advantages, to stay in the salary competition indefinitely.

Baseball's confrontation with rival leagues came in 1959, when Branch Rickey announced formation of the Continental League with franchises in New York, Houston, Denver, Toronto, Minneapolis, Buffalo, Atlanta, and Dallas. Major league owners, like their counterparts in the NFL, were worried about the impact of the rival league, not only because of the potential it had for raising player salaries but because it would cut the National and American Leagues out of valuable television markets. They decided to expand to protect their position. The American League moved first, allowing Calvin Griffith to relocate the Washington Senators in Minneapolis and creating a new expansion team for the nation's capital. Gene Autry, the singing cowboy turned media multi-millionaire, purchased rights to an American League expansion team and placed them in Los Angeles as the Angels. The National League got into the act in 1962, giving Houstonian Roy Hofheinz the Colt-45s, who became the Astros in 1965, and moving back into New York with the Mets franchise.

With ten teams in each league, the majors stayed intact, except for the move of the Milwaukee Braves to Atlanta and the Kansas City Athletics to Oakland, until 1969. The American League expanded to twelve teams in 1969, establishing the Kansas City Royals and the Seattle Pilots; the Pilots lasted only a year before moving to Milwaukee as the Brewers. The National League followed suit that same year, giving San Diego the Padres and establishing the Montreal Royals. The Padres survived on a shoestring until McDonald's hamburger king Ray Kroc bought the franchise in 1974. The Washington Senators became the Texas Rangers in 1971, and in 1976 the American League expanded again, placing the Blue Jays in Toronto and the Mariners in Seattle's new "Kingdome" stadium.

The flurry of rival leagues, new franchises, and franchise shifts in the 1960s and 1970s changed the structure of professional sports. The American League had gone from eight teams to fourteen; the National League from eight to twelve; the National Hockey League from six to twenty-one; the National Basketball Association from eight to twenty-three; and the National Football League from eleven to twenty-seven. Even new sports had entered the ranks of professional team competition in the 1970s—the North American Soccer League and the World Tennis Association—but both failed after a few years.

In addition to bringing about a rapid expansion in the number of professional sports teams, the combined influence of television, federal tax laws, and the booming economies of the South and West transformed the nature of team ownership and management. During the 1970s and 1980s the value of sports franchises increased far more quickly than the consumer price index, and the tax advantages made it easier for extremely wealthy individuals or corporations to own a team than merely a well-to-do individual. Not only did the rising price of sports franchises make it impossible for any but the very rich to buy a team, but the tax advantages could be exploited only by those capable of writing them off other income sources. The days of Art Rooney sustaining the Pittsburgh Steelers from race track winnings, or George Halas or Calvin Griffith or Bill Veeck using teams as their sole source of income were over. Except for Green Bay, where the city still owned the Packers, a new generation of owners came in to professional sports—wealthy individuals like George Steinbrenner, Jack Kent Cooke, Edward Kauffman, and Ray

Kroc, or powerful corporations like CBS Broadcasting or Anheuser-Busch. They changed the game.

Sports was not like other businesses. Losing could actually be winning, because of tax implications. In 1975, only half of the major league baseball franchises broke even or made money, and it was even worse in basketball, where twenty-two of the twenty-seven franchises ran in the red. Hockey was somewhat better off, with "only" ten of twenty-eight major league teams operating at a loss. Eight of twenty-six pro football teams were losing money. But despite the losses, franchise values kept climbing. The Anaheim Amigos in the American Basketball Association is a good example. Chartered in 1967 for a price of $1.7 million, the Amigos never turned a profit, but Salt Lake City investors moved the team to Utah in 1971 at a price of $5 million, all because of the possible tax write-off.

The tax implications of team ownership directly affected sports management. Most owners had other profitable businesses; the principal advantage of team ownership is tax deductions, not operating profits. Even if the team lost money, the losses could be deducted from other profits, saving millions in taxes. But the benefits of ownership last only as long as the IRS depreciation schedule, after which the team must be sold to another buyer interested in sheltering income. Uninterested in long-range planning, some owners sacrificed the future for the present, trading draft choices for aging players. Instead of the stability coming from an interested owner committed for a lifetime to the team, professional sports management in the 1970s and 1980s was characterized by instability and change. Gary Davidson's success in establishing the American Basketball Association, the World Football League, and the World Hockey Association had more to do with tax savings for would-be investors than serious hopes of running successful franchises or creating a stable league. The ability to make money while losing money also eliminated, for some owners, any serious drive to invest the funds necessary to make some teams competitive. So what if they languished in the cellar, as long as they produced tax savings.

Unlike earlier generations of team owners, the new breed of the 1970s and 1980s often had more on their minds than making money in the business. Tax advantages and public relations issues attracted large corporations into sports, and bureaucratic management replaced the individual leadership of the past. In 1964, for example, the Columbia Broadcasting System purchased the New York Yankees from Del Webb and Dan Topping, primarily for the public relations coup of listing the team as a glamorous addition to the CBS investment portfolio. But CBS's expertise was in broadcasting sports events, not in managing a professional baseball team. The Yankees won the pennant in 1964, but in the next nine years the team slipped from first to last, becoming a perennial loser in the American League. In the process the team became a public relations liability; CBS did not like the image of presiding over the demise of the greatest sports franchise in American history.

CBS sold the Yankees in 1973 to a syndicate headed by shipping magnate George Steinbrenner III and people like Nelson Bunker Hunt, brother of AFL founder Lamar Hunt, and Jesse Bell, president of the Bonne Bell cosmetics firm. They represented another dimension of modern sports ownership: people whose business success had given them money and power but not fame. Although they often lacked experience in professional sports and were too busy with other business interests to acquire much expertise, they cavalierly interfered in the day-to-day affairs of running the team. Steinbrenner quickly got rid of general manager Mike Burke, hired and fired manager Billy Martin regularly over the next ten years, and ranted and raved over team and individual player performances. Owning the Yankees gave Steinbrenner what the anonymity of corporate business, no matter how successful, could never provide—a "bully pulpit," a public profile, a reputation in American popular culture.

Sometimes huge conglomerates acquired sports franchises as part of their drives for asset diversification. Instead of the colorful figures of the past like Tim Mara and Art Rooney or entrepreneurial barons like Horace Stoneham or Phil Wrigley, anonymous bureaucratic managers took over teams, and owners became nebulous stockholders. Madison Square Garden, for example, had owned the New York Knicks and the New York Rangers, which Art Wirtz and Jim Norris controlled through their 40 percent interest in the Garden. By 1968, when the new Madison Square Garden opened, Gulf & Western, a huge conglomerate in oil, tin, zinc, sugar, iron ore, and entertainment, had purchased the arena and, indirectly, its basketball and hockey teams. Nobody knew who really controlled the team anymore.

The new owners, whether corporate or individual, often had less loyalty to particular cities and communities than the earlier generation. Walter O'Malley—who decided in 1957 to move the eminently profitable Dodgers out of Brooklyn to Los Angeles—was a forerunner of later owners who cared little about their fans, even when those fans bought tickets in record numbers. O'Malley had given birth to the phenomenon of the "carpetbag" owners. In the 1970s it was the National Football League which produced the most notorious of the carpetbaggers. The move of the Los Angeles Rams to Anaheim and the Oakland Raiders to Los Angeles are good case studies. Carroll Rosenbloom, the late owner of the Los Angeles Rams, set in motion the chain of events which culminated in the move of the Raiders from Oakland to Los Angeles. On July 25, 1978, he announced his plans to move the Rams from Los Angeles to Anaheim. Although he claimed the move was for the benefit of fans, Rosenbloom's real reason was money. In much the same way as Los Angeles attracted O'Malley, Anaheim offered Rosenbloom a sweetheart deal. Not only did city officials promise to enlarge Anaheim Stadium and build more luxury boxes, but they also agreed to give Rosenbloom ninety-five acres adjacent to the stadium, which was prime real estate for commercial development.

NFL Commissioner Pete Rozelle supported Rosenbloom's decision, and the other franchise owners sanctioned the relocation. Los Angeles officials were angry but were caught in a difficult position. After all, this was the city which had lured the Dodgers from Brooklyn, the Rams from Cleveland, and the Lakers from Minneapolis. To complain now would be at best ironic. Los Angeles decided to get even by convincing another NFL team to relocate in their city. Franchise owners fully understood the Los Angeles Coliseum Commission's plans, and they used the threat of relocation as a club to win valuable concessions from their respective home cities. This led to a series of quasi-blackmail capers by several owners.

First Robert Irsay, owner of the then Baltimore Colts, expressed interest in relocating in Los Angeles. To keep the Colts in Baltimore, city officials offered $24 million for stadium improvements. It also granted Irsay a desirable short-term lease. So Irsay stayed in Baltimore for five more years; the short-term lease expired, and he moved the team, literally in the dead of night, out to Indianapolis. After briefly trying to convince Joe Robbie to bring his Miami Dolphins to Los Angeles, the Coliseum Commission courted Max Winter, owner of the Minnesota Vikings. Winter listened, at least until Minneapolis officials agreed to build a domed stadium for his team. It took a $55 million bond issue to satisfy Winter.

Thus even before Al Davis and the Oakland Raiders arrived on the scene, several things were apparent. Major cities were committed to professional sports; they believed that the loss of a franchise represented a real financial and psychological setback. Franchise owners knew this and readily used the threat of relocation to win concessions from their home cities.

In 1979 the Los Angeles Coliseum Commission approached Al Davis, the managing partner of the Oakland Raiders. Davis had a deserved reputation as a renegade. Forceful, brash, and often charming, Davis's life was filled with a series of conflicts and successes. Sam Rutigliano, former coach of the Cleveland Browns, captured the essence of Davis's complex personality when he observed, "He'll take your eyeballs and tell you you look better without them."

In Oakland, Davis had built a winning team in his own image—confident, bold, and unpredictable. The Oakland Raiders played in a good stadium before consistently packed houses and had strong community support. But Davis worried about the future. If, he emphasized, free agency came to football and cable television revenues were not included under the general NFL revenues-sharing arrangement, then the most competitive teams would be the richest teams, and the richest teams would be those that occupied the best media markets. Davis was one owner who had to win. He decided to leave Oakland and move to Los Angeles.

Rozelle opposed Davis's move, and in March 1980 the other league owners voted down the proposed relocation of the Raiders. Undaunted, the Los Angeles Coliseum Commission and the Oakland Raiders sued the National Football League. Their case centered on section 4.3 of the NFL constitution, which stipulated that at least three-fourths of the owners had to agree to any franchise relocations. Davis claimed that the rule was in restraint of trade and thus a clear violation of the Sherman Antitrust Act. Rozelle and the NFL countered that the teams comprised a single entity—a partnership of sorts—and were not ordinarily economic competitors. On May 7, 1982, after a five-week trial, the U.S. District Court in Los Angeles ruled in Davis's and the Coliseum Commission's favor. The Raiders were free to move to Los Angeles.

The ownership changes in recent years and the franchise shifts precipitated a major debate in professional sports circles. Some people wanted the federal government to move in and regulate the sports business. To former ABC sports commentator Howard Cosell, "Sports today is deals, always deals. Tax abatements, luxury boxes, a bigger slice of the concessions pie, and land, lots of land, to facilitate increased revenues from parking and perhaps the construction of a glistening new training complex." In 1972 the New York Giants left New York City, eventually to relocate to East Rutherford, New Jersey, at the new Meadowlands sports complex. In 1984 Sonny Werblin took the Jets out there too. And in the spring of 1986, the city of Pittsburgh agreed to purchase 40 percent of the outstanding stock of the Pirates to keep the baseball team in the city. Behind all these moves, like those of the Dodgers and Raiders, was a series of intricate financial deals. There was little concern about the financial loss to the cities involved or about the loyal fans. Cosell began calling for congressional regulation of the sports business.

Critics like Cosell felt the team owners were playing a game with the public. On the one hand, they had argued for years that professional sport was special and unique, and that to protect the "integrity of the game" the leagues needed special exemptions from antitrust laws. The court-ordered antitrust exemption for baseball, the special antitrust exemptions for the football television pool in 1961 and the AFL-NFL merger in 1966, along with the reserve and option clauses, had given owners virtually monopolistic control over the labor markets. But at the same time, team owners insisted they should be able to do anything they wanted to do "with our property," as if they were operating in a free, competitive market. When questioned about his 1983 decision to move the Colts out of Baltimore to Indianapolis, owner Robert Irsay said simply: "This is my team. I own it, and I'll do whatever I want with it."

That was hardly a unique point of view in American business. But neither was congressional regulation unique. Beef producers were simultaneously demanding relaxed federal meat standards *and* higher tariffs on foreign beef imports, and Lee A. Iacocca, head of

Chrysler Motors, was calling for a postponement of federal fuel efficiency standards just as he was negotiating federal multi-billion dollar loan guarantees for the troubled company. Those demanding
regulation of professional sports viewed it simply as a natural step in
the evolution of the industry. To protect the loyalties of fans as well
as urban tax bases, Howard Cosell argued that a federal commission
be established to set guidelines for franchise shifts. The guidelines
could include "such factors as population, geographic balance, financial liability, quality of facilities, fan loyalty, and location con-
tinuity." The need for congressional scrutiny was particularly essential if cable television continued to grow. Team owners would be
even more tempted to move their clubs to lucrative media markets in
order to remain competitive. Congress could accept the notion that
professional sports have an important emotional as well as economic
impact on their home cities. Sports fulfill public needs. In addition,
Congress could protect cities from carpetbagger owners whose only
concern was how and where they could make more money.
Owners, critics argued, should not be permitted to bargain with city
officials using the threat of relocation as a loaded gun. Government
control would both save money and protect the fragile emotional
balance of cities.

But opponents of congressional regulation also made compelling arguments. Nothing in life stays the same, particularly in economics and politics. In the course of a generation, New York City
lost the Dodgers, the Jets, and both the Giants to other cities, but
during that same generation it also lost hundreds of thousands of
citizens, who moved to the suburbs or to the South and West; hundreds of thousands of jobs, which headed in the same direction; and
hundreds of corporations. H. Ross Perot, the billionaire entrepreneur who founded EDS systems in Dallas, even tried to move New
York's prized American Indian Museum to Texas. New York City's
loss of sports franchises was simply one dimension to a long-term
decline it was undergoing.

Advocates of a free market in sports also argued that the sports
business is not terribly different from other businesses. Chambers
of commerce in every city and town across the country actively en-
gage in bringing new businesses to their communities. More jobs
mean more money. City industrial parks offer free land, cheap
leases in city-built factory facilities, low property taxes or even prop-

erty tax exemptions, and county access roads to factory sites. State governors, congressmen, U.S. senators, and state legislators shamelessly court company presidents and boards of directors to convince them to relocate to their environs. Every major city in the United States with visions of grandeur wants major league baseball, football, basketball, and hockey franchises, a topflight symphony orchestra, a decent fine arts museum, a good university or two, and a performing arts center. Serious cities pay to get them. For every team owner willing to take a club away from one city, there is another city anxiously bidding to get it. Congress should leave well enough alone, according to those who still believe in the efficiency of market forces.

The controversy over the business of professional sports came to national attention in the spring of 1986 when the United States Football League brought a $1.32 billion antitrust suit against the National Football League. Arguing before a five-woman, one-man jury in the U.S. District Court in Manhattan, the USFL charged that the NFL had conspired to destroy the new league. Acknowledging that television revenue is the lifeblood of professional sports, USFL lawyers claimed that the NFL had successfully convinced the American Broadcasting Corporation to end its broadcasts of USFL games. Between 1983 and 1985, the USFL enjoyed television contracts with ABC and ESPN worth $35 million a year. The National Football League was nearing the end of its five-year, $2 billion contract with ABC, NBC, and CBS. Intending to play a fall schedule in 1985, the USFL could not negotiate a network contract that year and decided that the NFL, by offering ABC only a mediocre schedule for "Monday Night Football," had forced ABC to drop USFL games. After a trial lasting several months, the jury found that the NFL had worked to put the USFL out of business, but they awarded the United States Football League only $1 in damages. The USFL was forced then to cancel the 1986 season.

Franchise-shifting and owner shenanigans were matched in the public mind only by the revolution in player salaries which took place in the 1970s and 1980s. Television revenues poured billions of dollars into professional sports and raised player expectations. Expansion teams and rival leagues created new demand for player services, and team owners often found themselves caught in bidding wars with one another. The image of musical chairs in franchise lo-

cation had undermined owner credibility in some circles, particularly in those cities with losing teams, and public perception of
owner sincerity was no longer as strong as it once had been.

The changes in league structures and management relations
transformed the labor markets in professional sports. Three developments in particular contributed to skyrocketing player salaries
in the 1970s and 1980s: favorable decisions in federal courts, increased solidarity among the major players' associations, and the
use of professional agents in negotiating individual player contracts.
By the late 1980s, the balance of power in professional sports had
finally tilted toward the players, at least to the point that they could
negotiate successfully for themselves. The monopoly owners had
enjoyed in labor relations for more than a century had finally broken
down into a more competitive arrangement.

Baseball led the way, with Marvin Miller heading up the Major
League Baseball Players' Associaltion. One of his first achievements
was a general contract with Topps Chewing Gum Company, which
had been paying each major leaguer $125 a year for rights to picture
him on bubble gum cards. Miller told Topps the old days were over
and by 1968 had negotiated a multimillion-dollar contract providing
royalties and bonuses. Far more important was conclusion of baseball's first Basic Agreement in 1968. The Basic Agreement provided
for grievance procedures, a joint player-owner study of the reserve
clause, and an increase in the minimum salary to $10,000. The mini-
mum salary had been $5,000 in 1946 and only $7,000 in 1966 when
Miller arrived on the scene. When Miller tried to get improved
health and life insurance and a better pension plan in 1969, the
owners balked and there was talk of a strike in spring training. Only
the intervention of Bowie Kuhn, a National League attorney, averted
the crisis. Kuhn advised the owners to compromise, and the season
was saved. Kuhn's sage advice also won him a promotion: he became commissioner of baseball.

The assault on the reserve clause came in 1969 when Curt
Flood, star center fielder of the pennant-winning St. Louis Cardinals, protested August Busch's decision to trade him to the Philadelphia Phillies. Busch paid his players well by major league standards, but in labor relations he was another Henry Ford: benevolent
but adamant about the "place" of his employees. His Budweiser
beer empire had provided him enormous prosperity, but his per-

sonal and political conservatism could hardly countenance the general rebellion against social values in American society and the specific militancy of the Players' Association. Yet Flood did not want to be traded, especially after twelve years in the major leagues.

Flood considered his options carefully and talked with a number of players, with Marvin Miller, and with Bowie Kuhn. Kuhn, after listening to Flood's claim that he was not another person's property, said: "I certainly agree with you that you, as a human being, are not a piece of property to be bought and sold. That is fundamental to our society and I think obvious . . . . [But] I cannot see its applicability to the situation at hand." Miller did, and the Players' Association agreed to finance a lawsuit. The case went to trial in May 1970, and in the meantime Miller used the threat to the reserve clause to the player's advantage. Club owners agreed to a Second Basic Agreement, this one raising the minimum salary to $12,000 in 1972 and $15,000 in 1975, reducing the maximum cut in salary to 20 percent instead of 30 percent a year, and providing for impartial arbitration of grievances.

The Flood case finally reached the Supreme Court in 1972, and the Players' Association lost in a 5–3 decision. The justices decided to leave the 1922 antitrust exemption in place. It was a short-term victory for the owners, however. On April 1, 1972, the Major League Baseball Players' Association called a general strike, and the players walked out of spring training. At issue was owner refusal to provide cost-of-living increases in pension and health benefits. The strike went thirteen days into the regular season and cancelled eighty-six games before the owners capitulated. Flood's unsuccessful attack on the reserve clause and union solidarity had their effects: in March 1973 Miller got a new Basic Agreement out of baseball management. Although there was no change in the reserve clause, the minimum salary went up to $16,000, the "Flood" rule gave ten-year major league veterans with at least five years on the same club the power to veto all trades, and players won the right to impartial salary arbitration.

The next year Catfish Hunter, the star pitcher for the Oakland Athletics, found himself immersed in a contract dispute with owner Charlie Finley. Hunter's 1974 contract called for deferred compensation of half of his $100,000 salary. For tax reasons Finley wanted Hunter to accept full salary payment, but the pitcher refused.

Hunter took his case through formal arbitration procedures and won. The arbitrators decided Finley had violated the contract and that Hunter was a free agent. He quickly signed a $3.75 million, five-year contract with the Yankees.

Marvin Miller decided then to test the reserve clause and asked Andy Messersmith, a pitcher for the Los Angeles Dodgers, and Dave McNally of the Montreal Expos to play out the 1975 season without signing a contract to see if the reserve clause had only a one-year duration. They agreed, and a three-man baseball arbitration panel upheld the one-year lifespan of the reserve clause. So did the Supreme Court when it decided not to interfere with the arbitration decision. The reserve clause was dead. The owners tried a lockout at spring training in 1976 to get a new agreement, and Marvin Miller, with the support of most players, decided to compromise. Instead of a lifetime reserve clause, owners would have a six-year "control" period over a player, after which he would become a free agent and enter a "re-entry draft." This compromise became part of the Basic Agreement of 1976, which also raised minimum salaries up to $21,000 by 1979. Players were no longer slaves. Indeed, by 1979 they enjoyed average salaries of $100,000 and had the best pension plan in sports.

The rise of free agency, however, troubled the owners, and they insisted that some form of compensation be awarded to teams losing a player. If it cost a team one of its better players to sign a free agent, the owner might be more conservative. The cumulative effect would be to limit salaries. In 1981 the team owners announced their own plan. If a team signed a free agent who had been ranked in the top half of his position in the major leagues, the club losing the player could claim a player from the signing team's roster, after the team had "protected" eighteen people. Marvin Miller blasted the proposal, filed an unfair labor practices suit with the National Labor Relations Board, and took the players out on strike on June 12, 1981. The owners were prepared, with a $50 million Lloyds of London strike policy and a $15 million strike fund. Still, the players held strong, striking for fifty days and cancelling 713 games. In the final settlement, a compromise compensation arrangement was worked out, with signing teams being able to protect twenty-four players and the losing club gaining an amateur draft choice and one of the unprotected players from the signing team's roster. The court cases and players' association solidarity had a dramatic affect on salaries in the major leagues. By 1985 the minimum salary was up to $60,000 a year, and the average player salary had reached more than $310,000 a year. That average salary reached $420,000 in 1988. On opening day in 1988, there were fifty major league players with salaries exceeding $1 million a year.

Yet owners still clung to their old ways. Between 1982 and 1984, baseball team owners signed free agents with passion. Between the World Series of 1984 and spring training of 1985, sixteen of the twenty-six major league clubs signed free agents who had been playing for other teams. Something happened the next year. Kirk Gibson, the star outfielder of the Detroit Tigers, became a free agent at the end of the 1985 season. He expected to be wined and dined by several teams before signing a contract that would make him an instant multimillionaire. The Kansas City Royals even started the bidding by offering him a fancy hunting trip in October. The club owners met at the end of the month, and it became immediately apparent that Gibson was not going to get any offers except the one from the Tigers. Home-run hitter Bob Horner of the Atlanta Braves, also a free agent, similarly received one offer—from his own team. By the beginning of the 1986 season, no free agents had been signed to contracts with other teams except for Horner, who quit American baseball and headed for Japan.

The Major League Baseball Players' Association was more than a little suspicious. In 1986 it sued the club owners for restraint of trade, and the case went to arbitration early in 1987. On September 21, 1987, the arbiter, Thomas T. Roberts, found for the players, claiming that the owners had conspired to limit the signing of free agents. Not until January 6, 1988, when the New York Yankees signed St. Louis Cardinal slugger Jack Clark to a two-year, three-million dollar contract, did the owners reopen the free agent market.

Similar changes were underway in professional basketball, and to a much lesser extent in hockey and football. In 1971, average salaries in basketball were the highest in professional sports, averaging $50,000 a year, and that figure rose to more than $510,000, still the highest, by 1988. In 1976 the NBA and the National Basketball Players' Association reached a free agency agreement; any team signing a free agent had to compensate the losing team with draft choices, current players, cash, or a combination of all three. If the two teams could not agree on the settlement, the NBA commissioner would arbitrate the controversy and decide. A 1981 agreement between the NBA and the NBAPA gave the losing team the "right of first refusal," allowing a team about to lose a free agent the right to match any offer by another team. Player salaries were increasing so rapidly that in 1983 the NBA decided on a salary cap—a maximum amount a team could spend on player salaries. The 1988 agreement between the NBA and the NBAPA gave absolute free agency to all players with seven years in the league who were completing their second contract. They were free to negotiate with any NBA team, and the franchise signing them did not have to compensate their former team. The contract raised the salary cap to a maximum of $6.2 million for each NBA franchise in the 1988–89 season.

In professional football the owners, coordinated during the quarter-century tenure of Pete Rozelle as NFL Commissioner, have maintained a much more united front on the issue of free agency than team owners in baseball and basketball. In 1979 there were 106 professional football players claiming free agency, but only 6 of them signed contracts with a new team; the rest opted to remain with their old franchise. If free agency had come to professional football, it was not having nearly the impact it had in baseball and basketball. In addition, average salaries in the NFL were well below those in baseball, basketball, and hockey. In 1982 the average NFL salary was $90,000, and it had risen to only $230,000 in 1987. The bidding wars so common in baseball and basketball skipped the National Football League.

For two generations the National Football League, under the leadership of Bert Bell and Pete Rozelle, had displayed a united front against the players, and the NFL Players' Association had been riddled by internal bickering. The 1970s and 1980s were not much different. Technical free agency had existed for years in professional football because the option clause in a contract operated for only one year after the expiration date. But under the so-called Rozelle Rule, established by NFL owners in the mid-1960s, any club signing a free agent was required to pay fair compensation to the losing team, and if the two parties could not agree on just compensation, the NFL commissioner would make the decision. Rozelle interpreted the rule literally and insisted on awarding losing teams valuable players or first-round draft choices from the signing teams. The prospect of losing a player as valuable as the one signed made team owners less likely to bid for free agents.

In 1975, in the *Mackey v. NFL* case, federal courts decided that the Rozelle Rule was an illegal conspiracy in restraint of trade by denying football players the right to negotiate freely for their services. The Rozelle Rule constituted a boycott or refusal to deal with players. It was a major victory for the NFLPA but the union made a major bargaining mistake in the 1977 negotiations with the league by accepting a modification, rather than elimination, of the rule. That agreement allowed a player to play out his option at 110 percent of his previous year's salary to achieve free agency. His own team had the right of first refusal to match the offer of any bidding team. The signing team was required to surrender one first-round draft choice to the losing team if the signed player's salary had been under $129,000, and two first-round draft choices if the salary had been over $129,000. Relatively few free agents were worth that price, and only six out of a total of more than five hundred free agents signed with different teams under the 1977 agreement.

When time came for the 1982 contract negotiations, the NFLPA demanded changes in the 1977 agreement—specifically seeking distribution of 55 percent of all team revenues to players and allowing a player to become a free agent every three years unless he chose voluntarily to stay with his team. The owners bitterly opposed both demands, and on September 21, 1982, the NFLPA struck the National Football League. The strike lasted fifty-seven days and nearly cancelled the season. In the end, the players surrendered their demand for 55 percent of gross revenues in return for new minimum salaries of $50,000 for rookies in 1985 and at least $10,000 annual increments for veterans; severance pay ranging from $2,000 to 140,000 based on seniority in the league; bonus money ranging from $10,000 for rookies to $60,000 for veterans of four years and more; and higher pay for play-offs. The players also traded off the three-year free agency demand for a five-year arrangement, but signing teams still had to compensate losing teams through draft choices. The strike had improved player compensation, but professional football salaries were still the lowest in any of the four major sports.

By 1987 those salaries had reached an average of $230,000 a year, but the players were still dissatisfied with the way free agency worked. Because of the equal compensation arrangement, teams were unwilling to sign highly talented free agents for fear of losing equally talented players in the compensation settlement. Between 1979 and 1987 nearly two thousand NFL players became free agents, but only one of them was able to sign with a new team.

The players then committed the unforgivable sin of labor relations: they called a strike they weren't certain they would win. On September 22, 1987, Gene Upshaw, executive director of the NFL Players' Association, cancelled the Sunday game and set up picket lines outside club offices, demanding the elimination of the compensation requirement so that free agency would really exist. He miscalculated at every turn. Fans overwhelmingly supported management, expressing a complete inability to empathize with the economic problems of people averaging $230,000 a year in wages. By the second week of the strike, club owners had fielded "scab teams" of semi-pros, former college players, and professionals like Mark Gastineau of the New York Jets who refused to go out on strike. The quality of play ranged from comical to barely acceptable, but the networks televised the games and enough fans watched to undercut the players' bargaining position. By the third and fourth weeks of the strike, some premier players like Danny White and Tony Dorsett of the Dallas Cowboys crossed the picket lines and broke the strike. The owners hadn't budged on the free agency issue. On October 25, 1987, the strike was over.

Unlike the other sports, hockey did not have a collective bargaining agreement until 1975 and has never had a strike. The prevailing conservatism, both political and ethnic, of most hockey players worked against union militancy over the years, as did the fact that the National Hockey League has been virtually under the control of two autocrats—Arthur Wirtz during the formative years of the 1940s and 1950s and R. Alan Eagleson, czar and head of the National Hockey League Players' Association. A militant anti-Communist and fervent Canadian nationalist, Eagleson was born in 1933 at St. Catharines, Ontario, to working-class immigrant parents from Northern Ireland. Brash and ambitious, Eagleson went to law school and took over the NHLPA in 1967. He rules it with an iron hand, and most of the players want to be ruled. In Eagleson's own words, NHL players are "not a series of Einsteins." His own management company represents many of the best players in the league; he negotiates television contracts for the NHL; he promotes hockey contests between the NHL and foreign countries; and he gets the players to sign a contract each year without a strike. The owners love him and defer to him, and the players go along as well. NHL contracts provide for free agency, but in reality Eagleson does not allow it. Still, average player salaries have risen from $19,133 in 1967 to $178,000 in 1987.

Times have indeed changed. In 1953–54, Al Rollins won the National Hockey League's Most Valuable Player Award working as a goalie for the last-place Chicago Black Hawks. With the Hart Trophy in hand, he went to Black Hawk general manager Tommy Ivans for a new contract and had to fight for a $1,500 raise. Twenty years later Bobbie Hull signed a ten-year, $2.75 million contract with the Winnipeg Jets of the new World Hockey Association. Or, in 1946 Stan "The Man" Musial, the best hitter in baseball, was enjoying a $13,000 contract from the St. Louis Cardinals. A generation later pitcher Rick Sutcliffe signed a lucrative contract as a free agent with the Chicago Cubs. From his "Rookie of the Year" as a Dodger in 1979, Sutcliffe had fashioned a reputation as one of the best pitchers in baseball. The Chicago Cubs believed him. They signed Sutcliffe to a nine-year contract beginning with the 1985 season. The contract provided for $720,000 in 1985, all of the money to be deferred for tax reasons. In 1986 he began to earn $700,000 a season with annual deferred payments of $290,000, $560,000, $830,000, and $1,100,000. Earlier deferred salary plus earnings in the later stages of the contract would provide $1.5 million in 1990, $1.5 million in 1991, $1.34 million in 1992, $305,000 in 1993, and $305,000 in 1994. On top of that he had a signing bonus of $2.7 million plus interest, totaling $700,000 in 1985, $165,000 in 1992, $1.2 million in 1993, $1.2 million in 1994, $926,000 in 1995, and $940,000 in 1996. The team also agreed to an annual $500,000 interest-free loan for Sutcliffe. Forty years had passed since Robert Murphy had unsuccessfully organized major league baseball players. Demographic change, federal tax codes, and billions of television dollars had completely altered the structure of professional sports, giving players more money than their predecessors could ever have imagined. The irony with Sutcliffe, of course, was that in 1986 he won only four games. Each win cost the Cubs $350,000.

Successors to black champions like Joe Louis found in their celebrity status an opportunity to promote civil rights, economic equity, and social acceptance. (Credit: University of Notre Dame)

# • The Black Rebellion in American Sports

*I don't want to be what you want me to be, I'm free to be who I want.*
—MUHAMMAD ALI

If the rebellion of white athletes caught America off guard in the 1960s and 1970s, it was nothing compared to the new demands of black athletes. A photograph foretold the whole story to an incredulous nation. Spread across the morning newspapers and evening television shows was the "pretty face" of Cassius Marcellus Clay. To a nation of whites the "Louisville Lip" was an omen of the future of sports. Hoisted on the shoulders of ringside handlers Angelo Dundee and Drew "Bundini" Brown at the Convention Hall in Miami Beach, Clay's arms were raised in triumph, his mouth wide open, upper lip pushed back by a still-in-place mouth protector, eyes bulging in exultation. Heavyweight champion Sonny "The Bear" Liston had failed to come out of his corner for the seventh round. Exhausted and battered, he quit. It was February 25, 1964, and Cassius Clay was on the top of the world. America seemed at peace at home and abroad.

Despite the assassination of President John F. Kennedy in 1963, America was still in a postwar innocence compared to what was soon to come. The Keynesian consensus was holding firm in economics; government spending and taxation policies could maintain the balance between price stability and full employment. The inflation rate in 1964 was less than 2 percent, and the unemployment rate only slightly more than 4 percent. The "stagflation" about to unfold was, quite literally, inconceivable. On the other side of the world, the United States had 20,000 military advisers and support

**163**

personnel in South Vietnam, but talk was of a negotiated settlement and phased withdrawal similar to the Laotian agreement of 1962. Few people could see the ugly war looming on the horizon. The racial situation at home was still tense, but President Lyndon B. Johnson was promoting the Civil Rights Act of 1964. The dream of Martin Luther King, Jr., seemed close to fulfillment, even though the black rebellion in Harlem was only six months away and the conflagaration in Watts eighteen months away. John Kennedy was dead, but America still hoped and believed that Camelot would live on among "the best and the brightest"—liberals committed to a vision of freedom, equality, and brotherhood. Stagflation, Vietnam, and Watergate would shatter those dreams.

Cassius Clay became a lightning rod for the American struggle over civil rights and Vietnam. The black power movement forced Americans to reevaluate their identity as a people. Although the civil rights crusade had achieved its major goal with passage of the Civil Rights Act of 1964, outlawing racial discrimination in public facilities, expectations for real and rapid progress had been hopelessly raised. When ghetto life remained unchanged, frustrations mounted. "Black power" appeared in two guises, one spontaneous and emotional, the other deliberate and ideological. In August 1965 the Watts ghetto of Los Angeles erupted when thousands of black youths rioted after a teenager was arrested for reckless driving. Black mobs looted white businesses, snipers fired at police, arsonists destroyed $40 million in property, and thirty-four people died. More than a thousand blacks were wounded. Another race riot broke out in Newark, New Jersey, in 1967, and in the summer of 1967 Detroit was engulfed in a major riot, with angry blacks turning on police and white-owned businesses. The explosions were unpremeditated uprisings against the hopelessness of ghetto life. White America was outraged, confused, and scared.

The ideological dimension of black power appeared in 1966 when James Meredith, the black who integrated the University of Mississippi in 1962, decided to prove he could march to Jackson, Mississippi, during voter-registration week without harassment. One day into the march, he was wounded by a shotgun blast, and civil rights leaders from all over the country descended on Mississippi to complete the "freedom march." A younger generation of black leaders had run out of patience. While Martin Luther King, Jr., called for nonviolent civil disobedience, Stokely Carmichael, the leader of the Student Nonviolent Coordinating Committee, ridiculed nonviolence and cried out for black power, electrifying black audiences wherever he spoke. On the other side of the country, Eldridge Cleaver and Bobby Seale established the Black Panthers in Oakland, California, and called for black control of the urban ghettos. The age of black power, of Afro haircuts and black studies programs and black pride, had arrived. It came to sport, too.

But sport was not just a mirror reflecting the racial tensions running through American society; it also became a primary vehicle for expressing the darker side of black folk culture. During slavery, when blacks had little control over their own destinies, folk culture had revolved around the trickster tales, where animal surrogates for people acted out elaborate struggles over power. In the most enduring of the stories, Br'er Rabbit, though smaller and weaker than his enemies, relies on wit and cunning instead of strength and constantly triumphs over them. Slaves understood the message of the tales: that their own cultural and emotional survival was more a function of cleverness and guile than power. They could not destroy white people, only fool and outwit them.

But emancipation transformed black folk culture. The animal trickster gradually disappeared, only to be replaced by a more ominous figure, at least as far as whites were concerned. By the late nineteenth and early twentieth centuries, black folk heroes were "bad" men and toughs who survived through the use of remorseless violence, humiliating and killing their enemies. Physically strong, sexually virile, and emotionally neutral, they acted instinctively and guiltlessly, almost pathologically. The most legendary of the "bad men" were Po' Lazarus, Dupree, Bolin Jones, Shootin' Bill, Bad Lee Brown, Devil Winston, Toledo Slim, Dolomite, the Great McDaddy, Staggerlee, and Railroad Bill. Folk hero Railroad Bill was based on Morris Slater, an Alabama turpentine worker who killed a policeman in 1893 and escaped aboard a freight train. He survived by robbing trains of food and supplies for three years. Slater killed a white sheriff in 1895, and died in 1896 after being ambushed in Atmore, Alabama. In the tales surrounding him, Slater supposedly had magical powers to change himself into various animals when he needed to escape. Many southern blacks refused to believe he was dead and celebrated his exploits in song, jokes, and rhyme. He was tough, ruthless, and unafraid of authority.

Until the transition from nonviolence to black power in the civil rights movement, the "bad men" of black folk culture were confined to the ghetto side of the color line, circulating in the huge black communities of the North and West and throughout the rural South in the 1950s and 1960s. But as the civil rights movement became more aggressive after 1965, the "bad men" surfaced in popular culture, primarily in music and films. Former pro football players Fred Williamson and Jim Brown starred in a number of "black exploitation" films in the early 1970s, and Richard Roundtree's *Shaft* portrayed a black man winning in head-to-head confrontation with whites. Ron O'Neal's "Superfly" films offered the same image. The character of Clubber Lang in Sylvester Stallone's *Rocky III* in 1983 provided another image of a ruthless, "bad" black man avenging his frustrations on whites. Jim Croce's 1973 Top Ten hit "Bad, Bad Leroy Brown" celebrated a ghetto black who was "meaner than a junkyard dog" and inspired the creation of Junk Yard Dog, the black heavyweight touring with the World Wrestling Federation in the 1980s.

But all these were fictional creations, not nearly as threatening as the real life "bad men" sports produced in the 1960s and 1970s. Eventually there were a host of them, such as defensive back Johnny Sample of the Baltimore Colts and New York Jets in the 1960s or Dallas Cowboy halfback Duane Thomas in the early 1970s. They were accused of violence, sullenness, and disloyalty—anything but the "credits to their race" white America still wanted from its black superstars. The most notorious of the "bad" black men to surface into the national consciousness was Cassius Clay's first championship opponent. Charles "Sonny" Liston was born to cotton farmers near Little Rock, Arkansas, around 1933. Even he didn't know the exact year. Liston was one of twenty-five children. When his parents divorced in 1944, he went with his mother to St. Louis, where he grew up mean. Restless, illiterate, and unable to tolerate school, he went to work as a petty criminal and thug, spending two years as a teenager in the Missouri State Prison for armed robbery. Upon his release, Liston became an enforcer, a leg-breaker, for St. Louis mobster John Vitale. Between 1950 and 1957, when he went to prison again for assaulting a policeman with intent to kill, Liston was arrested a dozen times. He started boxing in prison, and by 1962 had a record of 33 and 1. At 6 feet, 1 inch, and 214 pounds, Liston was a hulking figure whose Stepin Fetchit, droopy eyes concealed the personality of a "bad" man. Liston was said to have two moods— "neutral and ugly"—and he was positively scary to most Americans, black or white.

The reigning heavyweight champion was Floyd Patterson, a kind, devoutly religious Roman Catholic who had first won the title in 1956, lost it to Ingemar Johannson in 1959, and regained it from Johannson in 1960. Liston became the leading contender after that, and Patterson finally agreed to fight him in 1963, even though the NAACP opposed the match. The last thing middle-class blacks wanted was a hoodlum to replace another Joe Louis–type "credit to his race" as heavyweight champion. Even after being forced to testify before the Kefauver organized crime hearings in 1960, Liston was arrested twice, once for verbally assaulting a Philadelphia policeman and again for forcing a white woman off the road in her car. Sonny Liston was "bad." The fight, billed as a struggle between good and evil, was no contest. Evil knocked out good in the first round. The next day a disappointed sportswriter suggested a ticker-tape parade for the new champion through the streets of Philadelphia with his shredded arrest warrants supplying the confetti.

As the title match with contender Cassius Clay approached in 1964, a *New York Times* sportswriter predicted an easy Liston victory, claiming that "Liston, mean and cruel by nature, might even let Clay linger for a few rounds so that he could deliver a merciless beating to his tormentor before flattening him for keeps." Equating Liston with the likes of Railroad Bill or Staggerlee, most boxing observers, black as well as white, expected the champion to "waste" the young upstart, to annihilate him and walk sullenly away. Because Clay had been so brassy and loud in predicting victory, most Americans were even hoping the champion would administer a thrashing. They were astounded when Clay danced circles around Liston, beating him to the point of surrender.

The next day, Clay and Liston were headlines for more than the fight. Liston acted true to form. After flying home to Denver he was stopped for speeding, arrested for carrying a loaded handgun, and charged with resisting arrest. His run-ins with the law had not stopped since they had begun when he was thirteen, and they were not about to stop now. Clay, however, stunned the country. Fresh from a meeting with Black Muslim Malcolm X, Clay announced that he had joined the Nation of Islam, renounced his "slave name," and taken the name of Cassius X. A few weeks later he dropped Cassius too, and insisted on being addressed as Muhammad Ali.

Founded in 1930 by Wallace D. Fard, the Black Muslims rejected the word "Negro," Christianity, and white values, arguing that human civilization began with blacks, who were the chosen people of Allah. The white race, according to Fard, was the devil and embodied pure evil. The English language, Anglo names, and Christianity were all badges of slavery. Puritanical in their values, the Muslims preached frugality, hard work, obedience to the laws of the land, and sexual fidelity. Elijah Poole, the son of a Baptist who had moved to Detroit in the 1920s, joined the movement and changed his name to Elijah Muhammad. When Fard disappeared in 1934 Muhammad inherited leadership of the Black Muslims. By 1960 there were eighty Muslim temples scattered throughout major cities in the United States. Muslims demanded equality of opportunity, release of black prisoners, an end to police brutality, black teachers in ghetto schools, a federal jobs program for blacks, black exemption from taxation and military service, and creation of a separate territory for blacks as reparation for the pain of slavery. In their cosmology, the Muslims predicted the imminent destruction of all whites and the triumphant return to power of Allah's people—black people—in the United States.

Muhammad Ali was their most illustrious convert. A descendent of slaves who worked the plantation of slaveowner-turned-abolitionist Cassius Marcellus Clay in Kentucky, Ali was born in Louisville in 1942. He began boxing at the age of twelve, and by the time he was eighteen he had won two national Golden Gloves championships, two national AAU titles, and a gold medal in the 1960 Olympic light heavyweight division. At 6 foot 3, and 200 pounds, Ali was a classic athlete but hardly a classic heavyweight: he punched like one but moved about like a bantamweight. He defied boxing rules, dancing around the ring, hands dangling at his side, head pulling away from punches, fists delivering a flurry of counterpunches, bewildering his opponents and fans with his speed. "Float like a butterfly, sting like a bee" was the poetic phrase which stuck.

Between the gold medal in 1960 and his title bout with Liston in 1964, Ali became infatuated with the Muslims, particularly Malcolm X, the brilliant, fearsome spokesman for Elijah Muhammad. Before the first Liston fight, Malcolm X came down to Miami to preach and teach the challenger, and the lessons took. Islam provided Ali with an external pride and certainty to match his feelings about himself, a spiritual antidote to the passivity and subservience white society had long demanded of blacks. He exuded pride in his body and skills, and Islam gave him the same pride in his people and heritage.

Ali's conversion to Islam, along with the heavyweight championship, elevated him to the level of folk hero in black culture, legitimizing the "bad" black by giving him supremacy in the sports arena. He became larger than life, bigger and "badder" than Jack Johnson, Joe Louis, and Sonny Liston, a composite figure in black folk culture, a symbol of courage, rebellion, and skill. Black folk culture had always celebrated the "bad" man whose strength and style allowed him to defy the conventions and limitations imposed by white society. Black bandits like Staggerlee and Sonny Liston fell into that category, as did social rebels like heavyweight champion Jack Johnson, whose flamboyant dress and white wives and mistresses outraged American society and whose taunts and devastating punches humiliated white opponents like Tommy Burns and Jim Jeffries. The image portrayed by Johnny Sample in the 1950s and early 1960s did the same; he remarked that Americans expected a professional football player to "be a nice, clean-cut guy who always smiles at the right times and gives his team the credit for his own performance. I don't buy that."

But there was another dimension to the "bad nigger" in black folk culture, the "hard moral man" who defeats white society on its own territory, by its own rules, according to its own standards. Joe Louis and Jesse Owens pioneered the "hard moral man" who accepted the limitations of white society but carved out a place of prominence in it by defeating whites at their own game. Both men were law-abiding, avoided the material symbols of rebellion, and did not threaten white social values. Black people throughout the country thrilled at their victories, but white people could take some pleasure in them as well, or at least not feel totally alienated by them. The whole phenomenon of black athletic prowess in the postwar world became a vicarious victory for black people throughout the country.

Muhammad Ali was both the "bad nigger" and the "hard moral man," a beautiful contradiction symbolizing the black rebellion in modern America. He was his own man, solicitous of neither blacks nor whites, and his career after defeating Sonny Liston in 1964 exposed the cultural ethos of black America—its alienation from the larger white society as well as its own internal divisions. At the press conference after the first Liston fight, when Ali announced he was a Muslim, several reporters kept pressing him about the social and political implications of Muslim theology, about black separatism and the responsibilities of being heavyweight champion of the world. Frustrated with questions about civil rights, superstardom, and black progress, about being a symbol of America, like Joe Louis and Jesse Owens before him, Ali set the tone for the rest of his career and neatly stated the suppressed attitudes of black people when he finally remarked: "I don't have to be what you want me to be, I'm free to be who I want." And he was.

The white reaction to Ali's new religion was intensely negative; Black Muslim rhetoric frequently referred to white people as "devils," and many whites reacted as if Elijah Muhammad and Malcolm X were latter-day Nat Turners plotting the apocalypse. It was 1964, a good year for America, a time when the promise never seemed brighter, and here was Muhammad Ali saying just the opposite—that the country was wallowing in materialism, racism, and hate, and that he would have none of it. "I go to a Black Muslim meeting and what do I see? I see there's no smoking and no drinking and no fornicating and their women wear dresses down to the floor. And then I come out on the street and you tell me I shouldn't go in there. Well, there must be something in there if you don't want me to go in there."

America didn't want him in there. Despite its emphasis on marital fidelity, chastity, honesty, and loyalty to the law, the Muslim faith was anathema, an indictment of white people, white values, and white society, of America in general. The editors of the *New York Times* refused to print the name "Muhammad Ali," insisting on "Cassius Clay" until Ali legally changed it. At Madison Square Garden a few weeks after the Liston fight, the heavyweight champion of the world was sitting at ringside, but the management refused to introduce him unless he would go by Cassius Clay. Ali refused and sat there stoically. In 1966, when Ali was in England for a title defense against Henry Cooper, the State Department convinced British prime minister Harold Wilson to break off a scheduled appointment with the champion. Ali was a thorn in the American side, a symbol of controversy and disaffection at a time when there was a national premium on unity. Entertainment and advertising companies avoided him like the plague, not wanting the least identification between their products and Muslim theology. It wouldn't be good for business. Ali was philosophical about it all: "It's funny. If I changed my name to Jimmy Jones or Calvin Washington nobody would say nothing. Muhammad Ali. Worthy of all praise most high. They wouldn't introduce me in Madison Square Garden the other night."

Escalation of the war in Vietnam in 1965 put Ali further at odds with the white establishment. In the summer of 1964, after North Vietnamese patrol boats allegedly attacked American destroyers, Congress authorized large-scale bombing of strategic and military targets in North Vietnam, and in the spring of 1965 President Lyndon B. Johnson made the fateful decision to send regular ground troops to South Vietnam. The war became a source of great anxiety in the black community. Because of poverty and lower education levels, blacks were drafted in greater percentages than whites and more frequently found themselves assigned to high-risk, front-line combat units in Vietnam. In 1965 and 1966 black soldiers accounted for more than 20 percent of all battlefield deaths among American troops in Southeast Asia.

To militant blacks engaged in a struggle for civil rights and economic opportunity, the Vietnam casualties seemed especially cruel, another example of the deadly consequences of institutional racism in the United States. Dying abroad for a country unwilling to extend full civil rights to all its citizens at home was a tragic irony for blacks. Martin Luther King, Jr., began protesting involvement in Vietnam in July 1965, arguing that it diverted resources from badly needed domestic programs and made black "boys" cannon fodder for a white man's war. He openly joined the antiwar movement in 1967.

White Americans roundly criticized King for his attempt to link the antiwar and civil rights movements, but the most famous black opposing the war in Vietnam turned out to be Muhammad Ali. From the time he was eighteen, Ali had been classified 1-Y by the Selective Service, enjoying a deferment from military service because of mental deficiencies on standardized tests. But when the war escalated and draft calls increased, Ali was reclassified 1-A.

What America wanted out of its heavyweight champion was what Joe Louis had done in World War II and Rocky Marciano in Korea—traveling about the country and the combat zones giving exhibition bouts and preaching patriotism and sacrifice. But when asked at a press conference in 1966 what he thought about the war in Indochina, Ali remarked innocently, "I ain't got nothing against them Vietcong." Although most of the country would feel the same way in a few years, his honesty in 1966 raised a storm of protest.

Ali unsuccessfully appealed his reclassification, tried to secure a ministerial deferment, and finally argued that his religion prohibited him from taking up arms in the war. As the clock ticked away before his induction, Ali tried to explain his feelings at a press conference on April 26, 1967. When told he could do exhibitions on behalf of the soldiers, Ali retorted: "What can you give me, America, for turning down my religion? You want me to do what the white man says and go fight a war against some people I don't know nothing about, get some freedom for some other people when my own can't get theirs here?" Two days later, at an induction center in Houston, Texas, Muhammad Ali refused to enter the army. Three hours after his refusal to take the required one step forward and oath, the New York State Athletic Commission and the World Boxing Association stripped him of the heavyweight title. Other state boxing commissions quickly fell in line. They also withdrew his boxing license. The State Department refused to allow Ali to travel abroad, effectively taking away from him his livelihood. But among black people, Ali was an unparalleled hero, the most spectacular national figure in Afro-American folk history.

Ali's status as a hero exposed ideological cracks in the black community which had been widening ever since the rise of the black power movement. Middle-class black groups like the NAACP and the National Urban League had campaigned for years on the white man's terms, using the federal courts and white philanthropy to promote equality of opportunity. New groups like the Southern Christian Leadership Conference, the Student Nonviolent Coordinating Committee, and the Congress of Racial Equality enjoyed meteoric rises to prominence in 1966 and 1967, and they resorted to civil disobedience, political insurgency, and the rhetoric of rebellion to protest discrimination. Black activists were not playing by the old rules anymore. Suddenly, to increasingly large numbers of black students and intellectuals, the NAACP and the Urban League seemed anachronistic and conservative, even reactionary, too accommodating to white expectations. Even Martin Luther King Jr.'s dedication to nonviolence was under attack by young radicals such as H. Rap Brown, Roy Innis, and Stokely Carmichael.

For the black masses, the rift in the black community was expressed in the fights of Muhammad Ali, in and out of the ring. Ali did not play by the old rules either. In the words of black militant Eldridge Cleaver, Ali was an "autonomous man." He fancied himself a modern Jack Johnson, without the attraction for white women, and flaunted white rules and expectations. When he defeated Jerry Quarry in his comeback fight in 1971, Bundini Brown kept shouting in the ring that "Jack Johnson here. Jack Johnson here. Ghost in the house. Ghost in the house." Between 1965 and 1967 he easily dispatched a series of white opponents—Henry Cooper, Brian London, George Chuvalo, and Karl Mildenberger—usually toying with them before putting them away. His poetic antics, first used in 1963 when he promised that "Archie Moore will go down in four," were in the best tradition of the ghetto "dozens," the "cutting" verbal repartee young blacks used against each other to prove themselves. Verbal art was as important as physical prowess in defining status in the black community, and Ali had both.

But Ali's jibes were not reserved for whites. Black militants were also turning their wrath on "Uncle Toms" and "Oreos"—black on the outside, white on the inside—to ridicule black people still playing by white rules. Middle-class black organizations had always put a premium on integration and assimilation—the discarding of Black English, the dozens, premarital sex, and partying—so that whites would find them more acceptable and be less inclined to discriminate. By the late 1960s, however, black militants were talking about black pride and black power, about not suppressing Afro-American culture to satisfy white people.

In many of his fights Ali cast his black opponents as "Uncle Toms." The Floyd Patterson fight of November 22, 1965, was billed as a battle between "the Crescent and the Cross," between the Islam of Ali and the Roman Catholicism of Patterson. Despite his two first-round knockouts at the hands of Sonny Liston, Patterson in 1965 was the darling of the liberal establishment—devoutly religious, personally conservative, appropriately active in the NAACP, and a "friend" to people like Dr. Ralph Bunche, Roy Wilkins, and Robert and Ted Kennedy. In several press conferences before the fight, Patterson promised to "bring the title back to America," as if Ali were some kind of alien. Ali was livid, and he punished Patterson for twelve rounds, refusing to knock him out, even when Patterson injured his back, so that the beating could continue. In the words of the *New York Times*, it was an "exhibition of cruel and senseless tragedy." When he fought black heavyweight Ernie Terrell, who insisted on referring to him as Cassius Clay, in 1966, Ali kept taunting the challenger with "What's my name, Uncle Tom" while punishing him unmercifully. Later in his career, after his 1971 comeback, Ali regularly managed to cast his black opponents—Joe Frazier, George Foreman, and Ken Norton—as the latest of the "great black, white hopes."

Ali's refusal to enter the U.S. Army in 1967 became part of a larger black protest surrounding the Olympic Games in Mexico City in 1968. The leader of the boycott was Harry Edwards. Born in the black ghetto of East St. Louis in 1942, Edwards had been raised by his father, a construction laborer. At first his only assets were physical—excellent coordination and a 6 foot 8, 240-pound body. Edwards went to San Jose State University in California on an athletic scholarship in 1960 and starred there as a discus thrower, all-conference lineman, and captain of the basketball team. But Edwards was also blessed with an incisive mind, and instead of accepting a pro football offer after graduation, he went to Cornell University as a Woodrow Wilson Fellow to study sociology. At Cornell, Edwards focused on the sociology of sports and the problems of black athletes. He returned to San Jose State as an assistant professor of sociology in 1967.

By that time Edwards was already in the national consciousness. He was organizing a boycott of the New York Athletic Club's 100th anniversary track meet at Madison Square Garden because the club itself was not open to black members. The idea of inviting black track stars to perform for the glory of a segregated organization seemed the height of hypocrisy. Floyd McKissick of CORE and Martin Luther King of the SCLC endorsed the boycott, as did militant H. Rap Brown (who also suggested blowing up Madison Square Garden). The New York Athletic Club went ahead with the meet in

February 1968, but a number of black athletes failed to compete, and attendance at the Garden was way off.

The success of the New York Athletic Club boycott encouraged Edwards, and he joined an African demand for a boycott of the 1968 Mexico City Olympic Games. Thirty-two African nations had formed the Supreme Council for Sport in Africa in 1966 and demanded the expulsion of South Africa and Rhodesia from the 1968 games because of apartheid. Athletic protest against discrimination was gaining momentum of 1968. At such major universities as Ohio State, Michigan, and Kansas, black student athletes were demanding more black coaches and trainers; an end to "stacking," where several black athletes were forced to compete for the same position while less talented whites made the team; unwritten quotas on the number of blacks on college rosters; and prohibition of interracial dating on campus. Some black athletes at the University of Wyoming, Texas Western, and Arizona State University refused to compete in football and track against Brigham Young University, or wore black protest armbands because of the Mormon Church's unwillingness to ordain blacks to its priesthood.

The time seemed ripe for an Olympic boycott, and Harry Edwards established the Olympic Project for Human Rights to advocate one. He insisted that black athletes stay away from the games unless South Africa and Rhodesia were excluded, Muhammad Ali's title was restored, black coaches were added to the U.S. team, and Avery Brundage was ousted as head of the International Olympic Committee. Brundage at first insisted on South African admission, and the Edwards campaign gained momentum. The member nations of the Supreme Council for Sport in Africa announced their boycott of the Mexico City games, and the IOC reversed its decision in April 1968 and excluded South Africa. In addition, the Mexican government refused admission to any person carrying a Rhodesian passport. The African nations then agreed to attend.

The decision to exclude South Africa from the Mexico City games broke the back of the boycott movement, especially after the black African nations agreed to participate. In the United States, however, Harry Edwards pushed his crusade to keep black athletes away. Expulsion of the South Africans had been only one of the original demands of the Olympic Project for Human Rights, and Edwards wanted all of them met. The assassination of Martin Luther King, Jr., in Memphis in April 1968, and the riots it inspired in ghettoes throughout the country, added intensity to Edwards's campaign. He spent most of the spring and summer of 1968 traveling around the country, speaking to black athletes, telling them to boycott the games unless the United States responded positively to their demands.

The United States Olympic Committee, of course, bitterly opposed the boycott. Jesse Owens, the winner of four gold medals at the 1936 games, was a member of the U.S. Olympic Committee, and he followed Edwards around the country opposing the boycott, arguing naively that politics should not be part of the Olympics, as if they really were not, and that sports was the one area in American life where true equality was being realized. Edwards looked on Owens the way Ali had viewed Patterson—as a black man doing the white man's bidding. To weaken the expected impact of the boycott, the USOC invited large numbers of athletes to complete at the trials in Lake Tahoe, especially in the sprints and hurdles, where the boycott stood to have the most effect. The committee prohibited athletes from giving interviews. The USOC also downplayed the boycott publicly, even though it caused the committee fits privately.

In the end Jesse Owens and the U.S. Olympic Committee were more successful than Harry Edwards and the Olympic Project for Human Rights. A few athletes, such as Tommie Smith, John Carlos, and Lee Evans, had worked with Edwards and the Olympic Project, but even they decided to go to Mexico City. Ferdinand Lewis Alcindor, the gifted center for the UCLA basketball dynasty, decided not to go, but claimed that academic pressures were too great to train and compete in the Olympics. Several of the most prominent black track and field stars, like Ralph Boston, Mel Pender, Bob Beamon, and Wyomia Tyus, were politically moderate and strongly antiboycott. As a long-jumper at Texas Western, Beamon had protested competing against Brigham Young University earlier in the year, but he did not believe boycotting the Olympics would serve any purpose. Few of them were as outspoken against the boycott as Owens, who frequently announced that the "Olympics should not be used as a battleground for civil rights," but they decided for a variety of personal reasons to compete.

The boycott collapsed into a few symbolic gestures at the

games. Several blacks wore black socks during trials, and Tommie Smith and John Carlos, after placing first and third in the 200-meters, raised their arms in clenched, black-gloved fists during the playing of "The Star Spangled Banner," so that young blacks in the United States would "have something to be proud of, to identify themselves with." Their salute created headlines in the United States. The USOC and IOC reprimanded and expelled both of them from Mexico City. A few days later, young George Foreman endeared himself to white America when, after winning the gold medal in the heavyweight boxing division, he paraded around the ring waving a small American flag.

By the early 1970s the tensions over civil rights had started to ease. The racial violence so common to the long, hot summers of the 1960s had subsided, and most whites in the North as well as in the South had accommodated themselves to the idea of integration. The Civil Rights Acts of 1964 and 1968 and the Voting Rights Act of 1965 eliminated the last bastions of *de jure* segregation. Across the Pacific, the Vietnam War had become such a quagmire that even more conservative middle-class Americans had joined the antiwar protestors of the 1960s in opposing the U.S. military commitment there. And the twin problems of inflation and unemployment, along with the political scandals of the Nixon administration, had distracted most Americans from their earlier fears about the future of the social structure.

The pace of integration in sports accelerated during the early 1970s. Lee Elder broke the color line at the Augusta National in Georgia in 1974 when the Masters Tournament invited him to play. Frank Robinson became the first manager of a major league baseball team in 1975 when he took over as skipper of the Cleveland Indians. Virtually all the major universities of the South integrated their football and basketball teams by the mid-1970s. Although blacks constituted only 12 percent of the American population, they were inordinately present on the rosters of professional teams. By 1972 they held down 38 percent of the positions on major league baseball teams, 45 percent in professional football, and 55 percent in professional basketball. Segregation, if not discrimination, was over.

More than any other dimension of American life, sports had projected black people into the white consciousness. Before the civil rights revolution of the 1960s, most Americans had seen blacks in terms of a couple of monolithic stereotypes—as helpless, happy-go-lucky incompetents like film character Stepin Fetchit or as loyal, talented, natural athletes like Joe Louis or Jackie Robinson. But the sports protest movements of the 1960s and early 1970s, as well as the continuing success of black athletes, had provided whites with a diverse set of images. There were still plenty of Jackie Robinsons—soft-spoken, intelligent competitors like halfbacks Calvin Hill and Tony Dorsett of the Dallas Cowboys, outfielder Jim Rice of the Boston Red Sox, or heavyweight boxer Ken Norton. And there were still gifted, inarticulate athletes in the Joe Louis mold—heavyweight champions Joe Frazier, George Foreman, or Leon Spinks. But there were also others. Wilt Chamberlain, the star center for the Los Angeles Lakers, and Jim Brown, the former all-pro fullback for the Cleveland Browns, were political conservatives, endorsing Republican candidates such as Richard Nixon in 1968 and 1972, Gerald Ford in 1976, and Ronald Reagan in 1980 and 1984. There were All-American men too—forward Michael Jordan of the Chicago Bulls or tailback O.J. Simpson of the Buffalo Bills and San Francisco Forty-Niners. A few seemed deeply angry and troubled—like Duane Thomas of the Dallas Cowboys or heavyweight Sonny Liston. Others were endearing and loveable—William "The Refrigerator" Perry of the Chicago Bears. They were people, just people, enormously talented to be sure, but just people nonetheless, and many whites began to see them in those terms.

Even the Black Muslims lost something of their hate stigma. Their black separatism struck deep into the American psyche during the 1960s, but by the late 1970s life had changed. A number of prominent athletes turned to Islam to cope with their own identity problems. Lewis Alcindor became Kareem Abdul-Jabbar after converting to the Sunni Moslems, the largest Islamic sect in the world. Sunnis did not accept the separatism and antiwhite rhetoric of the Black Muslims. Jabbar purchased a home in Washington, D.C., for the group to use as an American center, and in 1973 seven people were murdered there, allegedly by alienated Black Muslims. Soft-spoken, distant, and intelligent, Jabbar was obviously sincere in his conversion, and few people questioned his right to join the Sunnis. Bobby Moore, the talented wide receiver for the Minnesota Vikings in the 1970s, became Ahmad Rashad, and he converted his articulate understanding of football into a successful career as an NBC broadcaster after his retirement. In February 1975, Elijah Muhammad died and was replaced as head of the Black Muslims by his son Wallace Muhammad, who moved closer to orthodox Islamic doctrine by discarding black separatism and opening the movement to whites. He also got rid of the paramilitary guards surrounding Muslim officials and allowed his people to serve in the military. America and the Muslims had adjusted to one another.

The career of Muhammad Ali in the 1970s perfectly illustrates the changing fortunes of the black athlete in America. A federal jury in Houston convicted Ali of draft dodging in June 1967, sentencing him to five years in prison and imposing a $10,000 fine. Most Americans applauded the sentence at first, but in a few years Ali had almost become an underdog. Unlike Jack Johnson, who had threatened existing sexual and racial mores, Ali's Muslim separatism was as much political as social. Ali ended up rejecting white liberalism as well as white racism and stood up for what he believed. A number of white columnists and sportscasters, notably Robert Lipsyte of the *New York Times* and Howard Cosell of ABC, defended him. In 1970 the New York Supreme Court ruled that Ali's civil rights had been violated when the New York Athletic Commission stripped him of this title and license even before he had been convicted of any crime, an especially hypocritical move since the commission at the time had already licensed seventy convicted felons, many of them guilty of rape and murder.

Ali's comeback fight against Jerry Quarry in Atlanta in March 1971 inspired Georgia governor Lester Maddox to declare it a day of mourning, but by the time of his title fight against Joe Frazier in March 1971, Ali had become the public favorite. Sportswriter Peter Axthelm described the Ali of 1971 as a "folk hero." He lost the fight on a close decision but won another battle three months later when the U.S. Supreme Court ruled the Selective Service had violated his First Amendment rights by denying his ministerial exemption. But Ali remained Ali. When he went after the heavyweight title again in 1974 against flag waving George Foreman, Ali wanted to defeat the champion because he represented "Christianity, America, the flag. I can't let him win." He won the fight, regained the title, and became one of the most popular people in the country, not just among blacks. In what has to be one of the classic ironies in American history, President Jimmy Carter appointed Ali an "ambassador of good will" to try to get black African nations to honor his boycott of the 1980 Moscow Olympic games because of the Soviet invasion of Afghanistan. The Africans didn't listen, but it hardly mattered. Muhammad Ali, sixteen years after his TKO of Sonny Liston, was an American institution.

The contradictions inherent in American sports and the significance integration had on American values are perhaps best illustrated in Sylvester Stallone's series of "Rocky" films. Inspired by the courage and stamina of Chuck Wepner in his mismatched title fight with Muhammad Ali in 1975, Stallone wrote a screenplay in which an unknown club fighter, the "Italian Stallion" Rocky Balboa, gets a title fight with Apollo Creed, an Ali-like black heavyweight champion blessed with speed, power, and the gift of gab. The film was released during the Christmas season of 1976 and became an immediate hit, with the white challenger going the distance and losing the fight, but not before administering a frightful beating to Creed. A sequel was inevitable, since white audiences knew that the only time they were likely to see a white heavyweight defeat a black was if the fighters were actors following a script.

*Rocky II* came out in 1979 and was an even bigger hit. Balboa had matured somewhat, and Creed had become more human, a thoughtful, vulnerable person whose pride was hurt in the first fight. Of course, Balboa wins this time by taking the heavyweight championship from Creed in a fifteenth-round knockout. In 1982, *Rocky III* was released, with Apollo Creed now managing Balboa. In the third film they have become close friends, understanding one another's feelings and respecting one another's skills. The "bad" guy, literally, is Clubber Lange, an angry, Sonny Liston–like black heavyweight with a mohawk haircut and feathered earrings, who handily defeats Rocky in the first bout but loses the championship in the rematch after Creed has given Balboa the inspiration he needs—the "eye of the tiger"—to win. Finally, in 1985's *Rocky IV,* Balboa avenges the death of Apollo Creed, now a genuine American hero killed in an exhibition bout with Ivan Drago, a man-machine heavyweight created by Soviet sports medicine. Balboa goes to Moscow and knocks out Drago—a victory for Apollo Creed and for America. White audiences loved it.

Whites also tended to interpret problems in racial terms even when race was not a factor. In 1968, for example, Stan Wright had been hired to coach the sprinters on the U.S. Olympic team, one of the few black coaches on the team and in some ways a token reaction to the boycott threat. Wright was still coaching the team in 1972 at the Munich Games. But he failed to read the schedule of events carefully and did not get several American sprinters to their qualifying trials. One of them was Ray Robinson, a world-class sprinter regarded at the time as one of the fastest men in the world. Robinson was disqualified from the 100-meter dash, and many whites viewed the mishap as a perfect example of what could happen when blacks were given more responsibility than they were suited to handle.

Another example of how whites still tend to misinterpret the actions of black athletes came in 1978 when Kermit Washington, the black forward for the San Diego Clippers, nearly killed Rudy Tomjanovich during a game. Washington was a decent young man, eager to please, willing to work hard, and desperate for social acceptance. After floundering with the Lakers for several years, he had been traded to San Diego and immediately became more comfortable there. But when a fight broke out in a game against Houston, Washington glimpsed a fast-moving Tomjanovich out of the corner of his eye, assumed he was coming after him, and swung his fist around. Aided by the awful physics of a perfect punch, Washington leveled Tomjanovich, shattering his nose, jaw, and cheek bones. It was great television footage, and the incident was played and replayed a thousand times, with Washington portrayed as a vicious hoodlum. He was actually a quiet man, a kid from the ghetto who had managed to become a scholastic All-American. The NBA fined him $10,000 for the fight and suspended him temporarily from the league. In a society just recovering from the images of blacks rioting in the streets, the punch was a reminder of a frightening, violent age.

Another illustration of the ambivalence and contradictions in white racial attitudes came in 1973 and 1974, when Henry Aaron was chasing Babe Ruth's all-time career home run record of 714. A talented black athlete coming out of Alabama in the early 1950s, Aaron signed a contract with the Milwaukee Braves and for the next twenty years averaged more than thirty-five home runs a year. For four decades Ruth's record had seemed sacrosanct, not only because of his larger-than-life hold on baseball mythology, but because the record seemed so unreachable, so impossible to duplicate. Quietly over two decades, however, Aaron had chipped away at it, and by 1972 sportswriters were predicting its demise. For a white America which had once viewed black athletes as physically talented but tempermentally weak and lacking long-term drive and commitment, Aaron's success was undermining the myth of white athletic superiority. Detractors remarked that Aaron had played in more games than Ruth, that his slugging percentage was lower, that his ratio of home runs to at bats did not equal Ruth's. Ruth's widow, after congratulating Aaron when he broke the record in the first week of the 1974 season, added a final note, however: that "Babe was a pitcher as well as an outfielder, remember. He was a great all-round player. And really, he never thought so much about his home run record." People around the country lauded Aaron's feat, but there was more than a little ambivalence in their praise.

Other problems involving prominent black athletes in the 1980s were widely perceived as having racial roots—too much money in the hands of irresponsible people—even though white athletes frequently suffered similar difficulties. Steve Howe, the talented Dodger pitcher, was finally released unconditionally by Los Angeles when he repeatedly missed games and tested positive for cocaine. Keith Hernandex of the New York Mets also admitted he had overcome a drug problem. But it was the black athletes with drug addictions who garnered the most attention: David Thompson, the talented North Carolina basketball star who let drugs destroy his career with the Denver Nuggets of the NBA; Dave Parker, Pittsburgh Pirate superstar accused of using and dealing cocaine in the clubhouse; John Lucas, the Houston Rocket guard released after repeated bouts with cocaine addiction; Len Bias, the University of Maryland basketball star who died of a cocaine overdose the day after signing a multimillion-dollar contract with the Boston Celtics; and Don Rogers, the Cleveland Brown defensive back who died three days after Bias of a cocaine overdose.

Michael Ray Richardson's case was a perfect example. Raised in the Denver black ghetto, he accepted a basketball scholarship to the University of Montana. When his eligibility was up at Montana in 1978, Richardson signed a four-year contract with the New York Knicks of the NBA for $900,000—an annual salary of $190,000 and a $149,000 bonus. He went out and purchased sixteen automobiles in the next two years, went through six agents, and by 1980 was freebasing cocaine. In 1981 Richardson signed a new contract averaging $350,000 a season. But by the 1982 season he was missing games and practices because of drug use, spending his entire salary every month, and going in and out of drug treatment centers. The Knicks tried to work with him, thought he was cured again and again, but in 1986 the NBA suspended him for life. In eight years he had gone through three million dollars and was penniless. Large numbers of whites, although sympathetic with Richardson's problems, interpreted them as endemic to black professional athletes unprepared for the fame and money sports brought them.

The end of the bitter controversies of the 1960s and the continuing penetration of major sports teams and individual events by talented black athletes brought a confused introspection in white society. By 1970 sixteen of the previous twenty-two Most Valuable Players in major league baseball had been blacks. Twelve of the last thirteen MVPs in basketball were blacks. Blacks were also continuing to fill the rosters of professional teams. By 1980 more than 40 percent of professional football players, 45 percent of major league baseball players, and 75 percent of basketball players were black. But that athletic success was juxtaposed with the persistence of serious problems in the black community—poverty, divorce, teenage pregnancies, drug abuse, and low educational achievement. Despite more than a decade of Great Society programs, the social problems were only getting worse.

The combination of athletic prowess and social stress cried out for an explanation, and in the early 1970s many whites turned, in the guise of scholarship, to traditional racial explanations for the success differentials in sports and society between whites and blacks. In 1965, Daniel Patrick Moynihan, the Harvard sociologist, published *The Negro Family* and argued that the black family in America, especially in the urban ghettoes, was chronically unstable, characterized by weak father figures, rebellious children, and dependent mothers. Although the weakness of the black family was not immutable, it was the product of centuries of development and was "capable of perpetuating itself without assistance from the white world." Immediately labeled "racist" and "insensitive," the so-called Moynihan Report stimulated a powerful debate over black social problems.

But the debate over the Moynihan Report in 1966 and 1967 paled by comparison with the controversy raised by Arthur Jensen's

1969 article in the *Harvard Educational Review*. Jensen, an educational psychologist at the University of California at Berkeley, argued that lower scores of blacks on IQ tests were genetically, not environmentally or even culturally, based and that educators would have to tailor their programs to help black students get as much out of school as whites. At the same time, William Shockley, a Noble Prize–winning physicist from Stanford University, was making the speaking circuit throughout the country claiming that blacks had inferior intellectual abilities and that the government should provide monetary incentives to black women not to have children. Although the Jensen-Shockley thesis was not accepted by the larger academic community, it received wide press coverage and reinforced existing racist attitudes.

The sports equivalent of the Jensen-Shockley thesis was written by Martin Kane in a 1971 article for *Sports Illustrated*. Kane argued that black success in American sports was physiologically and psychologically based. He believed blacks were inherently better athletes than whites because they as a group had longer legs, narrower hips, wider calf bones, greater arm circumference, a higher ratio of tendon to muscle, a denser bone structure, and a basically elongated body structure enabling them to "function as more efficient heat dissipators." Psychologically, he thought they had a greater capacity "for relaxation under pressure" and that the high death rate of the "Middle Passage" had acted as a selective genetic screen, culling out weak blacks and leaving as survivors only the genetically stronger ones. Kane attributed black athletic success to those genetic factors.

Kane's article stirred up a bitter debate, as had the writings of Daniel Moynihan, Arthur Jensen, and William Shockley. Harry Edwards responded in *The Black Scholar* that Kane's article was essentially racist, that there was no empirical evidence confirming fundamental physiological and psychological differences between blacks and whites. Black athletic success, Edwards argued, was actually proof of the institutional racism inherent in American life. Trapped in economically depressed ghettoes with few other opportunities, blacks invested most of their energies in sports, playing basketball year round in city playgrounds and hoping and praying that a professional contract would pull them out of the ghetto and allow them to make a decent living to support themselves and their families.

In fact, sports success, according to Edwards, was playing a cruel hoax on generations of black youth. Fewer than nine hundred black people made a living in professional football, basketball, and baseball, yet hundreds of thousands of black young men were aspiring, against infinitesimal odds, to become one of those favored few. Although black enrollment at America colleges was only about 1 percent of the black population, blacks garnered more than 6 percent of all athletic scholarships, but were far less likely to graduate than white athletes. American universities were simply exploiting their talents for four years and then discarding them. In 1984, when the NCAA decided to permit scholarship grants only to high school graduates earning a minimum 600 SAT score, black activists claimed the move would discriminate against blacks because the tests were culturally biased. The answer, they argued, was not higher test score requirements but a greater institutional commitment to helping black athletes finish their college educations.

Numbers put together by the National Federation of State High School Associations in 1985 were particularly depressing. That year more than 700,000 young men played high school basketball, and more than one million played football. Across the country, NCAA colleges and universities offered 15,000 basketball scholarships and 41,000 football scholarships. The NBA drafted about 200 college basketball players a year, while the NFL brought 320 new rookies to summer camp. About 50 rookies actually made the roster of an NBA team, and approximately 150 got on an NFL team. The average NBA career lasts about three seasons, and the average professional football player survives only four seasons. So much for sports as a way out of the ghetto.

Edwards also claimed that "stacking" of blacks in certain positions was still high, that less talented whites were often retained in reserve positions, that black athletes did not get anywhere near the number of endorsements whites did, and that black coaches and front-office personnel were far less common than whites. The fact that professional all-star teams and college All-America teams were predominately black itself indicated that discrimination in the selection of secondary player personnel was probably biased in favor of whites. Because of the relocation of many professional stadiums to city suburbs and escalating ticket prices, black people in general were unable to watch their own people perform, turning sports into a facsimile of the Roman gladiator matches, where Christians had performed and died for an alien, pagan audience.

As far as Edwards was concerned, the world of sports was usually a cruel pipe dream for tens of thousands of black youngsters planning their lives around the hope of a lucrative professional contract. Instead of developing job skills and intellect, they dissipated all their energy on city basketball courts and playing fields, waiting for the magic moment when the NBA or the NFL or the major baseball leagues would come calling. For the vast majority of them, the call never came. The Kareem Abdul-Jabbars and Magic Johnsons were only a tiny minority. For each of them there were too many Earl Manigaults. Manigault was a playground legend in Harlem during the early 1960s, known for his ability to leap high above the basket, dunk the ball with one hand, catch it with another hand, and dunk it again before landing. But he never made it to college from Benjamin Franklin High School. For several years after quitting high school, Manigault continued his exploits on the playground courts, but by 1968 his heroin addiction took over his life. Earl stayed away from the basketball courts, spent some time in prison, went back to dope, and by the early 1970s was living life in a drug-induced stupor, his body wasting away. For Harry Edwards, Earl Manigault was more a reflection of the black sports reality than were superstars like Michael Jordan or Darryl Strawberry.

For many young black athletes who did make it to college the outcome was not much better. Billy McGill, for example, came out of Jefferson High in Los Angeles and accepted a basketball scholarship to the University of Utah, where he led the nation in scoring in 1961–62. He quit school when the NBA's Chicago Zephyrs made him their number one draft choice and offered him a $5,000 bonus and $17,000 a year on a two-year contract. McGill's career then went downhill quickly, primarily because, although gifted with an excellent touch, he was not strong enough to play the post with the likes of Wilt Chamberlain and Bill Russell. By 1970, when his professional career ended, McGill had played for seven teams and was dead broke. Unemployed and desperate, he even asked the president of the University of Utah if the school would grant him an honorary degree so he would have something to put on a job resumé.

The fortieth anniversary in 1987 of Jackie Robinson's assault on the color line in professional baseball reignited the controversy over black athletic talent. In April 1987, on opening day of the baseball season, ABC's "Nightline" focused on the question of continuing discrimination in baseball against blacks, especially in managerial and administrative positions. Ted Koppel interviewed Al Campanis of the Los Angeles Dodgers. Campanis attributed black underrepresentation in baseball management to blacks' own temperamental deficiencies: as a people they were just not managerial material. In the ensuing uproar, Campanis had to resign.

Early in 1988, during an interview on Martin Luther King, Jr., Day, CBS commentator Jimmy "The Greek" Snyder was asked why black athletes have been so successful. The guileless "Greek" knew the reason: "On the plantations, a strong black man was mated with a strong black woman. [Blacks] were simply bred for physical qualities." Snyder then loudly proclaimed what millions of whites were thinking: "If blacks take over coaching like everybody wants them to do, there is not going to be anything left for the white people." CBS fired Snyder from his $500,000 a year job two days later.

But for all the stereotypes and unfulfilled promises, sports had directly influenced the place of black people in American society, removing a few of them from ghetto streets and sharecropper shacks and placing them squarely in the center of popular culture. Although whites still had a distorted image of black culture, most took their images of black America from sports stars and were able to see a variety of personality types. By the 1980s it was not even newsworthy any more to have blacks like Reggie Jackson or Ahmad Rashad doing sports broadcasts, or Bryant Gumbel co-hosting the *Today Show*. White boys unconsciously looked to black superstars like Magic Johnson or Dwight Gooden as their heroes. The old white stereotypes of blacks—the Kingfish, Stepin Fetchit, Lightnin, Sapphire, and Aunt Jemima—had become irrelevent anachronisms by the 1980s, displaced in white minds by a host of diverse, hungry, and talented black athletes. In any survey of the attitudes of young whites toward blacks, new images had replaced the old: there were mental pictures of the quiet dignity of Kareem Abdul-Jabbar, the sheer joy of Michael Jordan, the consistency of Rod Carew, the competitiveness of Moses Malone, the good-natured decency of O. J. Simpson, or the articulate confidence of Tony Dorsett. Sports began the integration of American society in the 1940s and 1950s, and it completed the integration of American popular culture in the 1960s and 1970s.

The politics of third world countries insinuated themselves upon high level sports competition like the Olympics, and American viewers grew ever more conscious of political extremism.
(Credit: University of Illinois)

# ● In the Shadow of Munich

*We'll be back tomorrow with the memorial services . . . I know you'll enjoy them.*

—CHRIS SCHENKEL, after learning of the massacre of Israeli athletes at the 1972 Olympic Games in Munich

**B**efore the 1972 Olympics started, experts predicted that Duane Bobick of the United States would win the gold medal in the heavyweight boxing competition. At the Olympic Trials at West Point, Muhammad Ali called Bobick "the Great White Hope" of boxing and assured the television audience that Bobick would bring home the gold. At the Games, however, Bobick encountered several surprises. The three best heavyweights were in the same half of the draw, and Bobick's first fight was against an experienced Russian named Juri Nesterov. Bobick won, but the fight drained his energy. Two days later, on September 5, Bobick fought Teofilo Stevenson, a young and talented Cuban whom the American had defeated the year before. Stevenson had improved remarkably, and he convincingly defeated Bobick. It was a curious moment, not so much because Stevenson won but because the bout was contested as scheduled, for outside the stadium the Olympic movement was being held hostage in Building 31.

Early that morning eight young members of the Black September group, a radical Palestinian faction, had forced their way into the apartments shared by male Israeli athletes, coaches, and officials in the Olympic Village. A brief, violent struggle followed. Wrestling coach Moshe Weinberg and wrestling referee Yosef Gottfreund bought time for their roommates by throwing their bodies against their apartment doors. Palestinians machine-gunned both men.

**189**

Wrestler Joseph Romano attacked the intruders with a knife, and he too was killed. Most of the Israelis escaped. Nine didn't. The terrorists took them hostage. The twenty-hour ordeal had begun.

West Germany had planned the Munich Games as a celebration of the New Germany and an unstated apology for the Old Germany. Memories of the 1936 Berlin Games lingered still. Hitler was gone but not forgotten, and Munich had been the birthplace of the Nazi party. Outside Munich in the rich Bavarian farmland, Dachau stood as a stark reminder of the horror of the Third Reich. Howard Cosell remembered that the pomp and circumstance of the opening ceremonies left him with an eerie cold feeling. The Bavarian bullwhips sounded "unnervingly like gunfire." The German athletes, East and West, marched into the stadium "with a perfection of rhythm, in sharp contrast with the relaxed entry of the other nations." Images of Warsaw and Prague and the evils of World War II clouded Cosell's thoughts: "I couldn't shake it. Right then my whole background surfaced in me. I felt intensely Jewish."

Now it seemed it was happening again. Of course, the Germans were not to blame, but Jews were once more being senselessly killed in Germany. Aware of the symbolic and political impact of the events, West German chancellor Willy Brandt entered personally into the negotiations for the release of the hostages. At 9 A.M. the terrorists issued their initial demands: release of 200 Arab prisoners held in Israeli jails, release of other terrorists held in various prisons throughout the world, and safe passage for themselves and their prisoners to an Arab country friendly to the Palestinian cause. The terrorist leader promised to kill the hostages, two every thirty minutes, if the demands were not met within three hours.

Brandt telephoned Israeli Premier Golda Meir. Out of respect for the touchy political situation, he deferred to her. She absolutely ruled out any release of Arab prisoners, but in most other matters she passed the agony of choice back to Brandt. It was a German problem which the Germans had to handle. But Meir insisted that if the Germans allowed terrorists to leave Germany, the hostages had to be freed.

Police chief Manfred Schreiber, who dealt directly with the terrorist leader, entertained little faith that the hostages would be released safely. Brandt agreed. He decided not to allow the terrorists to leave Germany. Negotiators could and did promise concessions to the terrorists—including an unlimited amount of money—but the German government, like its Israeli counterpart, had already staked out an inflexible position.

Deadlines were reached, and passed. The world watched in horror. Peter Jennings, ABC's Middle East correspondent, sneaked onto the roof of the Italian building, which overlooked Building 31, and provided vivid and accurate details of the day's developments. And ABC cameramen documented the movements of the leading terrorist for American viewers. The tense, deadly drama of the crisis shot ABC's ratings upward.

But for most of the day the Games continued as if nothing out of the ordinary had taken place. Runners ran and fighters fought and athletes went peacefully about their daily business. Kenny Moore, an American marathoner, recalled that when he heard about the tragedy he rushed to his terrace: "Below, people played chess and Ping-Pong. The trading of Olympic pins continued. Athletes sunbathed by the reflecting pool." Moore cried, not only for the dead Israelis but also for the naive idea that sport was a world onto itself. "I shook and cried as that illusion, the strongest of my life, was shattered." Finally at 4 P.M., almost twelve hours after the deaths of the first Israelis, Olympic officials halted the day's competition.

Meanwhile, the crisis dragged on toward its tragic and seemingly inevitable conclusion. After a surprisingly short period of negotiations, the terrorists agreed to leave Germany in a Lufthansa 727 jet. Germans had no intentions of allowing the plane to take off; in fact, no crew could be found to fly a plane full of Palestinians and Israelis to some undisclosed Arab capital. Brandt simply wanted to move the political horror show from the Olympic Village to Furstenfeldbruck airport, where Peter Jennings and the ABC camera would be unable to televise the unimaginative German efforts to win the hostages' release.

At the airport five German sharpshooters waited for a chance to kill the eight terrorists. The opportunity never came, but the marksmen fired anyway. They killed three Arabs with their initial shots, but the other five reached sheltered positions. During the next hour of gunfighting, two more terrorists were killed. Finally the remaining three surrendered. But not before they killed all of the Israeli hostages.

Rumors spread. A local pub owner passed on the word that police had seized the terrorists. Early news reports claimed the hostages were safe. Munich went to bed feeling that a bad time had ended not too badly. After an indecent interval of four hours, German authorites admitted the truth. Trying to shift some of the blame, police chief Manfred Schreiber insisted that "the hostages were as good as dead from the minute the Israeli government refused to hand over the prisoners. We only tried to free some of the hostages . . . in the event that the terrorists made a mistake." Chris Schenkel, who was working in the ABC broadcast booth, received the news of the slaughter of the Israelis just before signing off the program. In his distinctive, warm pleasant voice, he insensitively said: "We'll back tomorrow with the memorial services. . . . I know you'll enjoy them."

After the truth was known, the International Olympic Committee faced a difficult decision. Should it continue the Games or not? Led by Avery Brundage, president of the IOC, the committee decided to suspend competition for a day, hold a memorial ceremony, and then continue business as usual. The ceremony was almost as poorly handled as the rescue attempt. The majority of spectators were ticketholders who had arrived at the Olympic Stadium to watch games, not remember deaths. They mingled uneasily and somewhat embarrassingly with Israelis in *yarmulkes* and mourning athletes. The Soviet Union chose to ignore the entire affair and didn't send a single representative. Close to the stadium, where the sad strains of the funeral movement of Beethoven's Eroica Symphony filled the air, the Russian soccer team practiced for its next match.

Brundage mouthed the final obscenity. After several other officials expressed their official sorrow, Brundage delivered the last address. The Munich Games would be Brundage's last; at 84 he was retiring as president of the IOC. But age had not mellowed his disposition or softened his rock-hard opinions. He still had a ruthless temper and reacted quickly against any attack on *his* Olympic ideal. "The bigger the Games, the more they are subject to commercial, political and now criminal activity," he told the mourners. This proved to be the theme of his talk—attacks on the Olympics, not the tragedy of the previous day. "The Games of the XXth Olympiad," he continued, "have been subjected to two savage attacks. We lost the

Rhodesian battle against naked political blackmail." The reference was to black Africa's threatened boycott of the Games if Rhodesia participated. Brundage's coupling of the killing of the Israelis and the threatened boycott gave the two threats to the Olympics equal weight and caused much official and unofficial uneasiness in the Olympic Stadium. Brundage quickly ended the discomfort, however, by boldly announcing: "The Games must go on." Cheers greeted his words. Although a few people in the stadium felt, as Howard Cosell said, "unclean" after the ceremony, most seemed pleased that the Games would continue. Asher Lubelski, a German Jew, described the entire ceremony: "The people came not in memory of the Israelis. They came to see if the Olympics would go on."

After a day's delay, the Games continued as planned. But in Israel the deaths were not forgotten. The day after Brundage's speech, Israeli planes raided Lebanon. The next day they hit Syria and again Lebanon. The peace movement in the Middle East, which had been slowly gaining strength, deteriorated rapidly. The year after the Munich Olympics, Egypt and Syria launched a surprise attack against Israel during the Jewish holy day of atonement, Yom Kippur. When the United States provided economic aid for Israel, Arab members of the Organization of Petroleum Exporting Countries (OPEC) retaliated with oil embargos. Although the terrorist attack at the Munich Olympics was not the only cause of the problems in the Middle East, it certainly was an important catalyst.

The Munich Games shattered any illusion that sport was a world apart. As athletes became spectators, terrorists performed for the television cameras. The Games became their stage for political expression. It was, sadly, unfortunate but not really unexpected. The Olympics had always contained a symbolic message. During the late 1940s and 1950s this symbolism was tailored to fit Cold War realities. But starting in the mid-1960s the Games became a real political tool which could be used for almost any purpose. Terrorists, presidents, black nationalists, and premiers would use the tool. Since each faction defined the rules of the Games anew, it became increasingly impossible for the Olympics to represent any concrete ideal.

Signs of the future were apparent as the IOC prepared for the 1964 Tokyo Games. The site of the summer Games was important. Not only was it to be the first Olympics held in Asia, but it was also meant to signal Japan's recovery from World War II. And Japan prepared for the peaceful Olympic festival with the same attention to detail that it had displayed in its preparations for Pearl Harbor. Expense was of no concern. Japan spent over $2.7 billion in building projects and other preparations for the Games. The Olympics were planned as a showcase for Japanese pride and technology. To conform to Western standards, Japanese temporarily shelved the time-honored tradition of urinating in the streets, and for the sake of world harmony the Japanese press underplayed a shoplifting spree conducted by Western athletes. Journalists devoted far more attention to electronic timing devices—the first to be used in the Olympics—and the friendly hosts.

But solemn bows and warm smiles could not erase the fact that deep divisions divided the world and the IOC, and sport had become a political tool for world leaders. Division within the IOC was hardly a unique phenomenon. Since arriving on the Olympic scene, the Soviet Union had effectively politicized the IOC. Much to the chagrin of Brundage and the other Western European members of the IOC, Russia and its Eastern European allies had initiated bloc voting. Of course, the Russian members of the IOC denied the existence of bloc voting. On one occasion, a French delegate remarked that when Soviet members made a proposal, Eastern European members rose "one after the other . . . to punctuate their assent." Nonsense, replied leading Soviet delegate Konstantin Andrianov. Then, one after another, the Eastern European delegates rose to support Andrianov's position that bloc voting was a figment of Western imaginations.

Yet the Cold War rivalry between Russia and the United States was not the only problem confronting the IOC. Third World countries had also learned the benefits of voting en masse. What was more, Third World leaders had grown weary of taking orders from their former imperial masters. At IOC meetings African and Asian officials were tolerated more than welcomed, and their wishes and problems, no matter how beautifully expressed, were generally ignored. In practice, the IOC was still controlled by wealthy Europeans, who bent their rules for powerful countries but were quick to punish weaker nations for the slightest infractions.

Revolt was inevitable. In 1962 at the IV Asia Games, the host country, Indonesia, refused to issue visas to athletes from Taiwan and Israel. Such political actions were not new to Regional Games. In 1952 Israel had been barred from the Mediterranean Games. However, when the Indonesian Olympic Committee failed to protest its government's action, the IOC suspended Indonesia from Olympic competition. Angered and insulted, Indonesian president Achmed Sukarno withdrew his country from the Olympic movement.

Maneuvering behind the scenes was China. Although the People's Republic of China had withdrawn from the Olympic movement, it still recognized the political value of sports. Problems between Western and Third World countries encouraged China to organize a competition which would rival the Olympics. China, however, hoped to lead from behind the scenes. As the IOC moved against Indonesia, China saw its chance. An editorialist for *T'i Yu Pao,* the influential Communist Chinese biweekly sports journal, noted that "Indonesian public opinion has favored the proposed holding of Afro-Asian Games and the founding of an Afro-Asian Sports Organization." Such Games, the writer suggested, would represent the unity within the Third World struggle against imperialism and colonialism.

The idea intrigued Sukarno. In early 1963 he hosted a conference to officially organize the Games of the New Emerging Forces (GANEFO). Like the Olympics, the new Games would be held every four years, starting in 1963. Unlike the Olympics, these Games would be political in ideal and fact. "Let us declare frankly," Sukarno emphasized, "that sport has something to do with politics. And Indonesia now proposes to mix sports with politics." With the motto "Onward, No Retreat" GANEFO captured the spirit of countries emerging from or struggling against colonial domination.

The GANEFO torch, which was carried from Java rather than Mount Olympus, arrived in Djakarta in mid-November 1963. The Games began. Somewhere between 47 and 55 nations and 2,000 and 3,000 athletes (even the GANEFO officials were not sure of the exact numbers) took part in the competition. *Jen Min Jih Poa*, a leading Chinese newspaper, called the Games "a brilliant epoch-making event in the history of international sports." Another Chinese writer added that "in contrast to the imperialist-controlled Olympic Games, GANEFO has no discriminatory rules or regulations." Not to be outdone, yet another journalist hailed the Games as a victory for the people of the "whole world against imperialism and old and new colonialism, . . . a triumph of historical significance . . . in foiling the imperialist manipulation of international sports."

In truth, the Games were not quite so millenial. Twenty percent of the athletes came from Indonesia and China, and many of the teams contained only five or six athletes. In addition, most of the athletes at the Games did not actually represent their nations. Fearing reprisals by the IOC, countries such as the Soviet Union, Czechoslovakia, Poland, France, and the German Democratic Republic sent unofficial teams composed of third- and fourth-rate athletes. And the number of nations represented would have been far smaller had not China bankrolled much of the transportation costs to and from the Games for Third World athletes. In the end, GANEFO's threat to the Olympic Games remained more potential than real.

Still, for Olympic officials gathered in Tokyo the sacred movement seemed under attack, and battle lines apparently were being drawn between the West and the rest. Even the Western countries were not totally unified. France, the very home of the Olympic movement, sent athletes to GANEFO. Under the leadership of nationalist Charles de Gaulle, France was displaying greater independence in international athletics and politics.

For all the promise of problems, athletes happily dominated the Tokyo Games. To be sure, four Hungarians defected to the West, and a Nationalist Chinese pistol shooter defected to Communist China, but more attention was paid to the exploits of such athletes as Bob Hayes, Peter Snell, Billy Mills, Don Schollander, and Joe Frazier. As for Tokyo, wrote John Underwood, it survived "honorably, with dignity, having staged [the Games] with dispatch and with that extra little touch of precisional grace that characterize the Japanese. The Japanese had, as a poet once said of them, demonstrated 'the skill to do more, with the will to refrain.'" Such words— honor, dignity, grace, the will to refrain. They would rarely be used again to characterize an Olympics.

After 1964 the problems that the IOC had wrestled with— nationalist, commercialism, and racism—increasingly disrupted Olympic activity. As it prepared for the 1968 Mexico City Games, the IOC was forced to confront fully the question posed by South Africa. IOC officials might and did talk about the necessity of equality of opportunity and fairness of competition, but their words seemed empty when they allowed South Africa to compete in the Olympics. As South African minister of the interior Jan de Klerk stated in 1962, "The government policy is that no mixed teams should take part in sports inside or outside this country."

Before the Tokyo Games, South Africa's policy toward mixed competition was inflexible. Repeatedly the IOC attempted to convince the South African National Olympic Committee (SANOC) to change its apartheid approach toward sport, or at least to protest the official government position, but the South African officials rebuffed all appeals. Left with no alternatives, the IOC suspended SANOC before the Tokyo Games. It was a sad time for Brundage. As he would state again and again, he was not concerned about apartheid in South African society, only about apartheid in South African sport. The one was a political issue, and thus outside of the IOC's interest; the other went against the Olympic charter.

Brundage, ever the Olympic optimist, hoped that SANOC would alter its ways. The IOC had suspended, not expelled, South Africa, and the Olympic doors were left open for a reformed SANOC. On its part, SANOC promised to inch closer to the Olympic ideal. Brundage listened sympathetically to SANOC's proposed reforms and threw his considerable power behind reinstatement. He called for realism tempered with understanding of the difficult conditions in South Africa. Finally, in 1967 a three-man investigative committee from the IOC went to South Africa to evaluate the new SANOC. They were pleased by what they saw and recommended that the IOC reinstate South Africa. In 1968 the IOC did just that.

The decision insulted opponents of apartheid. Anti-apartheid leader Dennis Brutus told Brundage, "South Africa will not be at Mexico City." Other Africans agreed. Immediately after the IOC made its decision, the thirty-two nations of the Organization of African Unity called for a black African boycott of the 1968 Games. Considerable world support greeted the African action. Caribbean nations, much of the Islamic world, and the Communist bloc supported the boycott movement. And in the United States, Harry Edwards, a black activist, mustered Afro-American support for the boycott (see Chapter 8).

Tied to South Africa, the Olympic Movement faced the most serious crisis in its history. If the IOC lost the Communist world and the Third World to GANEFO or to some other organization, the

Olympics would die. There was, of course, a solution: dump South Africa; disinvite SANOC. But how does a gentlemenly organization like the IOC withdraw an invitation? Brundage turned to Mexico, suggesting that it announce that it could not adequately protect the South Africans. Mexico declined. Taking a slightly more direct approach, the IOC withdrew the invitation on the basis of the unhealthy political climate for South Africans travelling abroad. "We seem to live in an age when violence and turbulence are the order of the day," Brundage explained. Therefore, to save South Africans from a possible unpleasantness—and also to preserve Olympic unity—SANOC was once again barred from competition.

The exclusion of South Africa was no safeguard against violence and turbulence. Nineteen sixty-eight was a year of grief. In America, assassins murdered Robert Kennedy and Martin Luther King, Jr. In Vietnam the Tet Offensive undermined the optimistic predictions of President Johnson. Students rioted in Paris and New York. And in Czechoslovakia the possibility of "socialism with a heart" was crushed under the treads of Russian and East German tanks. Surveying his times, Brundage concluded, "The world, alas, is full of unjustice, aggression, violence and warfare, against which all civilized persons rebel, but this is no reason to destroy the nucleus of international cooperation and good will we have in the Olympic Movement."

But Brundage's last, best hope—the Olympic Games—created problems of its own. They were expensive to stage, and Mexico was a poor country. Many Mexicans felt that the money spent on the Games could have been better used. The poor, not athletes, needed to be fed. The homeless, not athletes, needed to be sheltered. In late September, students in Mexico City rioted. In early October, they rioted again. As many as 325 protestors were killed at the Tlatelolco massacre. Concerned, Brundage met with and was reassured by Mexican officials. Afterward, he commented that "nothing will interfere with the peaceful entrance of the Olympic flame into the stadium . . . nor with the competitions which follow."

The torch arrived without incident. The Games were not as lucky. Not all the protesters had been silenced by Mexican bullets. After Tommy Smith and John Carlos finished first and third in the 200 meters, they used the victory ceremony to draw attention to the plight of blacks in America. With black-gloved fists raised and heads lowered, they tolerated "The Star-Spangled Banner." Two days later, at the insistence of the IOC, the two joined South Africa and Rhodesia as Olympic outcasts. Commenting on the protests, Brundage noted: "Warped mentalities and cracked personalities seem to be everywhere and impossible to eliminate."

Other, less audacious protests followed. They seemed to overshadow the marvelous athletic performances. Lee Evans in the 400 meters and Bob Beamon in the long jump set world records, but the Mexico City Games are remembered more for being troubled than for being athletically unequalled. As one observer noted, "Politics has always been part of the Olympics, but in Mexico City the situation started to get uglier."

By 1968 the world was learning a lesson. The Olympics could be used as a forum for a variety of statements. Capitalists could use them to sell shoes and skis, and they did. Communists could use them to peddle the wonders of state socialism, and they did. But the Games could also be used by disgruntled students, angry athletes, and dissatisfied nations. The bigger the Games became, the more powerful the forum grew. In 1968 the IOC sold the United States television rights for the Mexico City games for $4.5 million. Politics, sports, and television had thus joined in an unholy trinity of awful possibilities. Just how awful was demonstrated in Munich four years later.

Munich was one of Brundage's favorite cities. He loved Bavaria, and several of his closest friends were German. He had been elected to the IOC in Germany, and he had defended Germany during the tense months before the 1936 Berlin Games. The Munich Games would be Brundage's last as president of the IOC, and the Bavarian capital seemed a fitting site to bid farewell to the IOC. The Games, German planners emphasized, would be upbeat—the *heitere Spiele* (cheerful games) they were dubbed. Munich, which was chosen to host the Olympics largely because it had a good security rating, welcomed the opportunity to display the new democratic Germany to the world.

As usual, there was a series of pre-Olympic problems. The South Africa issue surfaced again. The black African countries wanted South Africa expelled from the IOC. In 1970 by a vote of 35 to 28, the IOC did just that. It was the first time any member had been expelled from the Olympic Movement. Black Africa and her allies turned next to Rhodesia. Although Rhodesia undoubtedly had a racist government run by a white minority, its Olympic team was fully integrated. More black than white athletes made the team. In short, Rhodesia had not violated any IOC rule. Be that as it may, black Africa threatened to boycott the Munich Games unless Rhodesia was barred from the competition. Upset by the blatantly political maneuver, Brundage battled to keep Rhodesia in the Games. He lost. After a close vote, the IOC withdrew Rhodesia's invitation. Angered, Brundage told his colleagues that "it was obviously time . . . to leave the presidency."

And it was time. Howard Cosell once said, "There was a time for Avery Brundage, that of William of Orange." Perhaps Cosell was off by a century or so, but the point was well taken. Brundage continued to view sports in nineteenth-century terms. The words "amateur" and "professional" still meant something to him, when in fact they were irrelevant in the world of highly competitive sports. The best Olympic athletes were professional, full-time athletes. The state supported some, colleges supported others, and sporting equipment and clothes moguls supported the rest. The best track and field athletes were paid under the table, and the top skiers accepted their payments over the table.

Until the end, Brundage fought useless battles against the windmills of professionalism. In particular, he hated the Alpine skiers and would have been perfectly content to abolish the winter Games. In 1972 he announced: "If we confine the skiers allowed to compete in the Olympics to those who can meet the eligibility requirement of the IOC, then all the prominent skiers of the world—both Alpine and Nordic—must be disqualified." Of course, he could not disqualify all the skiers, but in 1972 he took his symbolic revenge against the entire sport. He convinced the IOC to bar Karl Schranz, the great Austrian skier.

Schranz complained. True, he took money from ski manufacturers, plenty of money. But, he said, "the Russians are subsidized by their own government, and all international athletes get help from one source or another. I think the Olympics should be a contest of all sportsmen, with no regard for color, race, or wealth." Increasingly the world and the IOC agree with Schranz. Once Brundage left office, the IOC gradually changed its amateur code.

The wars behind him, Brundage turned his attention to the Games themselves—to the Bavarian umpah-pah bands and Mark Spitz and Olga Korbut and the other gifted athletes. Then came September 5 and the greatest tragedy in Olympic history. Brundage's last fight was to ensure that Games would go on. They did. Then, as the scoreboard fights flashed "Auf Wiedersehen Avery Brundage," he passed the presidency over to Sir Michael Morris, Lord Killanin.

Killanin was no Brundage. That was probably why the IOC elected him. He was a friendly Irishman, Catholic in religion and liberal in politics. Unlike Brundage, who struck most observers as cold and stiff, Killanin radiated warmth and good humor. Also unlike Brundage, Killanin was a realist. "I try to deal with things as they are, not as we'd like them to be in a more perfect world," he said. Dealing with things as they are meant accepting that pure amateurs in international sport were as rare as innocence in politics. Under Killanin's leadership the IOC altered its amateur code to allow athletes to accept financial support while preparing for the Olympics.

To be sure, there were aspects of the Olympics that did not please Killanin. "I'd love to see the anthem-playing and the flag-raising go," he told a *Sports Illustrated* writer. But perhaps this was the Irish dreamer in him talking, for in reality the Olympic Movement mixed more than ever with chest-thumping nationalism. With each Games, the ends of state encroached further onto the playing fields and training rooms of athletes. During the 1976 Montreal Games, Killanin was unable to reverse the political direction of his beloved Olympics.

Before the opening ceremonies, two political battles disrupted the 1976 Games. The first concerned the reemergence of the People's Republic of China (PRC) onto the international sport scene. In 1965 the PRC mysteriously dropped out of all international sport. Trying to interpret China's great Cultural Revolution from a considerable distance, journalists speculated that many of China's best athletes—including three-time world table tennis champion Chuang Tse-tung and his teammate Li Fu-jung—had been victims of Mao's purges. Then in the 1971 world table tennis championship in Nagoya, Japan, the PRC returned to international sport. Led by an older but still effective Chuang, China defeated defending champion Japan for the world title.

Ping-Pong diplomacy had begun. It signaled China's renewed interest in the world beyond the Great Wall. In 1971 the United Nations expelled Taiwan and recognized the PRC. In 1972 President Richard Nixon made his historic visit to China and began the process of normalizing relations with America's heretofore unrecognized enemy. World sport federations also moved to welcome the PRC into their fold. China was anxious to extend its social ties. But it would not join any organization or attend any party that tolerated Taiwan.

Most organizations granted the PRC's request. The Asian Games Federation voted to admit the PRC and to revoke Taiwan's membership. Other international sports federations followed suit. The IOC, however, did not. The IOC wanted the PRC to join its movement, but it did not feel that it should have to exclude Taiwan. That was where matters stood when, eight days before the summer Games were scheduled to begin, Canada decided it would not allow Taiwanese athletes to compete in the Olympics under the flag of the Republic of China, a country it did not recognize. Once again, a national political issue had overridden the Olympic spirit.

Black Africa provided the second disruption. Successful before, it decided again to use the Olympics as an opportunity to isolate South Africa. True, it had successfully driven South Africa and Rhodesia out of the Olympic Movement. But the racist regimes still participated in other international sports forums. South Africa, for example, competed for the Davis Cup, and the New Zealand rugby team was planning a tour of South Africa. In fact, twenty-six nations maintained sports relations with South Africa.

Disregarding the other twenty-five countries, the Supreme Council for Sport in Africa announced that it would boycott the Games if New Zealand were allowed to participate. It was backed by the Organization of African Unity. The IOC stiffened. New Zealand had in no manner violated the Olympic charter, and besides, rugby was not even an Olympic sport. It refused to cave in under black Africa's last-hour boycott threat. As a result, thirty countries boycotted the Montreal Games. African athletes—including such world-class runners as Tanzania's Filbert Bayi and Kenya's Michael Boit, already in Montreal—received messages to return home. The pattern was painfully clear: the Olympics were for nations, not athletes.

Western journalists attacked the African boycott. It seemed so irrational. New Zealand was such an arbitrary target. Why not Great Britain or France or the United States, all of which had sports relations with South Africa? Even worse, they noted that participation is everything and nonparticipants are soon forgotten. The memory of Smith and Carlos's protest was vivid; those who protested by staying home became trivia questions. Surely, journalists speculated, the boycott was not a viable political solution.

Led skillfully by Killanin, the IOC prepared for the 1980 Games in Moscow. Politically, the IOC maneuvered about the muddy international waters with a greater sense of realism and confidence. Like its political counterpart, the United Nations, the IOC encouraged its members to further isolate Sourh Africa by refusing to participate in sports with the racist regime. Also like the United Nations, the IOC courted the People's Republic of China at the expense of Taiwan. USOC member Julian Roosevelt remarked that the "IOC has put itself into the political arena by taking orders from Peking," and other conservatives criticized the IOC abandonment of Taiwan. But the move was intelligently realistic and was strikingly similar to the United States' own dealings with Taiwan.

Even the choice of Moscow for the summer Games was good politics. It showed that the Olympics was not simply for Western or democratic countries but for all nations, regardless of their political orientation. In addition, Moscow was as secure as 1936 Berlin. Student riots, Israeli massacres, or other unexpected incidents could not happen in Moscow. Still, conservative Americans deplored the choice of sites. William F. Buckley, George F. Will, and Ronald Reagan felt that the United States should boycott the 1980 Games. But in discussing the idea of a boycott, Will concluded: "Two things are certain: The idea is excellent, and nothing will come of it."

Then, on Christmas 1979, the Soviet Union invaded Afghanistan. On December 27, Soviet troops captured and executed unpopular Marxist Afghan prime minister Hafizullah Amin and installed his rival Babrak Karmal. Within hours, more Soviet troops poured into Afghanistan to support the new Karmal government. A shocked and immobile world watched. Actually, Soviet actions should not have surprised anyone. Soviet invasions of Hungary and Czechoslovakia had demonstrated that Russian leaders would not permit Communist governments in neighboring countries to be overthrown.

For U.S. president Jimmy Carter, Russian timing could not have been worse. Even before the invasion, his support was dwindling. Conservatives said he was soft on Communism and attacked SALT II. Liberals claimed he had abandoned his domestic agenda. Consumers decried the rising cost of gasoline. Then on November 4, 1979, Iranian revolutionaries in Teheran stormed the U.S. embassy and took sixty-six American hostages. With an election less than a year away, Carter had to do something.

He did. On January 4, 1980, he called the Soviet invasion "an extremely serious threat to peace" and a "stepping stone to possible control over much of the world's oil supply." Within a week, he withdrew the SALT II treaty from the Senate and threatened to curtail relations between the Soviet Union and the United States. Grain sales, high technology and oil-drilling equipment, fishing rights, and athletic and cultural exchanges were all at stake, Carter indicated. As the weeks passed, Carter narrowed his focus. The idea of an Olympic boycott dominated his thoughts.

Of course, there were problems. The winter Games were scheduled to take place in Lake Placid in February. Carter did not want the Soviets to boycott our Games before he had a chance to boycott theirs. So Carter waited—on the pretext of giving Russia time to withdraw from Afghanistan. The Lake Placid Games took place as planned. Russia participated. In fact, the most memorable moment of the Games came when an underdog American ice hockey team defeated a favored Soviet Union team. While cynics commented that Russia gave America the win in exchange for Afghanistan, America exploded with nationalism. Chants of "U.S.A., U.S.A." filled the winter air. And in the locker room after the game, the American players sang "God Bless America." As Dave Silk recalled the scene, "We got to the part after 'land that I love . . . ' and nobody knew the words. So we kind of hummed our way to ' . . . from the mountains, to the prairies . . . ' and we finished it. It was great."

After the Games, Carter once again spoke out in favor of a Moscow boycott. He sent Muhammad Ali to Africa to gather black African support for his plan. Insulted by the idea of receiving a boxer-diplomat and remembering the lack of American support for their boycott, black Africa refused to follow Carter's lead. Nor did Carter receive much more support in Western Europe. Even the

USOC opposed the idea. Finally, American athletes themselves strongly opposed a boycott.

But Carter had the power of his office, which he proceeded to use. In late March he cut off exports to the Soviet Union of sporting goods and other Olympics-related products. If he could not get the Games moved out of Russia, then he wanted to destroy them for the Soviet Union. He forced the USOC to boycott and NBC to withdraw their television package. He cajoled other world leaders into joining the American boycott. In the end, sixty-two countries boycotted the Moscow Games.

Yet the Games went on as scheduled. Certainly fewer athletes competed, but the level of competition was remarkably high. More world records and Olympic records fell in Moscow than in Montreal. All Carter's boycott meant was that none fell to Americans. And while nationalism at the Lake Placid Games boosted Carter's popularity, the lack of American participation in Moscow hurt the president at the polls. In the end, the boycott did not affect Russia's foreign policy. The only troops withdrawn from Afghanistan were Olympic competitors. Senator Edward Kennedy was correct when he characterized Carter's boycott as "basically a symbol, and symbols are no substitutes for an effective policy."

The boycott did not change Soviet policy in Afghanistan, but it did chill its relations with Washington. History has amply demonstrated that Russia's national memory reached into the distant past. The threats and mistakes of Napoleon and Hitler have lingered and helped to mold Soviet foreign policy. It would be foolish to think that a country that remembers 1812 would soon forget the slights of 1980. As a Soviet official told Peter Ueberroth in 1980, "You sometimes call us the bear, the big bear. This time you can call us the elephant because we don't forget."

Somehow Americans and the IOC assumed that the Soviet Union would attend the 1984 Los Angeles Games. The 1980 election of Juan Antonio Samaranch to the presidency of the IOC was intended to ensure continued Soviet support for the Olympic movement. Samaranch, an elegant, articulate Spaniard, had once served as the Spanish ambassador to the Soviet Union. Warmly regarded behind the iron curtain, he had been elected president with the full support of the Communist bloc. But Samaranch knew that the American boycott of the Moscow Olympics had upset and embar-

rassed Russian leaders. "In 1980 and afterward," he said, "top people in the Soviet Union said to me that the word 'boycott' did not
exist in their dictionaries and that they would never use it, that never
would they use sport and the Olympic movement as a political
weapon. But I had always known that sport and politics did not live
on separate planets."

At first, Soviet leaders announced that they would send a team
to Los Angeles. After all, Leonid Brezhnev, the Russian premier in
1980, was dead, and the new Soviet leader, Yuri Andropov, was attempting to warm chilled Soviet-American relations. On December
7, 1983, Soviet sports minister and Olympic committee chairman
Macat Gramov remarked, "We do not see any reasons" why the Russian team would not travel to Los Angeles. And on February 6, 1984,
senior Soviet IOC official Konstantin Andrianov commended Peter
Ueberroth, president of the Los Angeles Olympic Organizing Committee, for the "excellent job" that he and his team had done.

Three days after Andrianov's lavish tribute, Yuri Andropov
died. Konstantin Chernenko, who had been one of Brezhnev's closest friends, assumed power. Old slights were once again remembered. Suddenly Soviet sports officials had reservations about the
job Ueberroth was doing. Publicly they fretted over security and the
overpublicized Ban the Soviets Coalition. Then on May 8, 1984,
Gramov announced that Russia would not participate in the Games.
Within days Russia was joined by Bulgaria, East Germany, Vietnam,
Mongolia, Czechoslovakia, Laos, Afghanistan, Hungary, Poland,
Cuba, and North Korea. Revenge was theirs.

The unflappable Ueberroth momentarily lost his sang froid.
He suggested that Chernenko, like Carter, was a hack politician. Later, after he had regained his equaniminity, he considered the Russian side: "The [1980] Olympic Games was their premier event
of . . . maybe, in Brezhnev's point of view, . . . their country's history, that and their astronauts, and there was a serious attempt to
damage it by Jimmy Carter."

The Communist boycott weakened the quality of competition
in Los Angeles. The best women track and field athletes were among
those who boycotted the Games. So were many of the best weight
lifters, gymnasts, swimmers, wrestlers, and boxers. In fact, the
quality of the Los Angeles Games fell far below the Moscow Olym-

pics. But the 1984 Games were an unqualified commercial success for ABC, which spent over $400 million to televise them, sold prime-time commercial slots for between $225,000 and $250,000 per 30 seconds, and reaped incredible revenues.

What ABC sold was not so much athletic competition as American nationalism. No previous Olympics—including the 1936 Berlin Games and the 1980 Moscow Games—had seen such nationalistic displays. ABC, which had almost 200 hours of air time to kill, consistently showed the award ceremonies when Americans won but seldom when another country's athlete captured the gold medal. Capturing the mood of the Games, Frank Deford wrote: "One night, at the volleyball competition, the P.A. announcer said he had a medal result. It was in some cycling event. The gold, he said, went to an American, and he gave the cyclist's name. Cheers! U!S!A! U!S!A! The bronze also went to an American, and he gave the name. Cheers! U!S!A! U!S!A! He didn't even mention the silver medalist's name. Foreigner. And so it continued, with Americans cheering on Goliath until the Games ended, neither with a bang nor a whimper but with a cry of U!S!A!"

After the Los Angeles Games there was talk about the future of the Olympics. Even during the weeks before the 1984 Olympics, scribes wrote that the Olympic movement was dead. "Better that the whole rotten mess be interred as quickly as possible," noted a *London Daily Express* editorialist. "It has been a terminal case for years." Others noted the history of recent problems: dead students in Mexico in 1968, dead Israelis in Munich in 1972, boycotting Africans not in Montreal in 1976, boycotting democrats not in Moscow in 1980, boycotting communists not in Los Angeles in 1984. Added to these human and political horrors were the squabbles over South Africa, Rhodesia, and China.

And in 1988—Seoul. Given the politicization of the Olympics, it would seem a heroically poor choice. As sport sociologist Harry Edwards commented, "How is it possible for [the IOC] to select Seoul and not expect trouble? The Soviets and their satellites do not recognize South Korea. North Korea is a client state of the U.S.S.R. The South Koreans accuse the North Koreans of shooting half of their government leaders in Rangoon. The Russian military shot down South Korea's Flight Seven. What a setting for terrorism." In

1964 Tokyo officials worried about Japanese offending Westerners by urinating in the streets. The problems, it seemed, had escalated since then.

Dire predictions for the Seoul Olympics fell woefully short of the mark. Few nations boycotted the Games, no major political issues disrupted them, and the level of performance was remarkably high. In fact, a few journalists remarked that the Olympics were entering a new age. Amateurism had ceased to be a problem. IOC officials allowed "professionals" to compete in some sports and "amateurs" to become millionaires through endorsements and other payments. Florence Griffith Joyner, for example, refused to sign an endorsement package until after the Olympics, banking that her performance would move her into a higher income bracket. It was a sound business strategy. By the end of the Games, teammates had stopped calling her Flo-Jo and begun refering to her as Cash Flo. Tennis agent Ian Tiriac noted the irony of the new Olympics: "You know, I think the millionaire tennis players are the only amateurs here. Steffi Graf wins this, and she doesn't earn a dime more. Same for Stefan Edberg. They have all their endorsements and money already. They are on a vacation from capitalism, and they want only the medal. But all the others, at least part of the reason they want to win is so that they can market themselves, make some money, do some economics. The tennis players are the true amateurs."

Settling the amateur issue and forcing politics into the background are signs of hope. Perhaps in a sad way, so too was the fact that sprinter Ben Johnson was stripped of his gold medal and world record for steroid use. Although drugs continue to be a major problem and drug testing is less sophisticated than drug use, the IOC has demonstrated that it is seriously addressing the issue. Reacting to Johnson's punishment, American distance runner Mary Decker Slaney said, "I think it's wonderful. Not because of Ben, but because I want a clean sport. The fact that a thing this big can't be swept under the rug is a sign of hope."

Even the television networks have gained some sense of proportion. For a time at least, the high-rolling days are over. The Seoul Olympic Organizing Committee hoped to sell television rights for as much as $1 billion. It opened bids at $600 million and set its bottom line at $500 million. After several embarrassing negotiation sessions, NBC purchased the rights for a modest—Seoul felt indecent—$300 million, or slightly less than ABC paid for the 1988 Calgary winter Games.

But if the financial luster of the Olympics had dimmed, their symbolic light, for better or worse, was as bright as ever. The world was a much smaller place than it had been when Avery Brundage first appeared on the Olympic stage. Multinational corporations, transcontinental communications, and the appearance of an international marketplace had created a global village. Around the world people were consuming the same products and engaging in the same processes for manufacturing those products. English had become the language of commerce and the second language for the entire world. American pop culture—television programs, fashions, films, music, and fast food—was steadily encroaching on regional diversity, ethnicity, and national cultures. Dallas Cowboys sweatshirts could be found not only on the backs of Texas teenagers but covering the shoulders of boys in Bangladesh or Senegal. T-shirts bearing the logos of American universities and Levis had almost become a uniform for young people around the world.

The Olympics was the sporting equivalent of the global village, the place where people from all over the world came together every four years to compete in the same games according to the same rules, to measure themselves and their societies against one another. In that sense, sports was rapidly becoming a cultural currency for much of the world, just as it had become for two generations of Americans. And when sports as cultural currency left the environs of the United States for a global arena, it was transformed. Avery Brundage, who died in 1975, would not be pleased by the changes. Realism and a sense of proportion were not his strengths. Idealism and blind belief were. The ideals were dead.

Like world business and popular culture, the Olympics had moved closer to the American sporting ideal, and not just in the introduction of basketball, baseball, figure skating, ice dancing, tennis, swimming, diving, or synchronized swimming as Olympic events. Amateurism had long since surrendered to professional demands, whether the state sports machines of the Eastern bloc or the wealthy "amateurs" tax accountant shenanigans produced in the capitalist West. Instead of being games to glorify competition and athletic triumph, the Olympics had degenerated into commercial extravaganzas financed by television and dominated by a show-business ethos. And the Victorian ideal of gentlemanly competition pursued by a cultured upper class had been eclipsed by the brutish immediacy of power politics. In America, sports were not games anymore, nor were they in Olympic competition. Ideologies, systems, religions, races, and nation states all turned to the Olympics for evidence—proof—that they were as powerful or as true or as inevitable as they claimed to be. The cultural currency of American sports—money, power, identity, and status—had colonized the Olympic Games. Avery Brundage would have raged against the dying of his light.

A generation of health-minded and fitness-conscious Americans cheered pentathlete Jackie Joyner-Kersee as she went faster and farther than her competition.
(Credit: Mary Ann Carter)

# • Sports and Self in Modern America

*Fewer and fewer people these days argue that running shortens lives, while a lot of people say that it may strengthen them. If that's all we've got for the time being, it seems a good enough argument for running. Not airtight, but good enough.*
—JIM FIXX

It was a perfect July day in Vermont—clear and cool. Jim Fixx, on the eve of a long-awaited vacation, put on his running togs and headed down a rural road for his daily run, expecting to do the usual twelve to fifteen miles. At fifty-two years of age, Fixx was a millionaire, the best-selling author of *The Complete Book of Running*, and the reigning guru of the American exercise cult. In 1968 he had weighed 214 pounds, smoked two packs of cigarettes a day, and worried about his family health history. Fixx's father had died of a heart attack at the age of forty-three. So Fixx started running and stopped smoking. He lost 60 pounds and introduced America to the virtues of strenuous exercise: longevity, freedom from depression, energy, and the "runner's high." He regularly ran 80 miles a week. When he hit the road on July 21, 1984, Fixx weighed 154 pounds and seemed the perfect image of fitness. Twenty minutes into the run he had a massive heart attack and died on the side of the road. A motorcyclist found his body later that afternoon.

Fixx's death shocked middle- and upper-class America. Of all people, how could Jim Fixx have died of a heart attack? Millions of joggers, runners, swimmers, cyclists, tri-athletes, walkers, weightlifters, and aerobic dancers had convinced themselves that exercise preserved youth and postponed death. It was the yuppie panacea; "working out" made them immune to the ravages of time.

The autopsy on Fixx was even more disturbing. In spite of all the running, his circulatory system was in a shambles. Fixx's cholesteral levels had been dangerously high. One coronary artery was 98 percent blocked, a second one 85 percent blocked, and a third one 50 percent blocked. In the previous two to eight weeks, the wall of his left ventricle had badly deteriorated. On that clear Vermont day, Jim Fixx shouldn't have been running; he should have been undergoing triple-bypass surgery.

Even more puzzling, Fixx had been complaining for months of chest pains while running—clear signs of a deadly angina, the heart muscle protesting lack of oxygen. Friends had expressed concern and urged him to get a check-up. He resisted, attempting to will good health. In January 1984 he had agreed to a treadmill test, but he skipped the appointment that afternoon, running 16 miles instead. Why had someone so committed to health ignored such obvious warnings? How had sports, exercise, and fitness become such obsessions in the United States?

Modern society was the culprit. In an increasingly secular society, church membership no longer provided the discipline to bind people together into cohesive social groups. Well-integrated neighborhoods with long histories and strong identities had given way after World War II to faceless suburbs. Corporate and professional elites tended to be highly mobile, relocating whenever a pay raise was offered. The new American community had become fifty suburban homes and a 7-11 convenience store. New organizations, especially business and government bureaucracies, had assumed power in the United States, but those were hardly places where most Americans could feel comfortable and in control. Blessed with money but deprived of community in the 1970s and 1980s, Americans began to use sports to rebuild their sense of community and fitness to define individual happiness and individual pleasure, creating a culture of competitive narcissism supported by a host of therapeutic panaceas, such as EST, psychotherapy, Scientology, and strenuous exercise.

For individuals, families, groups, and communities, sports had become a new cultural currency, a common ground upon which a diverse people could express their values and needs. Unlike European society, where such traditional institutions as the church, the aristocracy, and the monarchy had maintained order through established authority, America had been settled by lower-class working people and small farmers. The traditional institutions anchoring European society were absent. Without those same moorings, America had always confronted the centrifugal forces of individualism, capitalism, Protestantism, and ethnicity, using the culture of opportunity to stave off social disintegration. Social mobility, the westward movement, the abundance of land, and ruralism helped stabilize a highly complex society.

But in the twentieth century, when industrialization, urbanization, and the disappearance of the frontier changed the definitions of opportunity and progress, the values of individualism, community, and competition had to find new modes of expression, and sports became a prominent one. At the local, regional, and national levels, sports evolved into one of the most powerful expressions of identity. Outside observers marveled, for example, at the "religion" of high school football in the more than eleven hundred independent school districts of Texas. When viewed simply as sport, of course, the obsession with football seems absurd, but when viewed in terms of community identity, it becomes more understandable. In hundreds of rural areas, where scattered farms surround tiny county seats, the local high school, with its arbitrarily drawn district lines, was the central focus of community life. Rural Texans passionately opposed school district consolidations, even when it made good economic sense, because it threatened the high school, high school football, and community identity. For hundreds of small Texas towns—and rural areas throughout much of the rest of the country—high school athletics was literally the cement of community life.

It wasn't just high school sports which provided new identities in the United States. After World War II, social and economic pressures worked against the nuclear family. More and more women were working outside the home; more and more men were working at job sites long commutes from the suburbs; and divorce rates were way up. Childhood play became less spontaneous and more organized as schools, government, and communities assumed roles once played by the family. The most obvious consequence was the appearance of organized youth sports. Little League grew by leaps and bounds beginning in the 1950s; child's play, once the domain of the home and immediate neighborhood, became a spectator sport complete with uniforms, umpires, scoreboards, leagues, play-offs, drafts, and championships. By the 1980s, Little League was competing for time with Pop Warner football, Little Dribblers basketball, soccer, and swimming, with organized competition beginning in some sports at the age of three. In 1987 sports sociologists estimated that thirty million children under sixteen years of age were competing in organized sports.

Sports functioned as identity on the regional level as well. In an age when television, movies, and mass culture threatened regional distinctiveness, sports emerged as the single most powerful symbol of localism and community loyalty. That was obviously true of high school and college sports, but even in professional sports, when ownership shifted away from local businesses and entrepreneurs to conglomerates and national corporations, the regional identity of teams remained critically important to gate receipts and television revenues. The rivalries between the Chicago Bears and the Green Bay Packers, or the Boston Red Sox and the New York Yankees, or the Boston Celtics and the Los Angeles Lakers, filled stadiums, arenas, and living rooms with fans desperate for the home team to win. Five hundred years ago, European cities dedicated all their surplus capital over the course of 100 to 200 years to build elaborate cathedrals to God. In the United States during the 1970s and 1980s, the modern equivalent of the medieval cathedral was the domed stadium. For sports, not for God, American communities would sell bonds and mortgage themselves for the next generation.

Even on the national level, sports competition reflected and promoted American nationalism. Sports was a mirror of federalism, at once local in its community loyalties but national in its collective forms. The 1984 Olympic Games in Los Angeles did not just expose a rising tide of patriotism and national pride; they became a major force in stimulating a new American nationalism. Unlike the recent Olympic Games in Montreal, Moscow, and Seoul, the Los Angeles Games did not accumulate billion-dollar deficits and require the resources of national governments to prop them up. In 1984 "free enterprise capitalism" organized and conducted the Games, used existing facilities, and turned a profit. The Los Angeles Coliseum was filled with flag-waving Americans cheering every native athlete winning a medal. On television back home, Europeans watched the proceedings with astonishment and not a little fear, worrying about the burst of American patriotism, nationalism, and even chauvinism. Nearly a decade after the debacle in Vietnam, American pride and optimism was on the rebound, and the 1984 Olympic Games was center stage for the resurrection of the American sense of mission.

Modern sports in the United States also provided a sense of identity cutting across class, racial, and ethnic lines. In penitentiaries throughout the country, intense struggles were waged every evening over television and radio programming, black convicts wanting to watch soul stations and black sit-coms and whites demanding MTV or white sit-coms. But there was no trouble or debate on Sunday afternoon or Monday nights during the fall. It was football, only football, and blacks and whites watched the programs with equal enthusiasm. On Monday evenings in the fall, whether in the poorest ghetto tenement of the South Side of Chicago or the most tastefully appointed living room in the Lake Forest suburbs, televisions were tuned on to football, and discussions at work the next morning revolved around the game, who won and who lost and why.

For ethnic minorities and immigrants, sports similarly became a way of identifying with the new society, a powerful form of acculturation. During the 1980s, for example, Los Angeles became the second largest Mexican city in the world, behind only Mexico City in Spanish-speaking population and larger now than Guadalajara in terms of Mexican residents. At Dodger Stadium in Los Angeles, Mexicans and Mexican Americans became an increasingly large part of the evening box office, helping to sustain Dodger attendance at its three million–plus levels each year. In September 1986, when Dodger pitcher Fernando Valenzuela won his twentieth game of the season, the Spanish cable network SIN broke into its regular programming nationwide for live interviews. The fact that sports was making its way to the headlines and front pages of major newspapers was no accident in the United States. It had become, indeed, a new cultural currency in modern America, a way to interpret change and express traditional values.

Women, too, used sports as a vehicle in their drive for equality and identity. The development of women's and men's sports in America has varied considerably. From the first, men's sports have

emphasized fierce competition and the ruthless pursuit of expertise. Early male and female physical educators, however, believed
women were uncompetitive and decided that women's sports
should promote a woman's physical and mental qualities and thus
make her more attractive to men. They also believed that sports and
exercise should sublimate female sexual drives. As renowned nineteenth-century physical educator Dudley A. Sargent noted, "No one
seems to realize that there is a time in the life of a girl when it is
better for her and for the community to be something of a boy rather
than too much of a girl."

But tomboyish behavior had to stop short of abrasive competition. Lucille Eaton Hill, director of physical training at Wellesley College, urged women to "avoid the evils which are so apparent . . . in
the conduct of athletics for men." She and her fellow female physical
educators encouraged widespread participation rather than narrow
specialization. In short, women left spectator and professional
sports to the men. Indeed, not until 1924 were women allowed to
compete in Olympic track and field events, and even then on a limited basis.

During the 1920s the tennis careers of Suzanne Lenglen and
Helen Wills were used to demonstrate the proper and improper
pursuit of victory by athletic women. Tennis, for the great French
champion Lenglen, was not only a way of life: it was life. Her only
object on a tennis court was to win, and between 1919 and 1926,
when she turned professional, Lenglen lost only two sets of singles
and won 269 of 270 matches. But at what cost? Bulimic in her eating
habits and subject to dramatic swings in emotions, she suffered several nervous breakdowns and lived in fear of losing. In addition,
male critics noted that, far from keeping her looking young, tennis
cruelly aged Lenglen. Journalist Al Laney remarked that by the
mid-1920s Lenglen looked thirty years older than she actually was
and that her complexion had turned dull and colorless. Her friend
Ted Tinling agreed that before she turned twenty-five, "her face and
expression had already the traces of deep emotional experiences far
beyond the normal for her age."

In contrast, Helen Wills was a champion of great physical
beauty. Before Wills, Americans tended to agree with journalist Paul
Gallico that "pretty girls" did not excel in sports and that outstanding female athletes were simply compensating for their lack of

beauty. Summarizing this school of thought, Larry Engelmann observed: "Athletics was their way of getting attention. If Suzanne Lenglen were really beautiful, for instance, she wouldn't be running around like crazy on the tennis courts of Europe. She would have been quietly at home, happily married. Athletics proved a refuge and a last chance for the desperate female ugly duckling."

Yet Wills was beautiful, and she was great, winning every set of singles competition she played between 1927 and 1933. Journalists explained Wills' success and beauty by stressing the fact that tennis was only a game for her, not a way of life and certainly not life itself. Losses did not worry her. She always appeared composed. "My father, a doctor," she explained, "always told me not to wince or screw up my face while I was playing. He said it would put lines on my face." And no victory was worth a line.

Women were not fully emancipated from the older ideal until the 1970s, when they asserted their right to be as ruthless and competitive in athletics as men. Tennis champion Billy Jean King symbolized on the court as well as off this new attitude. Like Lenglen, she single-mindedly pursued victory. And she was no more concerned with sweating and grimacing than Pete Rose. Unlike Wills, King was not interested in art or starting a family. When asked why she was not at home, she replied, "Why don't you ask Rod Laver why he isn't at home?" It was as eloquent a statement of athletic liberation as could be asked for.

To develop fully as an athlete, King had to earn money. Along with Gladys Heldman and Philip Morris Tobacco Company, King helped to organize the Virginia Slims women's tennis circuit in 1971. That year she became the first female athlete to earn $100,000 in a single year. More importantly, she labored to get women players a bigger share of the prize money at the major championships. In the early 1970s women's purses at Wimbledon and the U.S. Open were about 10 percent of the men's. By the mid-1980s the prize money split was equal. As if to punctuate the point that women's tennis had arrived, King defeated the former Wimbledon triple-crown champion (1939) Bobby Riggs 6–4, 6–3, 6–3, in a highly publicized match in the Houston Astrodome in 1973.

Even more important than King for the future of women's athletics was Title IX of the 1972 Educational Amendments Act. It outlawed sexual discrimination by school districts or colleges and universities which received federal aid. Certainly, athletic budgets in high schools and universities are not equally divided between male and female athletics. But women have made significant gains. Before Title IX less than 1 percent of athletic budgets went to women's sports. By the 1980s that figure had increased to over 10 percent. No longer is there a serious argument over the road women's sports should travel. Instead, the battle is over what portion of the pie they should receive.

But it wasn't just countries, cities, colleges, small towns, high schools, and ethnic groups which turned to sports in the 1980s as the most powerful way of defining their values. The most extraordinary development in contemporary popular culture was the extent to which individuals turned to athletics, exercise, and body image as a way of finding meaning in an increasingly dislocated society. In the mid-1980s, a Louis Harris poll indicated that 96 percent of all Americans found something about their bodies that they didn't like and would change if they could. Harris said that the "rampant obsessions of both men and women about their looks have produced an obvious boon for the cosmetics industry, plastic surgery, diet doctors, fitness and shape advisers, fat farms, and exercise clubs." The cult of fitness and the cult of individual happiness went hand in hand. Politicians used international sports at the Olympic level to confirm the superiority of various political systems or prove the equality of their Third World cultures; they mustered professional sports to project the quality of life in major American cities; collegiate sports touted the virtues of different universities; and in the 1970s and 1980s, millions of Americans embraced the cult of fitness to discover the meaning of life, retreating into the fantasy that they are how they look.

The cult of fitness and the preoccupation with physical appearance first emerged in the United States during the John Kennedy administration. In the election of 1960, Kennedy used television as it had never been used before when he challenged Richard Nixon to a series of debates. Kennedy faced formidable odds. Young, handsome, and wealthy, he was considered perhaps too young, too handsome, and too wealthy to make an effective president. His Roman Catholicism seemed another albatross. Behind the polls, Kennedy needed a boost. The televised debates were perfect.

Nixon arrived in Chicago for the first debate looking tired and ill. He had injured his knee six weeks before, and a hospital stay had weakened him. On the eve of the debate a chest cold left him hoarse. He looked like a nervous corpse—pale, twenty pounds underweight, and haggard. Make-up experts suggested covering his heavy beard with a thick powder, but Nixon accepted only a thin coat of Max Factor's "Lazy Shave," a pancake cosmetic.

Kennedy looked better, much better. He arrived at Chicago from California with a suntan. He didn't need make-up to look healthy, nor did he need special lighting to hide a weak profile. He did, however, change suits. He believed that a dark blue rather than a gray suit would look better under the bright lights. Kennedy was right, of course, as anyone who watches a nightly news program must realize. Once the debate started, Kennedy intentionally slowed down his delivery and watered down his ideas. His face was controlled and cool. He smiled with his eyes and perhaps the corners of his mouth, and his laugh was a mere suggestion of a laugh. Although Nixon marshalled a mountain of facts and closely reasoned arguments, he looked bad. Instead of hearing a knowledgeable candidate, viewers saw a nervous, uncertain man, one whose clothes didn't fit and whose face looked pasty and white. In contrast, Kennedy *looked* good, scored a victory in the polls, and went on to win the election by a razor-thin margin.

The first president born in the twentieth century, Kennedy had claimed in his inaugural address that "the torch had been passed to a new generation of Americans . . . tempered by war, disciplined by a hard and bitter peace, proud of our ancient heritage." Life around the White House soon reflected the instincts of a new generation. It wasn't just little Caroline and later John-John frolicking on the White House lawn. The Kennedys were fiercely competitive and obsessed with sports. At the family compound at Hyannisport or Robert Kennedy's "Hickory Hill" home in Virginia, the days were filled with tennis, golf, sailing, isometric exercise, swimming, horseback riding, badminton, and a brutal form of touch football, which overweight and overaged visitors dreaded, since the Kennedys expected everyone to give it a try. An atmosphere of youthful virility surrounded the Kennedy administration. To impress the Kennedys, one associate remembered, you had to "show raw guts, fall on your face now and then. Smash into the house once in a while going after a pass. Laugh off twisted ankles or a big hole torn in your best suit."

The whole country became infatuated with the sense of vitality, and the fifty-mile hike became the symbol of fitness. Marine Corps commandant General David M. Shoup, whom Kennedy especially admired, accepted Kennedy's challenge to see if his marines could duplicate a feat of Theodore Roosevelt's 1908 marines—march fifty miles in less than twenty hours. Shoup met the challenge, as did Attorney General Robert Kennedy, who walked his fifty miles along the path of the C & O canal. Kennedy's secretaries took up the challenge, and once the newspapers had picked up the story, tens of thousands of Americans tried it too. The spring of 1963 became the season of the fifty-mile hike.

These were also years of giddy infatuation with the Mercury astronauts, whose crew-cut fitness first came to public attention at their introductory press conference in 1959. All of them were military pilots, and John Glenn of Ohio emerged as their leader. Square-jawed with ramrod perfect posture, Glenn had a personality and value system to match. He was the ultimate "goody-goody," and America loved him. The country was also astounded at his daily fitness regimen—vigorous calisthenics followed by a two-mile jog along the beach. Two miles—every day! Even when it rained.

If John Glenn was the leading jogger of the 1960s, the scientific father of running was Kenneth Cooper, an Air Force physician. A high school track star in Oklahoma City, Cooper finished medical school and joined the Air Force as a physician at the School of Aerospace Medicine in San Antonio. He tested fitness levels in thousands of potential Air Force pilots and in the process developed new standards of conditioning. To really benefit from exercise, Americans had to get their heart rate above 130 beats a minute for a sustained period. Jogging, running, racquetball, squash, cycling, walking and swimming were the best exercises.

To please an increasingly technical, postindustrial clientele whose faith in science was unrivaled, Cooper even charted fitness, providing a quantified methodology to guarantee fitness. An aerobically fit person had to "earn 30 points a week." He or she could do this by walking three miles in no more than forty-one minutes five times a week; by swimming 700 yards in fifteen minutes five times a week; or by running a mile in eight minutes only twice a week. To measure fitness, Cooper recommended the "twelve minutes test." If a person can run or walk less than a mile in twelve minutes, he or she is in "very poor shape"; 1 to 1.25 miles is "poor"; 1.25 to 1.5 miles is "fair"; 1.5 to 1.75 miles is "good"; and more than 1.75 miles is "excellent." Cooper also warned people to watch out if their pulse rate exceeded 80 beats a minute. Fewer than 60 beats was "excellent." Vigorous exercise would reduce the heart rate. In Cooper's own words, "You might just save your heart some of those 20,000 to 30,000 extra beats you've forced on it every day."

The country was more than ready for Cooper's message. Early in the 1960s the first of the baby-boom generation hit college. The "don't trust anyone over thirty" culture had appeared, protesting war and inequality and proclaiming the virtues of brotherly love and sexual liberation. In 1961 half the American population was under thirty. By 1964 the median age had dropped to twenty-seven and in 1966 to twenty-five. America fell in love with youth, health, sex, and pleasure. Hippies, protests, "love-ins," "teach-ins," Woodstock, drugs, rebellion, and loud, self-righteous rejections of materialism emanated from college campuses.

But in 1967 the first baby-boom class graduated from college. The transformation of hippies into "Yuppies" was underway. By 1971 those 1946 babies were twenty-five years old. The cruel tricks of gravity and heredity commenced. Bellies started to thicken, hairlines to recede. Women with babies looked despairingly at abdominal stretch marks and the faint beginnings of "crow's feet." The youth culture still survived, but individual youth was proving to be a temporary state. Middle age loomed as large as death.

Dr. Kenneth Cooper had the answer. Late in 1968, he coined a new word and wrote a book by the same name—*Aerobics*. By 1972 the book had sold nearly three million copies to anxious yuppies bent on postponing the inevitable. By the early 1970s, Cooper had an estimated eight million Americans, including astronaut John Glenn, adding up their weekly points, counting their pulse, testing their speed, taking their blood pressure, and weighing their bodies.

Throughout the 1970s and 1980s the cult of fitness reached extraordinary dimensions in the United States. More than twenty million Americans regularly exercised, and along with the running boom came a boom in racquetball, tennis, swimming, cycling, weightlifting, and "aerobic" dancing. In 1970 only 125 people entered the first New York City marathon, which took runners over a 26-mile course through all four boroughs; but in the 1986 marathon, 20,000 officially entered the race, and 19,412 finished it. The race was so popular that organizers had to reject thousands of applicants. Marathons became common events on every weekened all across the country.

The triathlon endurance was an even better gauge of the fitness cult. Known as the ultimate of the "ultrasports," the triathlon combined a 2-mile swim with a 112-mile cycle ride and a 26-mile run. In 1986 more than one million Americans competed in triathlon events around the country. And in what can only be considered the absurd limit of the fitness craze, Stu Mittleman won the "Sri Chinmey 1,000 Mile Marathon" in New York City in 1986. His time of just under fifteen days "was my best ever."

The cult of fitness was rivaled only by the obsession with youth and body image which swept through American culture in the 1970s and 1980s. To be sure, this was nothing new. Americans had long been preoccupied with their bodies, and attempts to stay young had centered on staying thin, as if slenderness were in itself a foundation of youth. In the 1860s Harriet Beecher Stowe had written: "We in America have got so far out of the way of a womanhood that has any vigor of outline or opulence of physical proportion, that, when we see a woman made as a woman ought to be, she strikes us as a monster. Our willowy girls are afraid of nothing so much as growing stout."

To stay thin, nineteenth-century American women dieted and corseted their bodies. "It ain't stylish for young courting gals to let on like they have any appetite," admitted one female. And through tightlacing their corsets, women could maintain the proper girlish waistline of eighteen inches, with only such acceptable side effects as headaches, fainting spells, and uterine and spinal disorders.

If tightlacing and dieting led to serious health problems, illness was in itself admired. Consumptive women were romanticized and imbued with spiritual qualities. Little Eva in *Uncle Tom's Cabin*, Beth in *Little Women*, Mimi in *La Boheme*—all were thin, romantic consumptives who radiated spirituality and sensuality. Perhaps the ideal was the romantic ballerina—thin, ethereal, pale, pure, as certain to die young as poor broken-hearted Giselle.

Throughout the twentieth century, thinness has largely remained the feminine ideal, although sickliness generally declined as an attractive characteristic. The Gibson Girl of the turn of the century touted athletics, and during the 1920s the flapper exuded energy, vitality, and youth. And if the breast-bound flapper did not survive the 1929 stock market crash, an emphasis on thinness did. Indeed, only during the 1950s, when Marilyn Monroe was at her height, was there a serious challenge to the slender ideal.

Post–World War II culture has enshrined both thinness and youth for men as well as women. Advertisers have aided the process. Since photographers maintain that clothes look best on lean bodies, leading fashion models have always been thin and generally young. But since the 1960s, advertisers have used youth and thinness to sell other products as well. The evolution of Pepsi-Cola slogans illustrates this point:

1935: "Twice as Much"
1948: "Be Sociable—Have a Pepsi."
1960: "Now it's Pepsi for those who think young."
1965: "The Pepsi Generation."
1984: "Pepsi: The Choice of a New Generation."

Appeals to abundance ("twice as much") and social interaction ("be sociable") were replaced by the promise of eternal youth. As if to reinforce this appeal, Pepsi paid magnificent amounts to two thin, youthful Michaels as spokesmen: Michael Jackson and Michael J. Fox. Far from being sociable, Jackson is a virtual recluse, obsessed with personality change through plastic surgery. And Fox, as sure as Peter Pan, is the perpetual adolescent.

To fit the culture's procrustean mold, advertisers encourage Americans to binge and purge, consume and diet. Consume because "you are someone special" and "you can have it all." Diet because "you can never be too thin or too rich." In his perceptive book *Never Satisfied*, Hillel Schwartz argues that "dieting is an essentially nostalgic act, an attempt to return to a time when one *could* be satisfied, when one *was* thinner, when the range of choices in the world neither bewildered nor intimidated. To restrict one's range of choices, as all dieters must do, is not so much deficient as it is regressive. . . . Imagining a miraculous future, the dieter is always looking back."

In a secular, materialistic age, dieting has become an ascetic religion. Seventeenth-century poet and preacher John Donne wrote, "The flesh that God hath given us is affliction enough, but the flesh that the devil gives us, is affliction upon affliction and to that, there belongs a woe." To be fat in America has become a religious as well as a secular sin. Christian diet books emphasize John 3:30: "He must increase, but I must decrease."

In 1957 Charlie Shedd in his *Pray Your Weight Away* confessed, "We fatties are the only people on earth who can weigh our sin." His book inspired some Christians to lose weight and others to write diet books. Such works as Deborah Price's *I Prayed Myself Thin*, Joan Cavanaugh's *More of Jesus and Less of Me*, Reverend H. Victor Kane's *Devotion for Dieters*, and Francis Hunter's *God's Answer to Fat—Lose It!* emphasized that godliness is in league with thinness. Capturing the temper of her times, columnist Ellen Goodman wrote in 1975 that "eating has become the last bona fide sin left in America." And on this point, religion and secular humanism are in complete accord.

The fitness boom and body-image obsession financed a huge growth industry. To support their new interest in fitness, Americans needed equipment and clothes—shoes, shorts, shirts, racquets, bicycles, balls, paddles, bats, cleats, gloves, goggles, weights, scales, blood-pressure cuffs, timing watches, clubs, socks, headbands, wristbands, and leotards. Between 1975 and 1987 sporting goods sales in the United States increased from $8.9 billion to $27.5 billion. Americans spent $4 billion on athletic shoes alone in 1987. Health clubs, once the domain of the wealthy and a small clique of bodybuilders, multiplied in number from 350 in 1968 to more than 7,000 in 1986. Gross revenues in 1987 exceeded $650 million.

Exercise and fitness revenues were matched by those of the weight loss industry. Jean Nidetch founded Weight Watchers in 1962 and eventually franchised it, making sure that group leaders had been through the diet program and reached "maintenance" levels. Attendance doubled between 1983 and 1987, and gross revenues went past $200 million that year. Sybil Ferguson's Diet Center, Inc., founded in 1969, had two thousand franchises in 1987 and nearly $50 million in gross revenues. Americans spent $6 billion for diet soda in 1986, $5 billion for vitamins and health foods, and $350 million for diet capsules and liquid protein. The President's Council on Physical

Fitness estimated that 65 million Americans were dieting in 1987. Diet Coke, Diet Pepsi, Diet Dr. Pepper, Lean Cuisine, Bud Light, Miller Lite, lite bread, sugarless gum, NutraSweet, Cambridge, and a host of other diet products entered American popular culture.

What dieting and exercise couldn't fix, plastic surgery could. Americans went on a plastic surgery binge in the 1980s—not to repair real damage to their bodies or birth defects, but to improve their appearance cosmetically and recapture the illusion of youth. In 1987 more than 500,000 Americans underwent cosmetic plastic surgery. The most popular procedures were abdominoplasty (tummy tucks), breast augmentation, liposuction (fat removal), blepharoplasty (eyes), and rhinoplasty (nose). Plastic surgeons were also beginning to perform "total body contour" procedures. To postpone middle age, yuppies made plastic surgery a $3 billion industry.

Americans also changed a number of their habits in the 1970s and 1980s. Cigarette consumption began to decline in 1982. In 1965, 52 percent of men and 34 percent of women smoked. By 1985 only 33 percent of men and 28 percent of women smoked, and at the end of 1987 the American Cancer Society estimated that only 27 percent of Americans were still smoking. Per capita whiskey consumption dropped nearly 20 percent between 1976 and 1986 as Americans turned to lower-alcohol-content beer and wine coolers. Beef and pork consumption dropped in favor of chicken and fish when cholesterol-conscious Americans turned away from "red meat." Caffeine was also suspect. Americans under twenty-five drank only a third of the coffee their parents did; sales of decaffeinated coffee and drinks like Pepsi Free and Pepper Free symbolized the new health consciousness.

The results were impressive, even though some of the gains had to be attributed to better drug therapy, the rise of heart bypass surgery, and improvement of cardiac care units in American hospitals. But the bottom line was that between 1950 and 1985, the death rate per 100,000 people from cardiovascular and cerebrovascular disease declined from 511 to 418, a dramatic improvement. The cult of fitness seemed to be paying dividends.

But there was an underside to the cult of fitness, an obsessive perfectionism which was the antithesis of good health. Jim Fixx and his daily runs in spite of chest pains were one example. Kathy Love Ormsby was another. The North Carolina State University junior, who held the U.S. collegiate women's record for 10,000 meters, had difficulty dealing with failure. In the 1986 NCAA championships, after 6,400 meters, she was struggling along in fourth place, running a bad race. Then, as she approached a turn, she decided to keep going straight. She ducked under a railing and ran straight past Wisconsin team coach Peter Tegen. "It was eerie," he said. "Her eyes were focused straight ahead." She kept going—out of Indiana University's track stadium in Indianapolis, across a softball diamond, over a seven-foot fence, down New York Street, toward the bridge that spans the White River. Seventy-five feet onto the bridge she stopped, climbed over the railing, and jumped. After falling thirty-five feet, she landed on the soggy ground close to the river. She broke a rib, collapsed a lung, and fractured vertebrae. The doctor who attended her said that she would be permanently paralyzed from the waist down: "Given the distance that she fell, she's very lucky she's not a quadraplegic," Dr. Peter Hall noted. "She could have easily died."

Why? Ormsby was a high school valedictorian, a straight-A student, the state record holder for the 800, 1,600, and 3,200 meters. At North Carolina State she was a track star and promising premed student. She was raised in a strong Christian family and was deeply religious herself. After her record-breaking 10,000-meter run, she told a reporter: "I just have to learn to do my best for myself and for God and to turn everything over to Him." Her leap had turned everything over to Him.

Some observers blamed Ormsby's consuming pursuit of perfection. Others blamed the pressure of world-class sport competition. Her father commented, "I believe . . . that it had something to do with the pressure that is put on young people to succeed." Certainly society's emphasis on the importance of sports places tremendous strains on young athletes. Often isolated from the world outside gyms and tracks and stadiums, they begin to think that their world has real, lasting meaning. Failure, then, becomes equated with death itself.

Such obsessive perfectionism also affected millions of other people, only a tiny fraction of whom were competitive athletes. For many people, exercise and weight loss became forms of psychological discipline, proof that the individual was in charge of his or her life. A 1986 Gallup Poll estimated that three million Americans, most of them women, suffered from eating disorders—anorexia nervosa and bulimia. In anorexia nervosa, victims virtually starve themselves to death, using laxatives, exercise, and absurdly low calorie intake to lose body weight. Most psychologists attribute the eating disorder to a sense of powerlessness in the victim. They strive for a sense of weightlessness, and in that weightlessness they find a sense of control missing from other areas of their lives. In 1984 the soft-rock vocalist Karen Carpenter brought the disease to national attention when she died of a heart attack induced by extreme weight loss. Even when their weight drops below 85 pounds and they resemble concentration-camp victims, anorectics still look in the mirror and see themselves as fat, with round faces and flabby skin. Breasts disappear, menstruation stops, and their bodies return momentarily, just before death, to preadolescence.

Bulimia is a related disorder. The Gallup Poll concluded that nearly 10 percent of all American women between the ages of sixteen and twenty-five practice bulimia, an eating disorder characterized by huge calorie intake followed by self-induced vomiting. The Food and Drug Administration said that bulimia may last up to eight hours, with an intake of 20,000 calories (an equivalent of 210 brownies, or 6 layer cakes, or 35 "Big Macs"), involve 25 to 30 vomiting episodes, and cost up to $75 a day for food purchases. If untreated, the disease causes irregular heartbeats, cramps, fatigue, and seizures by destroying the body's electrolyte balance. The gastric acid from vomiting will also erode teeth away.

In a country which historically has been keenly competitive and has periodically affirmed a belief in perfectionism, the idea of a better life through sports has been carried to obsessive lengths. Often the object of physical fitness has not been to produce health and well-being but to test or even to escape the limits of one's body. Ultra-distance runner Stu Mittleman, one of the leaders in his field during the 1980s, was the epitome of this tendency. For him a 26-mile marathon was unsatisfactory, a flat, almost meaningless endeavor. The 100-mile event was better, and in the early 1980s he established the American record with a 12:56:34 run. Better still was the six-day event, in which his 488 miles was also an American record.

In ultra-distance running Mittleman sees man rediscovering his lost past. "Our culture forces us to eliminate sensory input so that we can cope," he observed. "Sports re-sensitizes. I want to live life intensely. . . . Long slow running has a heritage in hunting and gathering. Sprinting is based on retreat, on flight." Life, then, is best experienced at the limits of endurance, well past what is good for one's health. Yet, sometimes even that does not seem enough. As Mittleman told an interviewer, "I plan to do a 12-hour run tomorrow. You know, it seems like so little now."

Among world-class athletes, performance is more important than health. During the nineteenth century athletes occasionally took drugs to enhance their performances. Cyclists, in particular, used drugs to extend their pain and endurance barriers. As early as 1869 some cyclists used "speed balls" of heroin and cocaine to increase endurance. Others used caffeine, alcohol, nitroglycerine, ethyl ether, strychnine, and opium to achieve the same effect.

Of course, not all athletes survived such experimentation. And in the twentieth century, as drug use became more frequent, the casualty rate climbed. In 1960 Danish cyclist Knut Jensen collapsed and died during the Rome Olympics. He had taken amphetamines and nicotinyl tartrate to improve his chances of victory. In 1967 Thomas Simpson died during the ascent of Mount Ventoux in the Tour de France. Amphetamines were discovered in his jersey pockets and luggage.

Since World War II, however, stimulants have done less damage than muscle-building drugs. During the 1920s American scientists isolated the male hormone testosterone. By the 1940s testosterone was being hailed as a potential fountain of youth. Science writer Paul de Kruif in *The Male Hormone* (1945) noted that the newly developed synthetic testosterone "did more than give [the subjects] more energy and a gain in weight. . . . It changed them, and fundamentally. . . . after many months on testosterone, their chest and shoulder muscles grew much heavier and stronger. . . . in some mysterious manner, testosterone caused the human body to synthesize protein, it caused the human body to be able to build the very stuff of its own life." There is evidence that during World War II testosterone was administered to German storm troopers to increase their strength and aggressiveness.

In 1945 de Kruif speculated, "It would be interesting to watch the productive power of [a] . . . professional group [of athletes] that would try a systematic supercharge with testosterone." By the 1952

Helsinki Olympics the Soviet Union had embarked on just such a campaign. That year Soviet weightlifters won seven Olympic medals, and U.S. Olympic weightlifting coach Bob Hoffman told reporters, "I know they're taking the hormone stuff to increase their strength."

At the 1954 World Weightlifting Championships in Vienna, a Soviet team physician confirmed Hoffman's belief. Upon returning home, Dr. John Ziegler, the U.S. team physician, acquired some testosterone and tested it on himself, Hoffman, and several American lifters. Concerned about the hormone's side effects—heightened aggression, increased libido, prostatic problems, and hirsutism—Ziegler approached the CIBA pharmaceutical company about producing a drug that would have testosterone's anabolic (muscle-building) effects without its androgenic (masculine characteristics) problems. The unsatisfactory result was the anabolic steroid Dianabol, a drug intended to aid burn victims and certain postoperative and geriatric patients.

Dianabol soon became the candy of the athletic world. By the 1960s nearly every world-class weightlifter was taking some form of anabolic steroid. In fact, steroids became the *sine qua non* of lifting. American superheavyweight weightlifting champion Ken Patera announced in 1971 that he was anxious to meet his Russian counterpart Vasily Alexiev in the 1972 Olympics: "Last year, the only difference between me and him was that I couldn't afford his pharmacy bill. Now I can. When we hit Munich next year, I'll weigh in at about 340, maybe 350. Then we'll see which are better—his steroids or mine."

Track and field athletes, football players, and bodybuilders similarly improved their performances with the aid of drugs. Jay Sylvester, a member of the 1972 U.S. Olympic track and field team, polled his teammates and found that 68 percent had used steroids to prepare for the Games. They believed that without them they would be at a competitive disadvantage. The same was true in football. One San Diego Charger player told team psychiatrist Arnold J. Mandell, "Doc, I'm not about to go out one-on-one against a guy who's grunting and drooling and coming at me with big dilated pupils unless I'm in the same condition."

Testosterone and anabolic steroids have led to athletes' experimenting with other performance-enhancing drugs. One of the more popular recent additions to this drug array is human growth hormone (hGH), a hormone manufactured from the pituitary. As the authors of *The Underground Steroid Handbook* claimed, hGH could "overcome bad genetics. . . . We LOVE the stuff." Of course, it may also cause elongation of the chin, feet, and hands; thickening of the rib cage and wrists; and heart problems.

Risk is part of taking drugs. Anabolic steroids can cause a rare, fatal type of kidney tumor, high blood pressure, sterility, intestinal bleeding, hypoglycemia, heart problems, acne, a deepened voice, and a change in the distribution of body hair. Steroids and testosterone also make users more aggressive and irritable. One NFL player confessed that testosterone "definitely makes a person mean and aggressive. . . . On the field I've tried to hurt people in ways I never did before. . . . A lot of guys can't handle it. I'm not sure I can. I remember a while back five of the guys on our team went on the juice at the same time. A year later four of them were divorced and one was separated. I've lost a lot of hair from using it, but I have to admit it's great for football. . . . I lost my family, but I think I'm a better player now. Isn't that a hell of a trade-off?"

By the 1970s steroids had become part of America's drug culture, and athletes asserted the right to decide what could or could not go into their own bodies. Frederick C. Hatfield in *Anabolic Steroids: What Kind and How Many* (1982) wrote: "As pioneers, these athletes carefully weigh the risk-to-benefit ratio and proceed with caution and with open minds. Can there be much wrong with getting bigger and/or stronger?" Users, then, have been transformed into pioneers, "adventurers who think for themselves and who want to accomplish something noble before they are buried and become worm food."

Ironically, however, most of the users are not world-class athletes. In the 1980s use of steroids expanded out of the realm of world-class athletes to college and high school playing fields. An estimated one million young American men and women were consuming large amounts of anabolic steroids in 1987. The praise they received for "bulking up" was irresistible. When they reduced steroid use and lost muscle tissue, friends immediately commented on how "much smaller you are," and they would return to the pills. Like bulimia and anorexia nervosa, anabolic steroids were addictions linked inseparably with body image.

Steroid use was most pronounced in the subculture of body

building. Most of these men and women are not competitive athletes trying to break a world record or win an Olympic gold medal—"to accomplish something noble"—but people who want to look "pumped." Like dieting and cosmetic surgery, steroid use has become a means to a better-looking body, and looks—not health—is the real objective.

The quest for the "ideal" body has been taken to its furthest pharmaceutical extremes by bodybuilders. Not only do they take steroids to build up muscle mass, but they also diet and take diuretics to achieve maximum muscular striation, or the "cut up" look. For weeks or even months before an important competition, bodybuilders eat as little as 1,000 calories a day and still work out eight or more hours a day. The result may be "the picture of health," but there is no reality behind the image. As one professional commented, "When we walk on stage we are closer to death than we are to life." And after a contest, in a bulimic binge, bodybuilders "pig out," often putting on fifteen pounds in one evening of eating.

Furthermore, to support their quest, many bodybuilders resort to homosexual "hustling." In theory, male bodybuilders have enshrined heterosexuality. Charles Atlas advertisements emphasized that the prize for the biggest biceps was the woman in the bathing suit. *Muscle and Fitness,* the leading bodybuilder magazine, reinforces this mythology by always picturing beautiful women hanging onto the biceps and thighs of "pumped," oiled men. "Ya know," said *Muscle and Fitness* editor Joe Weider, "in every age the women, they always go for the guy with the muscles, the body builder. [The women] never go for the studious guy."

In fact, gay men have been a continual source of financial support for bodybuilders. Since serious bodybuilding is a full-time pursuit, the men involved need some source of income. Anthropologist Alan M. Kline estimated that 50 to 75 percent of southern California bodybuilders "hustle" the gay community for living expenses. Hustling ranges from posing for "beefcake" photographers and dancing nude at all-male events to pornography and sexual acts. Most bodybuilders, however, insist that they are not homosexual, that they have to hustle only to finance their bodybuilding habit. And besides, they insist, almost everyone does it. "People don't realize," noted one bodybuilder, "that in any given line-up of 20 competitors 10 are hustling."

Many serious bodybuilders sacrifice heterosexual relationships as well as good health for their obsession. As one admitted,
"On any given time I can go out with a women, but it is not very
satisfying. . . . Women demand time. I don't have that right now."
Time, commitment, women, and even other men—all are obstacles
to be mastered or avoided in the pursuit of a narcissistic ideal. To
echo Michael Jackson's popular 1988 song, life for these bodybuilders starts and ends with the man in the mirror.

By the end of the 1980s, sports had become the secular religion
of America. The stadiums, tanning salons, health spas, and gymnasiums had become the new cathedrals; jogging, running, aerobic
dancing, cycling, weightlifting, and dieting the new rituals; and
televised events, newspapers, radio talk shows, and sports and
health magazines the new liturgies. The most obsessive athletes
have a disciplined devotion that even the most ascetic medieval
saints would have envied. Alberto Salazar, the world-class marathoner, bragged about his willingness to run 105 miles a week on
stress-fractured legs. In the heat of one marathon, he kept running
even when his body temperature had reached 108 degrees, collapsed in heat prostration, and while being packed in ice, received
the last rites of the Roman Catholic Church.

Sports in the 1980s holds out secular salvation for nations, communities, and individuals. In competition and fitness, they locate
the holy grail, the meaning of life in a world where god, church, and
state no longer reign supreme. In *The Complete Book of Running*, Jim
Fixx wrote: "It is here with my heart banging against my ribs that I
discover how far beyond reason I can push myself. Furthermore,
once a race has ended, I know what I am truly made of. Who can say
how many of us have learned life's profoundest lessons while aching
and gasping for breath?" On that Vermont road in 1986, with his
body aching, his lungs gasping for breath, and his heart pounding
against his ribs, Jim Fixx may have discovered the meaning of life.

# • Bibliographic Essay

For the past fifteen years it has almost become a ritual for historians writing on a sports topic to try contritely and apologetically to justify their reasons for selecting their particular subject. Many even deplore the lack of "serious" scholarship in the field of sports history. It is pleasurable to report that sport historians no longer have to resort to the traditional apologia. The field is alive and well, and if some areas have been better mined than others, that is to be expected. Like much of recent social history, the late nineteenth and early twentieth centuries have been more fully studied than the mid and late twentieth century. But even in this later period, sport historians, sociologists, psychologists, and journalists have been active. The following bibliography concentrates on the studies produced by sport historians and journalists.

### General Works

Academic journals demonstrate the growth in the field of sport history. Twenty years ago few articles in sport history were published in academic journals. Today a number of journals are devoted totally to sport history. Among the best are the *Journal of Sport History, Stadion*, the *International Journal of the History of Sport*, and the *Canadian Journal of History of Sport and Physical Education*. Other journals in sport studies also contain historical articles. See particularly the *Journal of Sport and Social Issues, Research Quarterly, Quest*, the *Journal of Sport Behavior*, the *International Review of Sport Sociology*, and *Arete: The Journal of Sport Literature*. Sport history articles in other journals can be followed in the *Journal of Sport History*; each issue devotes a section to surveys of periodical literature. Finally, some very good sport history can be found in the various magazines devoted to sport. *Sports Illustrated* heads the list. In fact, for a study in recent sport history it is probably the most important source. No news magazine is better written, and it deals critically with the important issues affecting sport.

Solid textbooks or overviews also indicate the growth in sport history. The best textbook on the history of American sport is Benjamin G. Rader, *American Sports: From the Age of Folk Games to the Age of the Spectator* (1982).

Soon to be reissued in a revised edition, it provides a useful paradigm for the study of sport history. Allen Guttmann, *A Whole New Ball Game: An Interpretation of American Sports* (1988), studies selected important issues. John A. Lucas and Ronald A. Smith, *Saga of American Sports* (1978), is also perceptive and sound, although not quite so sophisticated as Rader. Betty Spears and Richard A. Swanson, *History of Sport and Physical Activity in the United States* (1978), is also useful. Older but still important works include Foster Rhea Dulles, *America Learns to Play* (1940), and John Richard Betts, *America's Sporting Heritage, 1850–1950* (1974). The Betts survey is essentially a revision of his classic doctoral dissertation, "Organized Sports in Industrial America" (Columbia University, 1951).

Several overviews of the history of sport from ancient times to the present also contain sections on sport in America. William J. Baker, *Sports in the Western World* (1982), is an admirable, judicious synthesis. A bit more thematic but always full of insights is Richard D. Mandell, *Sport: A Cultural History* (1984). Other broad overviews include Peter C. McIntosh, *Sport in Society* (1963); Walter Umminger, *Superman, Heroes, and Gods: The Story of Sports through the Ages,* trans. James Clark (1963); and Earle F. Ziegler, *History of Physical Education and Sport* (1979). Finally, Robert J. Higgs, *Sports: A Reference Guide* (1982), surveys a number of different areas of sports studies and is particularly concerned with sport in the United States.

Historiographical articles have articulated themes and trends in the study of sport history. For American sport history see Melvin L. Adelman, "Academicians and Athletics: Historians' Views of American Sport," *Maryland Historian* 4 (1973): 123–37, and "Academicians and American Athletics: A Decade of Progress," *Journal of Sport History* 10 (1983): 80–106; Benjamin G. Rader, "Modern Sports: In Search of Interpretations," *Journal of Social History* 13 (1979): 307–21; Allen Guttmann, "Commentary: Who's on First? or, Books on the History of American Sports," *Journal of American History* 66 (1979): 348–54; Stephen Hardy, "The City and the Rise of American Sport: 1820–1920," *Exercise and Sports Sciences Reviews* 9 (1981): 183–219; Steven A. Riess, "Sport and the American Dream: A Review Essay," *Journal of Social History* 14 (1980): 295–301; David K. Wiggins, "Clio and the Black Athlete in America: Myths, Heroes, and Realities," *Quest* 32 (1980): 217–25; Peter C. McIntosh, "An Historical View of Sport and Social Control," *International Review of Sport Sociology* 6 (1971): 5–13; Peter Levine, "The Promise of Sport in Antebellum America," *Journal of American Culture* 2 (1980): 623–34; and Nancy Struna, "In 'Glorious Disarray' ": The Literature of American Sports History," *Research Quarterly* 56 (1985): 151–60.

A few scholars have attempted to apply an overarching theoretical framework to the history of sport. The most exciting and perhaps most useful is Allen Guttmann, *From Ritual to Record: The Nature of Modern Sport* (1978). In many ways Guttmann's *A Whole New Ball Game* (1988) is a continuation of his earlier pioneering study. Another important study by Guttmann that looks at change over time in *Sports Spectators* (1986). Richard Gruneau, *Class, Sports, and Social Development* (1983), looks at sport from a

Marxist perspective. Valuable theoretical essays by Norbert Elias and Eric Dunning are collected in *Quest for Excitement* (1986). Also important for the application of modernization theory to the study of sport is Melvin L. Adelman, *A Sporting Time: New York City and the Rise of Modern Athletics, 1820–70* (1986). The ideological and political uses of sports is detailed in John M. Hoberman, *Sport and Political Ideology* (1984). For an examination of the Neo-Marxist critique of sport, see Bero Rigauer, *Sport and Work*, trans. Allen Guttmann (1981), and Jean-Marie Brohm, *Sport—A Prison of Measured Time*, trans. Dan Fraser (1978). Much of the theoretical work of sport history has been written by German and French scholars and has not been translated.

Far afield from the theoretical studies are the numerous volumes on sport by journalists. Although the quality is dramatically uneven, a number of books are useful. For the recent period the best are Robert Lipsyte, *Sportsworld: An American Dreamland* (1975); James A. Michener, *Sports in America* (1976); Michael Novak, *The Joy of Sports: End Zones, Bases, Baskets, Balls, and the Consecration of the American Spirit* (1976); Paul Gardner, *Nice Guys Finish Last: Sport and American Life* (1975); Robert Boyle, *Sport: Mirror of American Life* (1963); Neil Isaacs, *Jock Culture, U.S.A.* (1978); Richard Lipsky, *How We Play the Game: Why Sports Dominate American Life* (1981); Leonard Shecter, *The Jocks* (1969); Joseph Durso, *The All-American Dollar: The Big Business of Sports* (1971); and Paul Hock, *Rip Off the Big Game: The Exploitation of Sports by the Power Elite* (1972). Of course, there are thousands of journalistic accounts of individual sports, issues, and athletes.

A final starting point for the study of sport history is the anthology. The most useful anthologies for American sport history include William J. Baker and John M. Carroll, eds., *Sports in Modern America* (1981); Donald Spivey, ed., *Sport in America* (1985); Steven A. Riess, ed., *The American Sporting Experience* (1984); George H. Sage, ed., *Sport and American Society: Selected Readings* (1970); John W. Loy, Jr., and G. S. Kenyon, eds., *Sport, Culture, and Society* (1969); and John T. Talamini and Charles H. Page, eds., *Sports and Society: An Anthology* (1972).

## International Sport

The centerpiece of international sport is the modern Olympics, and any study of the modern Olympics must start with the world and ideas of Pierre de Coubertin. The best study of Coubertin—and it is outstanding—is John J. MacAloon, *This Great Symbol: Pierre de Coubertin and the Origins of the Modern Olympic Games* (1981), which deftly combines history and biography with social science theory. Overly sympathetic to Coubertin is Marie-Thérèse Eyquem, *Pierre de Coubertin: L'Epoquée olympique* (1966). Focused more narrowly on the origins of the modern Olympics is Richard D. Mandell's readable *The First Modern Olympics* (1976) and John Apostal Lucas, "Baron de Coubertin and the Formative Years of the Modern International Olympic Movement, 1883–1896" (Ph.D. diss., University of Maryland, 1962). Eugen Weber surveys the French influences on Coubertin in "Gymnastics and Sports in *Fin-de-siècle* France: Opium of the Classes," *American*

*Historical Review* 76 (1971): 70–98 and "Pierre de Coubertin and the Introduction of Organized Sport in France," *Journal of Contemporary History* 5 (1970): 3–26. The role of Coubertin is deemphasized and the importance of the Greeks stressed in David C. Young, "The Origins of the Modern Olympics: A New Version," *International Journal of the History of Sport* 4 (1987): 271–300. Very critical of Coubertin in particular and the Olympic movement in general is John Hoberman, *The Olympic Crisis: Sport, Politics, and the Moral Order* (1986).

The period between 1900 and 1936 remains largely unexplored, but a few studies have yielded interesting results. Richard D. Mandell, *Paris, 1900: The Great World's Fair* (1967), sets the second Olympics in their proper place. The role of Jim Thorpe in the 1912 games is presented in Robert Wheeler, *Jim Thorpe: World's Greatest Athlete* (1975). Urban politics and the 1932 Games are examined in Steven A. Riess, "Power without Authority: Los Angeles' Elites and the Construction of the Coliseum," *Journal of Sport History* 8 (1981): 50–65. A series of English and German essays on international sports between the two world wars is collected in *Sport and Politics: 1918–39/40* (1986). International politics is also surveyed in Donald F. Fuoss, "An Analysis of the Incidents in the Olympic Games from 1924 to 1948 with Reference to the Contribution of the Games to International Good Will and Understanding" (Ed.D. diss., Columbia University Teachers College, 1951). Attempts to establish an international workers sport movement are discussed in David A. Steinberg, "The Workers' Sport Internationals, 1920–1928," *Journal of Contemporary History* 13 (1978): 233–51; Robert F. Wheeler, "Organized Sport and Organized Labor: The Worker's Sport Movement," *Journal of Contemporary History* 13 (1978): 191–210; and Gerhard A. Ritter, "Workers' Culture in Imperial Germany," *Journal of Contemporary History* 13 (1978): 165–89.

The literature on the 1936 Nazi Olympics is extensive. Still the best book is Richard D. Mandell, *The Nazi Olympics* (1971). It is especially good for its discussion of the role of sports and festivals in the political process. Aimed at a more popular audience are Judith Holmes, *Olympiad 1936: Blaze of Glory for Hitler's Reich* (1971), and Duff Hart Davis, *Hitler's Games: The 1936 Olympics* (1986). D. W. Kass, "The Issue of Racism at the 1936 Olympics," *Journal of Sport History* 3 (1976): 223–35, is an overview of the subject, which is treated in much greater depth in William J. Baker, *Jesse Owens: An American Life* (1986). The boycott movement is examined from different perspectives in Carolyn Marvin, "Avery Brundage and American Participation in the 1936 Olympic Games," *Journal of American Studies* 16 (1982): 81–105; Moshe Gottlieb, "The American Controversy over the Olympic Games," *American Jewish Historical Studies* 61 (1972): 181–213; George Eisen, "The Voices of Sanity: American Diplomatic Reports from the 1936 Berlin Olympiad," *Journal of Sport History* 11 (1984): 56–78; Arnd Krueger, "Fair Play for American Athletics: A Study in Anti-Semitism," *Canadian Journal of History of Sport and Physical Education* 9 (1978): 42–57; Bruce Kidd, "Canadian Opposition to the 1936 Olympics in Germany," *ibid.*, 20–40; Bruce Kidd, "The

Popular Front and the 1936 Olympics," ibid. 11 (1980): 1–18; and Ian Jobling, "Australia at the 1936 Olympics: Issue and Attitudes," ibid. 13 (1982): 18–27.

For the politics of the post–World War II Olympics and the career of Avery Brundage two books stand out. A detailed overview is Richard Espy, *The Politics of the Olympic Games* (1979; expanded edition 1981). Allen Guttmann, *The Games Must Go On: Avery Brundage and the Olympic Movement* (1984), is a superb biographer of the most important sports administrator in the twentieth century. Guttmann's "The Games Must Go On: On the Origins of Avery Brundage's Life-Credo," *Stadion* 5 (1979): 253–62, is also important, as are Richard Lee Gibson, "Avery Brundage: Professional Amateur" (Ph.D. diss., Kent State University, 1967), and David Benjamin Kanin, "The Role of Sport in International Relations" (Ph.D., diss., Fletcher School of Law and Diplomacy, Tufts University, 1976). Of interest for Brundage's personal life is William Oscar Johnson, "Avery Brundage: The Man behind the Mask," *Sports Illustrated*, August, 4, 1980; a sympathetic look at Brundage is found in Heinz Schöbel, *The Four Dimensions of Avery Brundage* (1968). The Avery Brundage Papers are housed at the University of Illinois; for a catalogue of the collection see *Avery Brundage Collection, 1908–1975* (1977), compiled by Maynard Brichford. Brichford provides a report of the collection in his "Avery Brundage—The Man and the Collection," in Norbert Müller and Joachim K. Ruhe, eds., *Sport History* (1985): 245–51.

The best book on sport in the Soviet Union is James Riordan, *Sport in Soviet Society: Development of Sport and Physical Education in Russia and the USSR* (1977). Also by Riordan are *Soviet Sport: Background to the Olympics* (1980); "The USSR and the Olympic Games," *Stadion* 6 (1980): 291–314; and "Marx, Lenin, and Physical Culture," *Journal of Sport History* 3 (1976): 152–61. Yuri Brokhin, *The Big Red Machine: The Rise and Fall of Soviet Olympic Champions*, trans. Glenn Ganelik and Yuri Brokhin (1978), presents a more sensationalized view of the subject.

The emergence of East Germany as a sports power has been carefully followed by historians as well as athletes. Doug Gilbert, *The Miracle Machine* (1980), details the East German scientific-sport complex. Two articles by G. A. Carr concentrate on the political impact of East German sports: "The Use of Sport in the German Democratic Republic for the Promotion of National Consciousness and International Prestige," *Journal of Sport History* 1 (1974): 123–36, and "The Involvement of Politics in the Sporting Relationships of East and West Germany, 1945–1972," *Journal of Sport History* 7 (1980): 40–51.

The Olympics have occasionally been used as a background for Third World nationalism. A general overview is provided in David B. Kanin, *A Political History of the Olympic Games* (1981). China and the GANEFO controversy is studied in Jonathan Kolatch, *Sports, Politics, and Ideology in China* (1972). The international reaction to apartheid is the subject of Richard E. Lapchick, *The Politics of Race and International Sport: The Case of South Africa* (1975); Richard Thompson, *Race and Sport* (1964); Peter Hain, *Don't Play with Apartheid* (1971); Chris de Broglio, *South Africa: Racism in Sport* (1970); and, at least in part, Harry Edwards, *The Revolt of the Black Athlete* (1969). The Israeli massacre at the 1972 Munich Olympics is recounted in Serge Groussard, *The Blood of Israel*, trans. Harold J. Salmeson (1975).

Not only Third World countries have resorted to boycotts. The U.S. boycott of the 1980 Moscow Games is discussed in Christopher Booker, *The Games War: A Moscow Journal* (1981), and Laurence Barton, "The American Olympic Boycott of 1980: The Amalgam of Diplomacy and Propaganda in Influencing Public Opinion" (Ph.D. diss., Boston University Graduate School, 1983). Boycotts and a variety of other issues are examined in the essays in Benjamin Lowe, David B. Kanin, and Andrew Strenk, eds., *Sports and International Relations* (1978), and Arthur T. Johnson and James H. Frey, eds., *Government and Sport: The Public Policy Issues* (1985). Especially good in the latter volume is James A. R. Nafziger, "Foreign Policy in the Sports Arena," and very critical of recent developments is Baruch A. Hazan, *Olympic Sports and Propaganda Games* (1982). Finally, every year sees more Ph.D. dissertations on international sports. Three of the most recent ones are Andrew Edward Stenk, "The Politicization of International Sport, 1945–1960" (Ph.D. diss., University of Southern California, 1983); Robin Tait, "The Politicization of the Modern Olympic Games" (Ph.D. diss., University of Oregon, 1984); and Martin Barry Vinokur, "The Politics of Sports: A Comparison of How Governments Use Sports to Advance Political Integration" (Ph.D. diss., American University, 1983).

Not to be ignored are the general popular histories of the Olympic Games. The most entertaining are William O. Johnson, Jr., *All That Glitters Is Not Gold: The Olympic Games* (1972); David Wallechinsky, *The Complete Book of the Olympics* (1984); and Michael Morris Killanin and John Rodda, eds., *The Olympic Games: Eighty Years of People, Events, and Records* (1976). Solid and well researched is John Lucas, *The Modern Olympic Games* (1980). And a fine collection of essays is provided in Peter J. Graham and Horst Ueberhorst, ed., *The Modern Olympics* (1976).

## Race and Sport

Although many aspects of black history have been studied during the late 1960s, the 1970s, and the 1980s, there has been no adequate overview of blacks in sport, a topic certainly in need of a synthesis. A few journalistic accounts are helpful. Jack Olsen, *The Black Athlete: A Shameful Story* (1968), is good for the 1960s. Ocania Chalk, *Pioneers in Black Sport* (1975), and Edwin B. Henderson, *The Black Emergence and Arrival* (1968), examine the lives of blacks who integrated various sports. Art Rust, Jr., *Get That Nigger off the Field: A Sparkling Informal History of the Black Man in Baseball* (1976), looks at blacks in one sport. Harry Edwards, *The Revolt of the Black Athlete* (1969), is also helpful for the 1960s. There is an interesting section on race in Daniel M. Landers, ed., *Social Problems in Athletics: Essays in the Sociology of Sport* (1976), which considers the "stacking" controversy and provides a good bibliography. Finally, Linwood G. Davis and Belinda S. Daniels, *Black Athletes in the United States: A Bibliography of Books, Articles, Autobiographies, and Biogra-*

*phies on Professional Black Athletes, 1880–1981* (1981), is a valuable bibliographical tool.

By contrast, the integration of professional baseball has been very well covered. For a history of the Negro Leagues, see Robert Peterson, *Only the Ball Was White: A History of Legendary Black Players and All-Black Professional Teams before Black Men Played in the Major Leagues* (1970), and Donn Rogosin, *Invisible Man: Life in Baseball's Negro Leagues* (1983). Rob Ruck, *Sandlot Seasons: Sport in Black Pittsburgh* (1987), recaptures segregated baseball and other sports in one city. The best book on the integration of baseball is Jules Tygiel, *Baseball's Great Experiment: Jackie Robinson and His Legacy* (1983); it is scholarly, sympathetic, and well-written. For a more personal view of the same subject, see Jackie Robinson, *I Never Had It Made* (1972). The Robinson-Robeson confrontation is covered in Ronald A. Smith, "The Paul Robeson–Jackie Robinson Saga and a Political Collision," *Journal of Sport History* 6 (1979): 5–27. Close examinations of the role of the press in the integration of baseball can be found in William Simons, "Jackie Robinson and the American Mind: Journalistic Perceptions of the Reintegration of Baseball," *Journal of Sport History* 12 (1985): 39–64, and David K. Wiggins, "Wendell Smith, *The Pittsburgh Courier-Journal*, and the Campaign to Include Blacks in Organized Baseball, 1933–1945," *Journal of Sport History* 10 (1983): 5–29. The feelings of other black players about Robinson and the integration of professional baseball can be discovered in a variety of places. John Holway, *Voice from the Great Black Baseball Leagues* (1975), is a fine collection of interviews. Charles Einstein, *Willie's Time: A Memoir of Another America* (1980), tells the story of Willie Mays very well. William Brashler, *Josh Gibson: A Life in the Negro Leagues* (1970), is a biography of the best player of the Negro Leagues. Roy Campanella tells his story in *It's Good to Be Alive* (1959). And Roger Kahn's *The Boys of Summer* (1971) is a baseball classic.

Integration in other team sports has not been as well studied as in baseball. There are a few good articles on football which suggest patterns. Especially see Ronald E. Marcello, "The Integration of Intercollegiate Athletics in Texas: North Texas State College as a Test Case, 1956," *Journal of Sport History* 14 (1987): 286–316, and Thomas G. Smith, "Civil Rights on the Gridiron: The Kennedy Administration and the Washington Redskins," *Journal of Sport History* 14 (1987): 189–208. Willie Morris, *The Courting of Marcus Dupre* (1983), is a wonderful look at changing attitudes in the South. For basketball see David Halberstam, *The Breaks of the Game* (1981); Bill Russell and William McSweeny, *Go Up for Glory* (1966); and Bill Russell and Taylor Branch, *Second Wind: The Memoirs of an Opinionated Man* (1979). David Wolf, *Foul! The Connie Hawkins Story* (1972), and Wilt Chamberlain and David Shaw, *Wilt* (1973), are also good on racial issues.

Blacks in individual sports have been well-covered. Two books by Randy Roberts, *Papa Jack: Jack Johnson and the Era of White Hopes* (1983) and *Jack Dempsey: The Manassa Mauler* (1979), deal with race in boxing in the 1900–1930 period. The career of Joe Louis is covered in Chris Mead, *Cham-*

pion *Joe Louis: Black Hero in White America* (1985); Gerald Astor, ". . . *And a Credit to His Race": The Hard Life and Times of Joseph Louis Barrow, a.k.a. Joe Louis* (1974); Joe Louis with Edna and Art Rust, Jr., *Joe Louis: My Life* (1981); Barney Nagler, *Brown Bomber: The Pilgrimage of Joe Louis* (1972); A. O. Edmonds, *Joe Louis* (1973); Alexander T. Young, Jr., "Joe Louis: Symbol, 1933–1949" (Ph.D. diss., University of Maryland, 1968); Dominic J. Capeci, Jr., and Martha Wilkerson, "Multifarious Hero: Joe Louis, American Society, and Race Relations during World Crisis, 1935–1945," *Journal of Sport History* 10 (1983): 5–25; and Jeffrey T. Sammons, "Boxing as a Reflection of Society: The Southern Reaction to Joe Louis," *Journal of Popular Culture* 16 (1983): 23–33. Race is also dealt with more broadly in Jeffrey T. Sammons, *Beyond the Ring: The Role of Boxing in American Society* (1988). Jessie Owens is studied fully in William Baker, *Jesse Owens: An American Life* (1986). Perceptive studies which touch on race in tennis are John McPhee, *Levels of the Game* (1969); Arthur Ashe and Neil Amdur, *Off the Court* (1981); Arthur Ashe and Frank Deford, *Arthur Ashe: Portrait in Motion* (1975); and Althea Gibson, *I Always Wanted to Be Somebody* (1958). No full biography of Muhammad Ali has been written, but a number of splendid books which examine aspects of Ali's career have been published. They include Norman Mailer, *The Fight* (1971); George Plimpton, *Shadow Box* (1977); Wilfred Sheed, *Muhammad Ali* (1975); Robert Lipsyte, *Sports World: An American Dreamland* (1975); Bud Schulberg, *Loser and Still Champion: Muhammad Ali* (1972); José Torres, *Sting Like a Bee: The Muhammad Ali Story* (1971): Howard Cosell, *Cosell* (1973); Malcolm X, *The Autobiography of Malcolm X* (1964); Frederic Cople Jaher, "White America Views Jack Johnson, Joe Louis, and Muhammad Ali," in Donald Spivey, *Sport in America* (1985); and Muhammad Ali and Richard Durham, *The Greatest; Muhammad Ali* (1975).

The debate during the 1970s over black athletic superiority was carried out largely in magazines and journals. To gauge the nature of the debate, see Harry Edwards, "The Myth of the Racially Superior Athlete," *Black Scholar* 3 (1971): 16–28, and Martin Kane, "An Assessment of 'Black is Best,' " *Sports Illustrated*, July 18, 1971.

## Labor, Business, and Sport

The literature on the business of sport and sport law is a healthy growth field. Much of it has appeared in specialized economic and legal journals. An early and important survey of the subjects was presented in the essays in Roger G. Noll, ed., *Government and the Sports Business* (1974), a Brookings Institution publication. Something of an update of the Noll volume is provided by Arthur T. Johnson and James H. Frey, eds., *Government and Sport: The Public Policy Issues* (1985). Both books contain essays on such subjects as antitrust legislation, broadcasting issues, tax policies, franchise relocations, labor relations, stadium subsidies, and other areas where sport and government policy intersect. Both books are also well-documented and provide convenient starting points for studying any of the issues in more depth. A more systematic treatment of these issues is provided in Robert C.

Berry and Glenn M. Wong, *Law and Business of the Sports Industries*, 2 vols. (1986); volume 1 is entitled *Professional Sports Leagues*, and volume 2 is *Common Issues in Amateur and Professional Sports*. The volumes are particularly good for their treatment of individual legal cases involving sports. Both are also fully documented.

Not until well into the twentieth century did professional athletes regard themselves as laborers, and even then only as a special type of laborer. But the attempt to organize professional athletes started much earlier. The story of the struggle to organize professional baseball players is told in Lee Lowenfish and Tony Lupien, *The Imperfect Diamond: The Story of Baseball's Reserve System and the Men Who Fought to Change It* (1980). The tale is also recounted in the two best multivolume histories of baseball: Harold Seymour, *Baseball*, 2 vols. (1960–71), and David Voigt, *American Baseball*, 3 vols. (1966–83). Paul Gregory, *The Baseball Player: An Economic Study* (1956), is an early look at the subject, and Jesse W. Markham and Paul V. Teplitz, *Baseball Economics and Public Policy* (1981), updates the topic.

Although labor relations are dealt with in the above books, this topic is also surveyed in Paul D. Staudohar, *The Sports Industry and Collective Bargaining* (1986), and Robert C. Berry, William B. Gould IV, and Paul D. Staudohar, *Labor Relations in Professional Sports* (1986). Both volumes examine football, basketball, and hockey as well as baseball. James B. Dworkin, *Owners Versus Players: Baseball and Collective Bargaining* (1981), focuses on a single sport, as does David Harris, *The League: The Rise and Decline of the NFL* (1986). *The League* is especially good on the personalities of the owners of professional football teams. The failures and brief history of the USFL are recounted in Jim Byrne, *The $1 League: The Rise and Fall of the USFL* (1986). And Gary Davidson and Bill Libby, *Breaking the Game Wide Open* (1974), details the histories of the ABA, the WHA, and the WFL. Bob Woolf, *Behind Closed Doors* (1976), gives the agent's view of sports. The best books on the economics of professional boxing are Thomas Hauser, *The Black Lights: Inside the World of Professional Boxing* (1986); Dean Allison and Bruce B. Henderson, *Empire of Deceit* (1985); and Art Fisher and Neal Marshall with Charles Einstein, *Garden of Innocents* (1972).

Franchise movements and legal issues are discussed with passion and insight in Howard Cosell with Peter Bonventre, *I Never Played the Game* (1985). An attempt to put the Dodgers' move to Los Angeles into proper perspective and a model study, is Neil J. Sullivan, *The Dodgers Move West* (1987). Various legal issues are dealt with in Warren Freedman, *Professional Sports and Antitrust* (1987), and Raymond L. Yasser, *Torts and Sports: Legal Liability in Professional and Amateur Athletics* (1985).

## Scandals and College Sport

The best book on the boxing scandals remains Barney Nagler, *James Norris and the Decline of Boxing* (1964), although Steven A. Riess, "Only the Ring Was Square: Frankie Carbo and the Underworld Control of American Boxing," *International Journal of the History of Sport* 5 (1988): 29–52, and

Jeffrey T. Sammons, *Beyond the Ring: The Role of Boxing in American Society* (1988), both cover the essential points. *Professional Boxing: Hearings before the Subcommittee on Antitrust and Monopoly* (1960–61), contains important evidence and a stark look at the sport. Two autobiographies are also helpful: Rocky Graziano, *Somebody Up There Likes Me* (1955), and Jake LaMotta and Pete Savage, *Raging Bull* (1970). Fraser Scott, *Weigh-In: The Selling of a Middleweight* (1974), demonstrates that crime persists in boxing. Fighters recount their own tales in Peter Heller, *"In This Corner": Forty Champions Tell Their Stories* (1973). Finally, Budd Schulberg covered the corruption in boxing as a writer for *Sports Illustrated*, and his stories are outstanding.

As with boxing scandals, the scandals in college basketball were generally well-covered by *Sport* and the *New York Times*. Two good books have been written about the 1951 basketball scandal. The most straightforward is Charles Rosen, *Scandals of '51: How Gamblers Almost Killed College Basketball* (1978). More personal is Stanley Cohen, *The Game They Played* (1977). Bert Nelli, *The Winning Tradition: A History of Kentucky Wildcat Basketball* (1984), and Neil D. Isaacs, *All the Moves: A History of College Basketball* (1975), also touch on the subject. David Wolf, *Foul! The Connie Hawkins Story* (1971), examines the 1961 scandal, as does the fine essay by William H. Beesley, "The 1961 Scandal at North Carolina State and the End of the Dixie Classic," in Donald Chu, Jeffrey O. Segrave, and Beverly J. Becker, eds., *Sports and Higher Education* (1985). More work needs to be done on college and amateur sports, especially in the middle and late twentieth century. For the earlier period, Ronald A. Smith, *Sport and Freedom: The Rise of Big-Time College Athletics* (1988), and Patrick Miller, "Athletes in Academe: College Sports and American Culture" (Ph.D. diss., University of California, Berkeley, 1987), are very good. Something of the politics of amateur sports is suggested in Arnold Flath, "A History of Relations between the National Collegiate Athletic Association and the Amateur Athletic Union of the United States, 1905–1963" (Ph.D. diss., University of Michigan, 1963). Several essays in James H. Frey, ed., *The Governance of Inter-Collegiate Athletics* (1982), deal with historical themes. Of the many critiques, Joseph Durso, *The Sports Factory: An Investigation into College Sports* (1975), and John Underwood, *The Death of an American Game: The Crisis in Football* (1979), are the best. John F. Rooney, *The Recruiting Game: Toward a New System of Inter-Collegiate Sport* (1987), calls for needed reforms.

### Television and Sport

Most of the studies which treat television and sport seem interested in placing blame for the "corruption" of the sporting experience. Certainly this is true of Benjamin G. Rader, *In Its Own Image: How Television Has Transformed Sports* (1984), the best overview of the subject. This transformation also dominates Donald Parente, "A History of Television and Sports" (Ph.D. diss., University of Illinois, 1974), which is particularly good on the rule changes in sports caused by television. Joan Chandler, *Television and National Sport: The United States and Britain* (1988), challenges this approach, arguing that sports have long been subject to rule changes and commercialization. An earlier book on the subject which set the nature of the debate is William O. Johnson, *Super Spectator and the Electric Lilliputians* (1971). Two books focus on the relationship of the networks to sports: Ron Powers, *Supertube: The Rise of Television Sports* (1984), and Bert Randolph Sugar, *"The Thrill of Victory": The Inside Story of ABC* (1978).

Several "insiders" have told their stories. Jim Spence with Dave Diles, *Up Close and Personal: The Inside Story of Network Television Sports* (1988), is helpful for understanding ABC. Three books by Howard Cosell—*Cosell* (1973), *Like It Is* (1975), and *I Never Played the Game* (1985)—give his point of view. Also of interest is Larry Merchant, . . . *And Every Day You Take Another Bite* (1971).

Several books consider individual sports. We were aided by Joe Williams, *TV Boxing Book* (1954), for boxing; Roger Angell, *The Five Seasons: A Baseball Companion* (1978), for baseball; David Halberstam, *The Breaks of the Game* (1981), for basketball; and Paul R. Lawrence, *Unsportsmanlike Conduct: The National Collegiate Athletic Association and the Business of College Football* (1987), for football. And several articles and interviews are important for understanding personalities: David Halberstam, "The Mouth That Roared," *Playboy*, December 1982, for Cosell; and for Arledge, "Playboy Interview," *Playboy*, October 1976, and Roone Arledge and Gilbert Rogin, "It's Sport . . . It's Money . . . It's TV," *Sports Illustrated*, April 25, 1966. Finally, the reporting of William Taaffe in *Sports Illustrated* keeps abreast of current trends in television sports.

## Sport and American Culture

The American obsession with sports can be traced in newspapers and the hundreds of popular magazines devoted wholly to athletics, health, and fitness. Harvey Green, *Fit for America: Health, Fitness, Sport, and American Culture* (1986), demonstrates that our concerns are not necessarily of recent origins. Hillel Schwartz, *Never Satisfied: A Cultural History of Diets, Fantasies, and Fat* (1986), similarly traces Americans' concern for their bodies, as does Lois W. Banner, *American Beauty* (1983), and Valerie Steele, *Fashion and Eroticism: Ideals of Feminine Beauty from the Victorian Era to the Jazz Age* (1985).

A good starting point for an examination of women in sports are the essays in J. A. Mangan and Roberta J. Park, eds., *From "Fair Sex" to Feminism: Sport and the Socialization of Women in the Industrial and Post-Industrial Eras* (1987), and Stephanie L. Twin, ed., *Out of the Bleachers* (1979). More sociological essays are provided in Ellen W. Gerber et al., *The American Woman in Sport* (1974), and in Mary A. Boutilier and Lucinda San Giovanni, *The Sporting Woman* (1983). The chapter on women in sports in Donald J. Mrozek, *Sport and American Mentality, 1880–1910* (1983), is particularly insightful, as is Larry Engelmann, *The Goddess and the American Girl: The Story of Suzanne Lenglen and Helen Wills* (1988). Bibliographical information can be found in Mary Lou Remley, *Women in Sport: A Guide to Information Sources* (1980).

The role of sports in American culture is discussed in Christopher Lasch, *The Culture of Narcissism: American Life in an Age of Diminishing Expectations* (1979). Drugs in sports is examined in Bob Goldman, *Death in the Locker Room: Steroids and Sports* (1984), and Allen Guttman, *A Whole New Ball Game: An Interpretation of American Sports* (1988). A particularly good article on the history of steroids is Terry Todd, "Anabolic Steroids: The Gremlins of Sport," *Journal of Sport History* 14 (1987): 87–107. Arnold J. Mandell, *The Nightmare Season* (1976), traces drug use in professional football. For the culture of weightlifting see Alan M. Klein, "Pumping Iron," *Sociology of Sport Journal* 3 (1986).

# ● Index